The Roots of Appeasement

The Roots of Appeasement

Martin Gilbert

Fellow of Merton College, Oxford

WEIDENFELD AND NICOLSON
5 Winsley Street London W1

© 1966 by Martin Gilbert

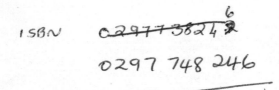
Printed in Great Britain by
Cox & Wyman Ltd., London, Reading and Fakenham

Contents

List of Maps

These maps were designed by the author and drawn by John Flower.

The aim is to get an appeasement of the fearful hatreds and antagonisms which exist in Europe and to enable the world to settle down. I have no other object in view.

Winston Churchill at the Imperial Conference,
7 July 1921

Appeasement in itself may be good or bad according to the circumstances. Appeasement from weakness and fear is alike futile and fatal. Appeasement from strength is magnanimous and noble, and might be the surest and perhaps the only path to world peace.

Winston Churchill, in the House of Commons
on 14 December 1950, during the Korean War

Introduction

In this book I trace the origins of appeasement, and follow its course from 1914–39. Often those who sought a lenient peace in 1919, or tried to bring Britain and Germany together during the inter-war years, are seen as misguided men who mistook weakness for charity. This was not so: appeasement was a policy of optimism and hope, even at times of strength. Those who believed that every possible effort should be made to improve Anglo-German relations did so, not because they feared German territorial ambitions, but because they respected German national aspirations and admired German cultural and scientific achievements. The arguments for and against appeasement were never simple ones, nor did the debate which raged with acerbity for twenty years fall into any clear categories of 'right' and 'wrong'. My aim is to examine the wide range of the appeasement argument, and to show that appeasement, both as an attitude of mind and as a policy, was not a silly or treacherous idea in the minds of stubborn, gullible men, but a noble idea, rooted in Christianity, courage and common sense.

During the inter-war years appeasement constantly changed in outlook and method. For Lloyd George it was a necessary counterweight to what he considered the excessive anti-Germanism of France. For Ramsay MacDonald it was an essential part of the restoration of European political sanity and economic progress. For Stanley Baldwin it sprang from the belief that tranquillity would come to Europe only if France and her eastern European allies could be prevented from isolating and 'encircling' Germany. Under Baldwin, Britain shunned close co-operation with France. Baldwin's Cabinet, much influenced by Churchill, in 1925 rejected a proposed Anglo-French alliance. Diplomats, politicians, and civil servants saw appeasement as the only path to permanent peace in Europe. Post-war frontiers were to be adjusted and post-war animosities whittled away.

Until 1935, the principal tenet of appeasement was concessions through strength. Even for Neville Chamberlain in 1938 appeasement was not so much based upon fear of Germany as upon the belief that further peaceful change in Europe was both desirable and feasible. Chamberlain believed tenaciously that constructive Anglo-German co-operation in and after 1938 could still preserve peace despite Hitler's growing advocacy of violence. In retrospect, appeasement towards Stresemann and Brüning seems to have been realistic, appeasement towards Hitler, folly. But although some contemporaries held this view, and held it strongly, Chamberlain denied that Nazism could not be appeased. He doubted that war was inevitable. The idea of the inevitability of war was contrary to the underlying assumptions of appeasement, assumptions upon which British foreign policy since 1918 had been based. Chamberlain was continuing the traditions of his predecessors. That he did so in radically different, unsuitable circumstances, may have been the fault of his judgement, but it was certainly not the fault of his intentions. His aim was to preserve peace in Europe. It was an honourable quest. No British Prime Minister in the inter-war years sought otherwise.

that rationale behind appeasement good.
but the Chamberlain didn't carry out the
policy properly or in the correct context

Acknowledgements

I have been helped in assembling material and in reaching my conclusions on the origins of appeasement and its course between the wars by a large number of people, both in conversation and correspondence. Among those who encouraged me to examine appeasement in a broad perspective and gave me an insight into its meaning and methods were Sir Norman Angell, Frank Ashton-Gwatkin, the late Lord Beaverbrook, Professor Max Beloff, Alan Campbell-Johnson, Alan Collingridge, Dr T. P. Conwell-Evans, Sir Colin Coote, Henry Drummond-Wolff, Dr Paul Einzig, G. E. R. Gedye, Sir Basil Liddell Hart, Sir Frederick Leith-Ross, Sir Reginald Leeper, Donald McLachlan, Julian Piggott, Captain George Pitt-Rivers, Lord Strang, Virgil Tilea, Dr Arnold Toynbee, Sir Horace Wilson, and A. P. Young.

In a subject so clouded by controversy it is at times difficult to separate passion and polemic from reality. I have tried to explain and do justice to all opinions, and seek to malign none. The 'Guilty Men' tradition in English historical writing has flourished for over a quarter of a century, and ought now to fade away. The inter-war years deserve to become the objects of more reflective inquiry. Historical assessments are best approached in an atmosphere of relative detachment. In seeking to present a new basis for the study of appeasement in Britain I have been influenced in particular by criticisms of my earlier opinions by Lord Strang and A. J. P. Taylor.

Chronology of Appeasement

1917: 22 January. President Wilson insists upon 'a peace between equals'.

1919: 25 March. Lloyd George's Fontainebleau Memorandum opposes a punitive peace.

1919: 16 April. Lloyd George explains his policy in the House of Commons.

1919: December. J. M. Keynes's *Economic Consequences of the Peace* published.

1920: 10 January. Ratification of the Treaty of Versailles.

1920: 12 February. First of a series of post-war Anglo-French conferences opens in London.

1922: April–May. Genoa Conference. Lloyd George fails to obtain a reparation settlement.

1923: January. Anglo-French clash over France's occupation of the Ruhr.

1924: 16 July. London Conference on Reparations opened by Ramsay MacDonald.

1925: 16 October. Locarno Agreements signed.

1931: May. European economic crisis intensifies international friction.

1931: November. The 'Sargent Chain' contemplates a wide-ranging settlement.

1932: January. Sir Robert Vansittart proposes Treaty revision in Germany's interest.

1932: June. Lausanne Conference, to end Reparations, opened by MacDonald.

1933: 30 January. Adolf Hitler becomes German Chancellor.

1933: 1 April. Anti-semitic pogrom in Berlin alienates British observers.

1935: January. Visit of Lord Lothian to Hitler.

1935: 21 June. The Anglo-German Naval Agreement signed.

1936: September. Visit of Lloyd George to Hitler.

1937: November. Visit of Lord Halifax to Hitler.

1938: 12 March. Economic and Colonial Appeasement checked by Hitler's annexation of Austria.

1938: 30 September. The Munich Agreements signed.

1939: 15 March. German occupation of Prague destroys popular appeasement.

1939: 1 September. German invasion of Poland halts remnants of appeasement policy.

1939: 3 September. Britain declares war on Germany.

CHAPTER I

The Challenge of War

For a hundred and fifty years the English public accepted war as a part of the natural order of events. From Marlborough's victories against France at the beginning of the eighteenth century, to the siege of Sevastopol in the Crimean war, the conflict in arms was accepted as both inevitable and expedient. By war, danger was averted, empire extended, and prestige enhanced. By war, reputation was maintained. Nor was this process considered a particularly ugly one. Armies were small, the devastation they caused was mostly limited to a narrow line of march and to battlefields which one man could survey at a glance.

For Englishmen, the impact of a hundred and fifty years of frequent wars was small. Those living on the verge of starvation suffered, particularly during the Napoleonic wars; but society, which provided the politicians and filled the salons with chatter, was hardly touched. Jane Austen's novels, written at the height of a prolonged war, give no indication of anguish or disgust. Edward Gibbon, wishing to travel from Geneva to London, could decide to go through Ostend instead of through France, because 'the long war has rendered even that polite people somewhat peevish'.[1] War was something that affected armies, not peoples; it was a political exercise, not a social and psychological catastrophe.

Yet even between Blenheim and Sevastopol voices were raised against the easy acceptance of war as no more than an item of political behaviour, of no more lasting consequence than a rigged election or the purchase of votes through patronage. There was, though in a minority, a feeling that war stood in a category of its own, and should if possible be avoided. Walpole was the first politician of modern times to make peace his firm object, and though he was finally forced into war with Spain in 1739 by pressure of the self-styled 'Patriots', he had made his mark as a man determined to avert war by a wide range of means.[2] Burke's judgement on Walpole is instructive, for Burke was later a leading advocate of war against revolutionary France. Of Walpole he wrote:

> He never manfully put forward the entire strength of his cause. He temporized; he managed. . . . They who stir up the people to improper desires, whether of peace or war, will be condemned by themselves. They who weakly yield to them will be condemned by history.[3]

Burke's appeal to history is important. He saw a moral issue, and the possibility of condemnation. He was concerned with posterity, and he made a distinction between just and unjust wars. His own changing views bear witness to the problem which he was among the first to recognize. In 1775 he condemned war against the American Colonies; in 1796 he demanded war against France. The arguments which he used on both occasions are the basis of the arguments used by the advocates and critics of appeasement before 1939. The theme of Burke's *Speech on Conciliation with America* was that:

> All government, indeed every human benefit and enjoyment, every virtue, and every prudent act, is founded on compromise and barter. We balance inconveniences; we give and take; we remit some rights that we may enjoy others; and, we chose rather to be happy citizens, than subtle disputants.[4]

Because he believed that Britain and America could be reconciled, he urged that they should be; that prolonged and strenuous efforts to procure peace were of greater value, and alone of moral value, than the politically easy resort to war.

In 1796 Burke saw no chance of reconciliation. The war against France, he insisted, was not a war of interests but of ideologies. It was morally right to take up arms against ideas which were subversive of liberty. It was a war, he wrote in his *Letters on a Regicide Peace*:

> . . . not with an ordinary community, which is hostile or friendly as passion or as interest may veer about: not with a State which makes war through wantonness, and abandons it through lassitude. We are at war with a system, which, by its essence, is inimical to all other Governments, and which makes peace or war, as peace and war may best contribute to their subversion. It is with an armed doctrine that we are at war.[5]

Such was Burke's analysis. It was, of course, a personal one. And it continued to be a personal one in the nineteenth and twentieth centuries. It is for the individual to decide, by means of whatever evidence is at his disposal, whether a particular war springs from a clash of interests which by better management could be shifted from the battlefield to the conference table, or from a conflict of ideologies which can only be resolved – indeed, some would say must be resolved – by war.

The personal dilemma creates a number of difficult problems. Can an individual, even a politician inside the government circle, know for certain that he has enough evidence at his disposal to make a valid judgement ? Can a politician, however much evidence is at his disposal, be certain that he is not unduly influenced by personal or popular prejudice, the result, perhaps, of decades of imperceptible yet insidious propaganda ? Can a man who is prepared, as Burke was in 1796, to make a definite claim for the absolute morality of his cause, be certain that later generations will not challenge the premises on which his judgement was based, and condemn the war which flowed from it ?

In this context of the morality of war, it is well to remember that when Britain declared war on Germany in 1939 both Neville Chamberlain, who had tried every means in his power to avoid war, and Winston Churchill, who had taken the Burkean view that Nazism and the British way of life could not co-exist, stressed in their speeches in Parliament that morality was on their side.[6] 'This is no war,' said Churchill, 'for domination or imperial aggrandizement or material gain. . . . It is a war . . . to establish, on impregnable rocks, the rights of the individual, and it is a war to establish and revive the stature of man.' Churchill told the House of Commons that Britain's efforts to preserve peace gave her a moral stature which would be a source of strength and energy: 'Our hands may be active,' he claimed, 'but our consciences are at rest.' Chamberlain asserted equally boldly that he had neglected no measure by which peace might have been assured.

In 1939 it was thus possible for Chamberlain, as in 1796 it had been possible for Burke, to see a particular war as morally justified; and this moral justification seemed so important that it overrode considerations of loss of life, damage to trade, the destruction of cities, bitterness between nations, and the difficulties, when war ended, of making a peace which would ensure the supremacy of the principles for which the war had been fought.

If, before every war, a nation could speak of its moral rectitude with the unanimity and conviction of a Burke or a Churchill, the problem of appeasement would never arise. If a war is just, and can, before its onset, be shown to be just, then attempts to preserve peace can have no justification, except to a pacifist who objects to all wars irrespective of their cause. But the British are not a pacifist people, and the conscientious objector has always been in a minority. How then can we explain the reluctance of the majority of Englishmen to contemplate a war in 1938 with a power which, in 1939, could be attacked, in the name of morality, with a unanimity of conviction probably unique in British history? The answer lies in the widespread doubt as to the morality of such a war; a doubt which led people to insist upon every possible effort being made to reconcile Britain and Germany. Appeasement was the instrument by which all doubts were to be allayed. If reconciliation were possible, it would be achieved. Appeasement was a search, by every means that politicians and even private people could find, to create a relationship between Britain and Germany other than that of war. It sprang from a belief, not that war itself was immoral, but that a war between Britain and Germany would be immoral. But in 1939 no grounds for such doubts remained.

This concern with the morality of any particular war had an imposing pedigree. The alarm bell which Walpole and Burke had rung, albeit in a minority, in the eighteenth century, was rung with increasing clamour in the nineteenth. In 1800 Charles James Fox had demanded peace with France, on the grounds that the war could no longer be upheld on moral grounds; indeed, he argued that British provocation had been as responsible for the outbreak of the war as French wickedness. We used morality as an excuse for war, not as the reason, he claimed, for when our allies had partitioned Poland, an act of 'infamy and disgrace', Britain had acquiesced. Fox urged the government to see the French viewpoint, to realize that the war was unjustified, and to end it. 'Is peace a rash system?' he thundered. 'Is it dangerous for nations to live in amity with each other?'[7]

Fox failed in 1800; the thought that a war might be immoral did not excite strong passions. Half a century later, John Bright succeeded where Fox failed. His denunciation of the Crimean War laid a firm foundation for subsequent doubt. A hundred and fifty years of easily accepted war was over; a hundred years of anguish and doubt were about to begin. The age when war was romantic, when alliances were skilfully manipulated for sudden gain, and patriotism was the ability to cheer on soldiers from the sideline – that age was dying. The age of conciliation and reconciliation, compromise and barter, realizing one's own faults, seeing both sides of any dispute, giving as well as taking, conceding as well as demanding – that age, the age of appeasement, had begun.

Bright began his political career, like his colleague Cobden, fighting domestic issues. Both he and Cobden became involved in foreign affairs as critics of particular policies. Bright was not a pacifist: he believed rather that the Crimean War was unjustified. 'Force is no remedy' he insisted; and, with Cobden, sought an improvement in international affairs through discussion and disarmament. Both men believed that all international change should be peaceful change; both believed that the balance of power was a phrase, in Bright's words, 'to be brought in on every occasion to stimulate this country to war' and that we ought 'to drive it from our minds'.[8] Bright stressed the flimsy reasons for which men would go to war, and their ignorance of the sufferings, economic and social as well as personal, which war would entail. His voice was prophetic as far as the First World War was concerned:

It is a painful and terrible thing to think how easy it is to stir up a nation to war . . . and you will find that wars are always supported by a class of arguments which, after the war is over, the people find were arguments they should not have listened to.[9]

Bright opposed war against Russia, Cobden[10] war against France, because the wars would create more problems than they could solve, more misery than they could cure, and more animosities than they could heal.

After 1854 European quarrels took on a new aspect. Wars became wars of national unity, not of conquest. It was for the liberation of Italy or the hegemony of Prussia that blood was shed. When Prussia defeated France she had not sought the wide territorial gains that marked earlier wars; she had not taken an acre of France's large empire overseas; and even the annexation of Alsace-Lorraine was caught up in Bismarck's reluctance to create too great a sense of grievance in French minds. It was outside Europe that war continued to flourish. Imperial conquest was clothed in the fine robes of civilizing missions and the spread of Christianity.

All Europe, being both civilized and Christian, could remain at peace: Africa and Asia could be the continents in which former enemies could search for glory and maintain a moral stance.

The alliance systems, which had, before 1854, been primarily preludes to war or balances intended to have a decisive influence upon the clash of armies and navies, were transformed, principally by Bismarck, into arrangements for preserving the existing frontiers, and creating a sense, not of impending conflict, but of security. Thus Prussia, Austria, and Russia co-operated, not to partition Rumania, as, in 1772 they had partitioned Poland, but to hold all existing frontiers together; not to fling the balance of armed might down upon the side of a particular combination of forces, but to make all such manipulations unnecessary. While Bismarck sought peace through a complex system of alliances, woven with the intricacy of a spider, Britain, in the age when Lord Salisbury's influence was paramount, preserved a cautious neutrality. Invitations to combine were gently rebutted. Arbitration was offered wherever Europe seemed in danger of exploding. Compromises were reached wherever conflict threatened. Diplomacy emerged as the honest broker: sometimes its language was threatening or brusque, but always its aims were clear – settlement, not slaughter. The policy known somewhat haughtily as 'Splendid Isolation' was something quite different; it was 'cautious manipulation' or 'subtle persuasion'.

Europe became, after 1854, more pragmatic; economic prosperity came to mean more than military might. Industrial and imperial prowess were the two criteria of a nation's might. In the forty-four years after 1870 the European powers shunned war. Only Turkey, the 'sick-man' of Europe whose place was considered to be outside Europe altogether, fought a desperate series of wars to preserve its Balkan lands. But Europe was Christian, Turkey was Muslim; Europe bursting with energy and technological discovery, Turkey Asiatic and backward. The growth of industrial expertise created a club of nations who, though often suspicious of each other, reserved their weapons for those who were beyond the pale altogether.

Imperialism was a substitute for European war. At the turn of the century European armies joined together to suppress the Boxer Rebellion in China and to rescue the Europeans trapped in the Legations. A German general led the force; a British general took charge of its observation balloons. Then each nation returned to pursue its own imperial aims – the Germans to suppress a rebellion in South-West Africa, the British balloon expert to lead a British force over the Himalayas and into Lhasa, the 'forbidden city' of Tibet.[11]

Conscious of the need for peace in Europe, the imperial powers pursued a policy of deliberate settlement overseas. So much land was available for imperial expansion that land squabbles would clearly be an absurd reason for war in Europe. African frontiers were first discussed by conference in 1884, when Bismarck was host in Berlin to all those with African ambitions. Sometimes the public mind was roused to a frenzy by the press or a demagogue, as when, in 1897, the British man-in-the-street shouted in favour of war in order to check French expansion in West Africa, but such outbursts of war-fever were soon calmed by diplomatic compromise. It was only when a non-European power blocked imperial ambitions that serious war threatened, as when the Boer Republics challenged British hegemony in Southern Africa in 1899. Soldiers paraded in Europe, but fought in Africa or Asia. Generals inspected each other's armies, admirals visited each other's fleets, monarchs watched each other's manoeuvres: then each went away and employed his forces to subdue or 'civilize' as he thought best.

The first fourteen years of the twentieth century saw a remarkable development in European affairs. Instead of allowing imperial rivalries to create national antagonisms sufficiently intense to lead to war, each country sought out its imperial rivals and tried to placate them. As it was becoming more and more inconceivable that war would ever again scar Europe, so non-European strife was eliminated. France and Britain, which in 1900 were snapping irritably at each other, hastened to settle all differences, and in 1904 signed the *Entente Cordiale*, whereby France recognized Britain's paramountcy in Egypt, and Britain promised to give France a free hand in her conquest of Morocco. Disputes between the two in Siam and off Newfoundland were also settled. Neither power committed itself to helping the other in Europe; but all obstacles to goodwill were removed. A similar agreement was signed between Britain and Russia in 1907: all Asian quarrels, over Persia, Tibet, and Afghanistan, were resolved. Compromise was in the air; conciliation was on the wing. No agreement was sought with Germany, because there was nowhere in Asia or Africa – and indeed nowhere

in Europe – where Anglo-German relations seemed to clash.
Despite the apparent lack of cause for dissension between Britain and Germany, mutual suspicion grew, and by 1912 the public and the press in both countries growled and grimaced at each other as if preparing for war. Yet diplomats on both sides of the North Sea saw no reason for alarm. They knew of no unsolvable problems between the two countries, and were confident that diplomacy, based as it was upon private, unhurried conversation and deliberate compromise, would always prevail. The circulation-boosting vitriol of the press had no place at the conference table. Sometimes an attempt was even made to staunch the flow of popular misconceptions, as when Noel Buxton, a Liberal MP, gave an interview to the *Daily Chronicle* in November 1912, and said:

I want to insist on the fact that there is no essential conflict of interest between the Germans and ourselves. Nowhere is there any conflict over territory. . . . There is ample room in the world for the commercial ambitions of both people.[12]

The widespread belief among politicians and diplomats that Anglo-German friction would never lead to war, and that public chauvinism would never influence governmental policy, lulled those responsible for the political and diplomatic decisions into an unwarranted complacency. Peace was thought to be assured as if by natural law, and not to need any special effort by individuals to guide it. In retrospect, this detachment seems incredible. Churchill captured its atmosphere when in 1923 he described the Agadir crisis of 1911. Germany sought a port on the Atlantic coast of Morocco; France said 'no'; Britain supported France; tension rose, and warning orders were sent out to the Royal Navy:

They sound so very cautious and correct, these deadly words. Soft, quiet voices purring, courteous, grave, exactly-measured phrases in large peaceful rooms. . . . It is nothing. It is less than nothing. It is too foolish, too fantastic to be thought of in the twentieth century. Or is it fire and murder leaping out of the darkness at our throats, torpedoes ripping the bellies of half-awakened ships . . . ? No, it is nothing. No one would do such things. Civilization has climbed above such perils. The interdependence of nations in trade and traffic, the sense of public law, the Hague Convention, Liberal principles, the Labour Party, high finance, Christian charity, common sense have rendered such nightmares impossible. Are you quite sure? It would be a pity to be wrong.[13]

On 4 August 1914, following Germany's invasion of France and Belgium, Britain declared war on Germany. All the confidence born of faith in diplomacy or belief in the impossibility of war between civilized states was destroyed. The impossible had happened: and even at that moment of intense patriotic excitement there were those who asked, in voices choked with sorrow and surprise – why had it happened? Why, despite all the rationalization of a common interest in peace, had the irrational happened? War had long ceased to be the distant glory and momentary thrill of a Blenheim or a Trafalgar; progress and conciliation had seemed to go hand in hand; diplomacy had been geared to compromise, and diplomats had become figures of national importance with an influence ten-fold that of a century before. And yet, with all these safeguards and certainties, war had come. On that day, amidst the anguished cries of 'why?', appeasement was born. Educated people in all walks of life, and of all political beliefs, knew that war between Britain and Germany was a tragic thing, that many lives would be lost, trade disrupted, society disturbed, empires threatened, and the international scene poisoned by hatred and recrimination. They determined that, when peace came, it should never again be broken; that all disputes should be settled without war, and all legitimate aspirations willingly granted.

Appeasement was born in the minds of those who said that the war need never have come, that it was accidental, and that neither Britain nor Germany was more responsible than the other for its onset. It was a determination to prevent by all means a second accidental, 'guiltless' war. Appeasement was created by a lack of confidence in the British case, and a resolve never again to drift or fall unwittingly into war.

CHAPTER 2

War Doubts

The shock of the outbreak of war in 1914 was accentuated by the contrast with the confidence of the previous six years that war with Germany could not take place. Many reasons were put forward as to why the unexpected and the unforeseen had become reality. Those who could convince themselves that German guilt was the cause could support the prosecution of the war with a clear conscience. But where one doubted German guilt, and saw the genesis of the war in any less clear-cut framework, there lay despair for the present, and hope that war could in future be averted by one's own exertions.

Such a desire to adopt a placatory attitude when the war was ended did not necessarily preclude total refusal to support the war once it had begun. Indeed David Lloyd George, who, in 1908, as a Liberal Minister, had declared that Germany meant no mischief for Britain, and who in 1933 gave his then authoritative voice to reinforcing the belief that the war had come by accident, was throughout the war itself one of the Ministers most active in its prosecution, and for its final two years, Prime Minister. He became the arch-appeaser in 1919, and yet, at the same time, was, without any doubt, a patriot.

Those who followed the statements of Liberal Ministers before 1914 would have seen repeated evidence of a desire to come to terms with Germany. Anti-Germanism was never a part of their policy. If any nation angered them, it was Russia, which, by its suppression of an embryo parliamentary system, called forth their suspicion, and by the persecution of Jews roused their disgust. France was considered harmless, even if republican; Turkey decadent; Austria, cumbersome but innocuous. Germany was the country nearest to Liberal approval, linked by ties of royal blood and cultural affinity, part of what was seen as an Anglo-Saxon tradition, young as a nation, ambitious, strident, but not a danger to Britain. If anything, Liberals strove to give Germany their sympathy rather than their suspicion, and Lloyd George expressed a wide-felt sentiment when he said in London in 1908:

Here is Germany in the middle of Europe, with France and Russia on either side, and with a combination of armies greater than hers. . . . Would we not be frightened; would we not build; would we not arm? Of course we should. I want our friends, who think that because Germany is a little frightened she really means mischief to us, to remember that she is frightened for a reason which would frighten us under the same circumstances.[1]

If one believed this to be true in 1908, there was a strong case to be made for it in 1914. Yet the logic of what Lloyd George said was clear: far from deliberately designing war, Germany had been propelled into war by fear. If this were so, what possible justification could there be for taking up arms against her? Those whose thoughts ran along these lines on 4 August 1914 were understandably disturbed when, as the war developed, and became more destructive, German guilt was stressed more and more loudly to justify the terrible nature of events. It was not the defeat of Germany in 1918, nor the severity of peace terms in 1919, which created the first guilty consciences on which appeasement was to grow: it was the outbreak of war.

In 1909 Norman Angell, a journalist who had worked in the United States, France, and Britain, and had been struck in each of these countries by the way in which patriotism and morality were linked in the public mind, published a book in which he stressed, not only that these conflicting patriotisms could not each be moral, but that their outcome, war, whatever its supposed morality, could not enrich or strengthen the countries which were victorious. His book, *The Great Illusion*, was hailed as the most revolutionary work since Darwin's *Origin of Species*. If war could not be profitable, the armaments race became futile, yet the rapidly increasing size of armies and navies was being pointed to on both sides of the North Sea as making war inevitable; there were no radical differences between European states to make war necessary, only a phenomenon arising from individual behaviour – 'I never noticed his collars were dirty till he got in my way'.

Co-operation, not war, led to riches; it was not the clash of empires but their development which led to imperial growth; it was not the confrontation of men taught to hate and to kill one another, but the long, slow, careful search for every possible sphere of joint-interest and joint action which led to the advance of welfare, learning, and human values.

Angell did not say that war was impossible; only that it was an absurdity on every conceivable ground, economic, political, national, and moral. If men could learn the lesson he was trying to teach, they might then abandon the idea of using war as an instrument of policy. The realization that this simple, yet seemingly foolproof line of reasoning had not been heeded, led after 1914 to a determination not to neglect it again. When, in 1918, it was clear that the war had destroyed on a massive scale, and that it would present a legacy of bitterness to succeeding generations, Angell's warnings were read again, and taken more to heart. If war could not pay, it should be avoided; if it brought devastation irrespective of the moral fervour of its combatants, it should be shunned; if it was the worst of all means of satisfying national ambition, it should be abandoned as a method of gaining national ends.

On 16 July 1914 Norman Angell, at a meeting in a private house, addressed a group of men and women in their twenties. He stressed the conflict between war and social reform, emphasizing how war could hold up, and even prevent, the development of a more egalitarian society. 'If you are to duplicate indefinitely international history as men have so far written it,' he said, 'all your own constructive labours will one day go up in the smoke of some grand military bonfire.' Angell believed that those to whom he was speaking were 'increasingly determined not to be the victims of that supreme futility'.[2] Within three weeks they were its victims. But his words had begun to make their mark, and his ideas, even while war, and the passions of war raged fiercely, began to trouble people's consciences.

Immediately before the outbreak of war, a gasp of astonishment arose in Liberal England. Were the social achievements of 1906–14, England's most intensive period of reform, to be jeopardized by the need to concentrate everything on war; was Irish Home Rule, now so nearly achieved after over thirty years of ever-mounting bitterness, to be postponed; were millions of imperial subjects to be asked to shed their blood in a European quarrel which might seem no cause of theirs? Writing to the *Daily News* on 3 August 1914, Gilbert Murray, Professor of Greek at Oxford, and an exponent of the liberal view, declared that he was confident that the Government would prevent England becoming involved in the war, while G. M. Trevelyan, the Cambridge historian, stressed that

... the ultimate danger must come from Russia. . . . I suggest that we should look both foolish and criminal if we now ruined our own civilization in order to help Russia more completely to ruin the kindred civilization of Germany.

Numerous pamphlets, particularly from the Independent Labour Party, urged neutrality. A wide range of arguments was mustered, which, in less hysterical times, would have commanded wide attention.[3] One said that, in helping Russia to defeat Germany, Britain would make Russia the dominant military power of Europe, 'possibly the dictator both in this Continent and in Asia'; that Britain had last gone to war in Europe to check Russia, and was now prepared to further Russian ambitions; that the Anglo-French *Entente* 'was certainly never intended by the British nation as a war alliance, but as an expression of goodwill', and that if war broke out, and Britain were involved, it would be impossible for London to remain the financial capital of the world, so that this inestimable advantage would be transferred, 'perhaps permanently ... to the other side of the Atlantic'. In another broadsheet the war was described as a plot by 'small but powerful cliques' whose economic interests were thought to lie in the stimulus war would give to armaments; it was the brain-child of a handful of Ministers who had deliberately set out to isolate and antagonize Germany, and who had created a powerful navy with the purpose of crushing Germany's legitimate imperial aspirations. One pamphlet asked bluntly:

Which is the greater peril to this country, 65 million civilized Germans, of our own race and blood, mainly engaged in trade and industry and peaceful occupations, or 140 million Russians, the slaves of a corrupt autocracy, and trained to the use of force alone?

Again and again, Anglo-German similarities were stressed. Britain had never fought Germany; Germany, like Britain, depended for her survival and prosperity upon a commercial and industrial life which war would throw into chaos; the Germans were 'racially allied to ourselves and with moral ideas largely resembling our own'. Finally, if these claims were unconvincing, there was a further appeal produced at the very last moment, after Germany had invaded Belgium, a curious mixture of expediency and morality:

> If Great Britain refrains from wasting her resources during the war and is the one great European power that remains unexhausted by the drain of war, she will be at the close in the best position to exercise her influence for the protection of Belgian interests; to see that justice is done and to act as arbiter in the general interest.

These arguments were of no avail. War fever swept the nation. It could not be controlled. But the doubts which the pamphlets put into words did not dissolve. Men brooded upon them, and continued to assert them, with growing confidence and conviction. Throughout the war the doubters denied that Germany was solely responsible for its onset, and strove to establish that Britain bore a large part of the burden of responsibility.

The first challenge to the popularly accepted view of the responsibility for the war came from Horatio Bottomley, who, for the rest of the war, led the anti-German publicists with unrivalled virulence. In the first week of the war, in his newspaper *John Bull*, he expressed strong doubts about the propriety of going to war.

On 11 July 1914 he claimed that he had documentary proof that the Serbian secret police had planned the murder of the Archduke Francis Ferdinand, and that Austria was right to take revenge. On 8 August, when Britain was already at war with Germany as a result of the chain of events leading from that murder, he reiterated his slogan in the headline: TO HELL WITH SERBIA, and he asked his readers: 'Why should Britain shed her blood to save a nation of assassins?' He concluded on a more profound note, one which he himself at once abandoned, but which others soon took up with strong conviction: 'It has been the doubtful diplomatic policy,' he wrote, 'of entering into continental alliances and understandings which has placed us in our present difficulty. . . . Let us hope when the crisis is over a saner view of our policy may prevail.'[4]

Immediately after the outbreak of war a Cambridge graduate of twenty-five challenged the basic concept of German guilt, in a speech which was published with the provocative title: *Is Germany Right and Britain Wrong*? Clifford Allen was a Socialist. He refused to believe that the failure of International Socialism to halt war meant that working-class solidarity was a myth. He believed that the war would finally expose the wickedness of capitalists who wished to use the war to create a sense of unity between classes whose interests were dissimilar and who, but for the war, were bound to be thrown against each other in violent conflict. 'War fills their pockets', he said bitterly. Such passions were part of a widespread socialist mood; just before the war H. N. Brailsford, in his outspoken book *The War of Steel and Gold*, suggested that if armaments firms were state-controlled the personal profit motive would be destroyed at a stroke and capitalists would have to turn to something more constructive for their profits. But Allen's pamphlet had a novel aspect. While his fellow-socialists were working themselves into a frenzy of anti-Germanism, with denunciations of German aggression, German atrocities and German territorial ambitions, Allen urged his readers to try to understand the German point of view. The Germans, he said, were 'encircled on all sides by great nations', one of whom, 'the great overpowering, sinister, tyrannous, ever-growing Russia' was Britain's ally. Not only did Germany need to defend herself against France and Russia but, Allen said, 'a man with his back to the wall has sometimes to break out upon his foes'. It was Britain, he claimed, which had ranged Europe into two camps; Britain which had excluded Germany from worthwhile imperial territory; Britain which had 'inspired the armaments race'; Britain which had used the German invasion of Belgium as an excuse to declare a war which she had always intended to fight; and it was Britain which, now war had begun, was maligning the German genius and inventing 'foul slanders' about German atrocities.[5]

Allen's doubts made some appeal. The change from peace to war had come too quickly for the imputation of Germany's sole guilt to be fully believed. Until June 1914 relations with Germany, shaken in 1906 and 1911 over Morocco, were improving. Politicians worried about Ireland, not Germany. In January 1914 Churchill's desire to spend more money on the Navy had split the Cabinet, and Ministers threatened to resign unless the Naval budget were reduced. Britain had sought no quarrel with Germany; the German government had hoped that Britain would remain neutral if France were attacked, even if, to make the attack on France more effective, Belgian neutrality were breached. It was

Gladstone who said, speaking of the guarantee to Belgium: 'I am not able to subscribe to the doctrine . . . that the simple fact of the existence of a guarantee is binding on every party to it, irrespective altogether of the particular position in which it will find itself when the occasion for acting on the guarantee arises.'

Liberals had never sought alliances which might commit them, in advance, to wars which arose from causes they had been unable to foresee or control, against nations towards whom they had no hatred. There were many who felt it wrong that Britain, which had avoided, despite French pressure, a formal alliance with France, was now, by the accident of a treaty 44 years old, in fact joining France as an ally against Germany. Even those who wished to uphold the obligation to Belgium were not overly anxious to commit themselves even more fully to France by the same action. The Treaty with France and Germany over Belgium included the clause that the Queen 'does not engage herself by this Treaty to take part in any of the general operations of the war beyond the limits of Belgium'. This was a clear pledge to help in the defence of Brussels or Antwerp, but not to rush to defend the line of the Somme or the Marne. Throughout the war there was great admiration for 'brave Belgium'; Churchill's sudden journey to Antwerp to supervise its defence was among the most dramatic moments of his career, and of the war: but for France there was less enthusiasm, less sense of debt. In *Goodbye to All That*, Robert Graves wrote of how anti-French feeling among the troops amounted 'almost to an obsession' by the time the war was over, and Colin Coote has recorded how the outbreak of war 'demanded a tremendous upset of traditional sympathies to transfer national dislikes from the French to the Germans'.[6]

Doubts as to Germany's exclusive guilt were strengthened by suspicion of France and Russia. E. D. Morel, a former shipping-office clerk who, together with Roger Casement, made his name by helping to expose the regime of terror in King Leopold's Congo, became the most prolific publicist of anti-Russian and anti-French opinion. In his letter of resignation to the Birkenhead Liberal Association two months after the outbreak of war, he wrote:

Germany is not peculiar in possessing a politico-militarist school whose influence is pestilential . . . we heard of Machiavelli before we heard of Nietzsche. Our Foreign Policy . . . has been fettered by a naval and military understanding which bound us to the side, not of France alone, but to that of Russia .... We had sacrificed our neutrality in advance by commitments secret and unsanctioned.[7]

Morel reiterated this theme throughout the war. He was even imprisoned for six months for sending one of his pamphlets to neutral Switzerland, in contravention of wartime legislation.[8] He argued that all alliances were wicked, and that our own secret commitment to enter into military talks with France in 1906 was the key to the origin of the war. By encouraging France to believe that Britain was her ally we gave her, said Morel, an interest in disturbing the peace of Europe, and, with the balance of power thus tilted in her favour, of avenging the defeat of the Franco-Prussian War. Morel claimed his argument was not emotional. It was based upon 'documentary evidence' – hence the strength of its appeal. He searched Hansard, and found 'evidence' of the government deceiving parliament over the nature of its commitment to France; he combed the diplomatic white papers, and produced 'proof' of French aggressive intentions. Through the Union of Democratic Control he sought to influence the Labour Party to his way of thinking: fair-play to Germany, suspicion of France; opposition to all armaments, support for post-war 'harmony' among all nations, whatever their part in the war. Among those who accepted Morel's arguments during the war were Norman Angell, Brailsford, and the philosopher Bertrand Russell, who had been deprived of his Cambridge fellowship on account of his outspoken hostility to war.

These intellectual doubts were not confined to publicists and pamphleteers. The Liberal Cabinet was divided over the need to go to war. Two Ministers, John Burns and Lord Morley resigned, rather than accept responsibility for the ultimatum to Germany. John Burns was the first Labour representative to sit in a British Cabinet. He felt that, as Britain was not formally allied to France, it should not act as if it were, for this would clearly be a challenge to Germans, an encirclement which they would be justified in resisting. Morley was a Liberal in the Bright and Cobden tradition – he had written a biography of Cobden – and had been a consistent opponent of armaments and alliances. He feared also the emergence of a strong Russia, and reminded the Cabinet that 'Germany is unpopular in England, but Russia is more unpopular still. And people will rub their eyes when they realize that Cossacks are their victorious fellow-champions for Freedom, Justice,

B

Equality of Man (especially Jew man) and respect for treaties. . . .'⁹
After long debate the Cabinet rejected Morley's arguments. When, in 1928, he published his *Memorandum on Resignation*, he revealed a deeper anguish than one born solely of a traditional dislike for commitment and involvement. Of the day before his resignation he wrote:

> What grounds for expecting that the ruinous waste and havoc of war would be repaid by peace on better terms than were already within reach of reason and persistent patience? When we counted our gains, what would they amount to, when reckoned against the ferocious hatred that would burn with inextinguishable fire, for a whole generation at least, between two great communities better fitted to understand one another than any other pair in Europe? This moral devastation is a worse incident of war even than human carnage, and all the other curses with which war lashes its victims and its dupes.[10]

Arguments based upon a sense of tradition, or upon documents, or upon the suspicion that diplomats had bungled, were not capable of a mass appeal. They certainly provided the material for a sustained intellectual assault upon anti-Germanism, but their market was limited. Even the appearance of Norman Angell, E. D. Morel, Clifford Allen, or Bertrand Russell on public platforms, and their versatile switch from written to spoken protest, reached only a small audience. Nor did the extremes of which they were at times capable help their cause. Thus Russell was cast into derision, as well as into prison, for his absurd, but sincerely held belief that American troops had been brought into the war, not merely to defeat German militarism in the trenches, but also to suppress working class discontent in England.[11] Such claims, however seriously put forward and however cogently argued, could not shock the conscience of a whole nation. It was the impact of the war itself that most disturbed the minds of patriotic men. It was the realization of the horror of war that caused men and women to question the basic beliefs upon which their support for the war, and their hostility to Germany, had been based.

This impact was vividly expressed by the poems of the war. The poems published initially, to stimulate patriotism, in *The Times* and the *Daily Express*, were poems of crude hate and derision. For six months a spate of vitriolic verse made its way into the newspapers. Not only the Germans, but also Englishmen who refused to volunteer on the grounds of a conscientious objection to war, were the object of poetic spleen. This Englishman with a conscience was singled out for insult by the popular poet, Francis Coutts, in his poem *A Preacher of Peace and Reconciliation*:

> Why do we suffer this traitor? Why
>   Suffer this gas-bag to pollute the air
>   And take poor lads and weaklings unaware?
> He is more noisome than the meanest spy
> Shot at the Tower, who dared at least to die
>   In service of his country; but no care
>   Has this man for his Motherland; why spare
> Cowards who propagate a treasonous lie?[12]

While poets in England could write of reconciliation as a treasonous lie, and find a market for their insensitivity and scorn, poets in the battle zones sought to come to terms with the slaughter in a more mature manner. They made an effort, neither forced nor shallow, to give a meaning to the ugliness and impersonal death-dealing of war. Thus Rupert Brooke could write in his sonnet *Peace*:

> Now, God be thanked Who has matched us with His hour,
>   And caught our youth, and wakened us from sleeping,
> With hand made sure, clear eye and sharpened power,
>   To turn, as swimmers into cleanness leaping,
> Glad from a world grown old and cold and weary....[13]

and in *The Dead*:

> Blow out, you bugles, over the rich Dead!
>   There's none of these so lonely and poor of old,
> But, dying, has made us rarer gifts than gold....
>
> Honour has come back, as a king, to earth,
>   And paid his subjects with a royal wage;
> And Nobleness walks in our ways again;
>   And we have come into our heritage.[14]

These heroic sentiments were sincere; answers to an urgent need to allay doubt and hesitation, and to show that there was a second side to war. They were not an attempt to gild war itself, but to find something golden among the dross. But as the war continued, as the casualty lists grew longer, as the number of homes from whom a son or husband or brother had been taken for ever, grew larger, the atmosphere of exaltation came to an end. The emotions could not take a surfeit of heroism. The growing doubts as to the rights and wrongs of the warring nations began to overshadow the early confidence in the sanctity of the British cause. More and more poems reflected these doubts, and spread them. Most outspoken were the poems of Charles Sorley, who served for five months in the trenches, before he was killed during the Battle of Loos in October 1915.

Sorley, who had spent the summer of 1914 in Germany, having left Marlborough and before intending to take up his scholarship to Oxford, refused to accept the view that Germany, the guilty nation, was being punished for her crimes by the innocent, God-blessed Britain. He commented wryly in September 1914 that justice was 'looked upon merely as an agent for winning battles.'[15] For him the central theme of the war was a tragic, not a noble one. Whereas for Brooke death was a transformation into 'a white unbroken glory', for Sorley it was 'no triumph . . . only an empty pail, a slate rubbed clean'. Sorley consciously rejected Brooke's enthusiasm. He was unable to put into his poems any assertions of death made noble by its association with national honour or a 'righteous' cause: for him questions of national honour were 'childish and primitive'. In his sonnet, *To Germany*, he introduced a plea for magnanimity towards the enemy. He looked on Germany, not as a sinner, but as a victim, needing, not abuse, but sympathy:

> You are blind like us. Your hurt no man designed,
> And no man claimed the conquest of your land.
> But gropers both through fields of thought confined
> We stumble and we do not understand.
> You only saw your future bigly planned,
> And we, the tapering paths of our own mind,
> And in each other's dearest ways we stand,
> And hiss and hate. And the blind fight the blind.[16]

Four years of war obliterated the romantic view of death. The trenches were squalid and stank; mechanically, the machine-gun mowed down line upon line of advancing men, tipping them into the mud; explosive shells turned quiet trenches into an acrid chaos of broken bodies; poison gas destroyed throats and lungs; disease and madness harvested their own crop. From the Channel to the

Vosges an almost static line of trenches drew nearly a million Englishmen to their death. Conscription replaced the voluntary system; every man available was dispatched to France.

The popular songs of 1914, with their optimistic lilt and supercilious smugness gave way, by 1916, to harsh songs filled with disillusion.[17] The four years of unrelenting horror wiped away the initial exuberance. The great battles of the past – Blenheim, Quebec, Trafalgar, Waterloo – had each become the focal point of stirring, exciting, sentimental sagas, of schoolboy romances and songs sung by timid children to visiting relatives. No such tradition sprang from Aubers Ridge, Loos, Passchendaele, or Ypres; and schoolboys of the nineteen-thirties, as of the nineteen-fifties, turned back to Byron for their poetry readings, and charged with the cavalry at Waterloo. The First World War found its chronicler in Siegfried Sassoon, whose volume *Counter-Attack* was published in the last year of the war, and whose poems explain why those who survived the war were determined that such a nightmare must never again burst upon men's minds:

> Lines of grey, muttering faces, marked with fear,
> They leave their trenches, going over the top,
> While time ticks blank and busy on their wrists,
> And hope, with furtive eyes and grappling fists,
> Flounders in mud. O Jesus, make it stop![18]

It was Neville Chamberlain's cousin Norman who, shortly before he was killed in France, set out what he hoped would be the message of the war, in a letter home; and the advice he gave no doubt impressed itself upon Neville Chamberlain's mind, for he published it after the war in a privately printed memoir of his cousin. 'Nothing but immeasurable improvements,' wrote Norman Chamberlain, 'will ever justify all the waste and unfairness of this war – I only hope that those who are left will *never, never* forget at what sacrifice those improvements have been won.'[19] This message made its mark in countless homes. It was not only the men who had been in the trenches who fled from the idea of a second war; it was the widows and mothers of those who had been killed.

War Guilt

The war created two quite distinct areas of doubt in the public mind. Its sudden onset, and the feverish circulation of anti-German propaganda, caused some people to wonder whether Germany had really been so wicked. The actual fighting, being so brutal, created, both among those who had fought and those who had stayed at home, a loathing of war itself unique in British history. These two doubts coalesced. If Germany had not been solely responsible for the war – if, indeed, the war had come, not by anyone's design, but by a series of accidents, surely the price of victory had been too high? If the war was not in fact a crusade of ideas of liberty against those of alien domination, was not the prolonged agony unnecessary, and would not the fairest answer once peace were assured be a peace treaty moderate in its demands and conciliatory in its tone? By the first months of 1919 the answer to all these questions seemed, to more and more people, to be 'yes': the intensity of the war had been a mistake; the sense of moral righteousness had been greatly exaggerated; the Germans ought now to be treated as friends, with whose co-operation a more lasting peace could be established, whose genius could flourish once again, in joint-enterprises rather than competition, and whose own desire to see their dead as heroes should not be upset by any insistence that the cause for which they had died was a wicked one.

Yet the Treaty of Versailles was not only severe in its demands; of greater consequence was the justification of its severity by a clause which was interpreted throughout Europe as an assertion of German guilt. Article 231 read:

The Allied and Associated Governments affirm and Germany accepts the responsibility of Germany and her allies for causing all the loss and damage to which the Allied and Associated Governments and their nationals have been subjected as a consequence of the war imposed upon them by the aggression of Germany and her allies.

This clause was at once seized upon by people in Germany as an intolerable insult to the German people. In England also there were people who felt uneasy about it. It charged the whole German nation with aggression; a nation which, it was pointed out, had repudiated its Kaiser and established a parliamentary democracy. Surely it was not intended to keep in front of a reformed Germany the spectre of Justice pointing an accusing finger? Two years before, on 22 January 1917, President Wilson told the United States' Senate:

It must be a peace without victory.... Victory would mean peace forced upon the loser, a victor's terms imposed upon the vanquished. It would be accepted in humiliation, under duress, at an intolerable sacrifice, and would leave a sting, a resentment, a bitter memory upon which terms of peace would rest, not permanently, but only as upon a quicksand. Only a peace between equals can last.[1]

These prophetic precepts were forgotten at the moment when they were most needed. Stung by the accusation of aggression, the German Foreign Office set up a special section whose task was to challenge the imputation of German guilt. Historians were encouraged to do research into the origins of the war. In 1923, during the height of the inflation, the War-Guilt Section, or Kriegsschuldreferat, was able to find the money to launch a periodical, the Kriegsschuldfrage, or War-Guilt Question, edited by an ex-army officer, Alfred von Wegerer, who, though posing as an independent editor, was actually employed by the German Foreign Office.[2] The periodical gave prominence to all evidence pointing to Russian, French, British, and even Serbian 'responsibility' for the war. The documents to which it gave prominence quickly found their way into the historical works of British historians who, from 1919, tended to be more and more critical of the British case. A book by a Serbian diplomat, Boghitschewitsch, *Causes of the War*, which gave 'evidence' of Serb complicity in the murder of the Archduke, was used by E. D. Morel as one of the bases for his refutation of German guilt in his three polemics, *Pre-War Diplomacy* (1920), *Diplomacy Revealed* (1921) and *The Poison that Destroys* (1922). In 1919 the German Minister in Berne had

arranged with the German Foreign Ministry for the payment of
Boghitschewitsch in gold francs, hardly a currency the German
Government could afford to distribute promiscuously in 1919.
The German Minister explained that Boghitschewitsch had not
even enough money to buy himself a new suit. For ten years he was
financed from Berlin, publishing between 1928 and 1931 a three-
volume documentary study of Serb 'duplicity', *Die Auswärtige
Politik Serbiens*, in which Serbia emerged as the tool of Tsarist
Russia, upon whose shoulders Boghitschewitsch put 'the largest
measure of responsibility for the war'.

Although Morel, like Boghitschewitsch, blamed Russia for
manipulating France, he felt that Grey bore a large part of the
responsibility because of Britain's commitments to France. It was
Grey who, according to Morel, had linked Britain with a European
power searching for revenge against Germany; Grey who, by
initiating Anglo-French military talks in 1906, gave both France
and Russia an essential ally, whose control of the seas was essential
to blockade and starve Germany and without whose support they
would not have been able to go to war; Grey who, by not revealing
Britain's commitments until the week before the outbreak of war,
deceived the British people, and turned them against a Germany
with whom they had no cause to quarrel and whose interests, both
European and imperial, in no way conflicted with their own. For
E. D. Morel 'war-guilt' for an Anglo-German war lay not with
Germany, but with Grey.

Even where the charge of guilt was made specifically against the
Kaiser, voices in England protested vigorously. The Kaiser had
fled to Holland, and would not leave; the Dutch Government
refused to force him out. The British Government put on an air
of enraged indignation, and the Dutch were given the clear impression that unless the Kaiser were handed over to them for trial
'the Allies might oppose the admission of Holland to the League
of Nations'.[3] But the emotions of war could not be kept at fever
pitch once war had ended, and these diplomatic threats, coming
fifteen months after the armistice, failed to make the impression
intended. The Kaiser was allowed to remain in Holland, and more
and more Englishmen grew ashamed that, in November 1918, the
cry 'Hang the Kaiser!' had been so loud.

The idea of laying all the responsibility for the war at Germany's
door had many drawbacks. Social unrest was leading to violence

throughout Europe, and communism, already well-established in Russia, despite Allied efforts to crush it, threatened to spread westwards. Germany was an obvious target; and if the German people were humiliated by Allied taunts of guilt, might they not be attracted to communism? This very argument was used in 1924 by a group of distinguished Germans who, in seeking British friendship, wrote, in a somewhat ominous tone:

> The German people unanimously repudiate the moral stigma of a criminal nation which in 1919 they were forced under duress to admit.
> The British people are, more than any other, in a position to check the anarchy and chaos of Europe. The fundamental condition for a sane reconstruction of European affairs is Justice to Germany.[4]

Among those signing this appeal were two industrialists, Robert Bosch and Carl von Siemens, the historian Erich Brandenburg, Hjalmar Schacht, President of the Reichsbank, and Thomas Mann, the novelist.

This, and similar appeals, found sympathetic hearers in England. In August 1925, Gilbert Murray could write without too much exaggeration to a German correspondent that 'hardly any reasonable person in England continues to talk of Germany as solely responsible for the war'; but he rebuked those in Germany who were writing books and pamphlets claiming that Britain, France, and Russia had themselves deliberately caused the war, for, wrote Murray, these writings 'will re-awaken all the old hatreds which we hoped were dying out'.[5] Yet it was only eight years since the war had ended. The Treaty of Versailles was still the instrument whereby Germany's actions were controlled and circumscribed; and Article 231, known as the 'War-Guilt clause', was still there. No effort had been made to alter or expunge it, and it remained in the Treaty after Germany's entry into the League of Nations in 1925.

Between 1925 and 1933 the cloud of war-guilt hung heavily over Anglo-German reconciliation. Englishmen visiting Germany could not help being struck by the German sensitivity on this point. It almost seemed as if, with the repudiation of war-guilt, international harmony would return. Some saw that the iron of this accusation had entered too deeply into the German soul, and had struck too forcefully at German pride, for mere cancellation of a five-line clause to change the course of European history. But in a decade when every possible solution to the rift between Britain and Germany offered itself for experiment, the obliteration of the war-guilt clause seemed well worth attempting, even if it could only be done on paper, and not in the mind. At the time, these differences were obscured: many people hoped that an open assertion of equal responsibility would be enough, and that words could alter the mood of Germany.

A full-scale attempt to alter the historical perspectives of 1914 came, in 1928, from Edith Durham. In her book, *The Sarajevo Crime*, she sought to prove that Pashitch, the Serbian Prime Minister, and his Government, had known of, and approved, the murder of the Archduke; that Austria's desire to punish Serbia was thus well-founded; and that for Britain to have become involved in a war aimed at chastising Austria was clearly absurd. By the use of documents and memoirs she seemed to point the finger of accusation at Serbia so completely, that a reader of her book might well ask why Britain had not intervened on behalf of Austria, rather than against her. Miss Durham's sincerity was beyond doubt, nor is there evidence to suggest that she was anything but an independent searcher for truth. As she wrote to a friend while her book was being finished:

> We know enough to nail the guilt absolutely to the Serb govt., which could have stopped the murder first. And afterwards could have arrested the criminals. . . . Think of the millions who died to save Pashitch and Co from the punishment they so richly deserved – & still deserve.[6]

If Germany were guiltless; if German involvement in the war was, like Britain's, part of a chain reaction, set off, according to Miss Durham by Serbia, according to E. D. Morel by Britain, France, and Russia, the only mental block to feeling a sense of brotherly love towards Germany was the knowledge of alleged German atrocities during the war, particularly in Belgium. Every Englishman had heard of Belgian babies who had had their hands cut off by German soldiers. To refute these beliefs Arthur Ponsonby, a former Liberal MP who had joined the Labour Party in 1918, published a short book in 1927, *Falsehood in Wartime*, which examined the best known German atrocity stories, and showed them to be allied propaganda, designed to stir up anti-German feeling. A chapter of the book was devoted to 'Germany's sole responsibility for the war', and by a judicious use of quotations showed how, during the war, Germany's guilt had been asserted and emphasized as a deliberate matter of policy. Ponsonby's conclusion was that:

None of the heroes prepared for suffering and sacrifice, none of the common herd ready for service and obedience, will be inclined to listen to the call of their country once they discover the polluted sources from whence that call proceeds and recognize the monstrous finger of falsehood which beckons them to the battlefield.[7]

A number of historical works abandoned altogether the idea of ascribing war-guilt to any one power or group of powers. Most important of these was G. Lowes Dickinson's *The International Anarchy*, which established itself as an important text book soon after its publication in 1926. He rebuked historians for concentrating upon 'the superficial occasions out of which this or that war happened to arise' and promised that he would seek 'the fundamental conditions which make war inevitable'. These conditions he described, not as the ambition of a particular nation or the duplicity of a particular group of people, but as pressures built up by armaments, public opinion, the press, considerations of national honour, and expansionist ambitions, all of which factors were present in all powerful states simultaneously, the result being an international anarchy leading to war. The anarchy was only possible, he thought, because individuals were gullible; because they allowed policies to be pursued 'in the dark by a very few men who, because they act secretly, cannot act honestly', and because they allowed the press to arouse 'primitive passions' in the public mind. The British Government in particular seemed to him to have played falsely with its people; to have accused Germany of seeking territorial aggrandizement, while itself using the war to make great increases in its territory; to have created secretly commitments to France 'which were like a suction pipe to draw her, whether she would or no, into the war'; and to have allowed the artificial and dangerous concept of the balance of power to create a situation in which Englishmen 'had become more afraid of Germany than of our traditional enemies, France and Russia'.

In 1928 H. W. Wilson, an expert on Naval Affairs, tried to reverse the ever-mounting denials of German war-guilt, and to show how much of Britain's sympathy was the result of systematic German propaganda designed to prove German innocence and thereby to obtain a revision of the Versailles Treaty. He was particularly critical of the validity of Miss Durham's 'revelations'. But whereas Lowes Dickinson's *International Anarchy* was quickly taken up in schools and universities, Wilson's *War Guilt*, although an important book, was ignored. People were not interested in a justification of attitudes which they regarded as outmoded.

In 1932 the Oxford University Press published a study of pre-war British policy by T. P. Conwell-Evans. His book, *Foreign Policy from a Back Bench*, was based upon the private papers of Lord Noel-Buxton and showed clearly the doubts that had existed in informed minds as to the wisdom of Grey's foreign policy. The book's use of documents marked it out as a serious contribution to the war-guilt controversy. Conwell-Evans chose extracts long enough not to admit of misinterpretation, and he set them in a context, which by 1932 was becoming increasingly familiar, of British responsibility. Conwell-Evans noted with sorrow that before 1914 those Englishmen 'who worked for an appeasement of the European situation, failed to arouse from the nation a deep seated response'; he felt that had Grey's secrecy been discovered 'the position would have been entirely changed and the country could have been effectively warned'.

He explored Grey's lack of knowledge of Germany, and what Haldane, in his *Autobiography*, published in 1929, showed to be the anti-German bias of Grey's advisers.

These historical studies were a plea for a rational discussion of the origins of the war. They were also attempts to free inter-war policy from any attachment to a belief in German war-guilt. Only by Englishmen getting away from what Conwell-Evans called 'a narrow patriotism harmful to itself' could Germany be treated fairly, and European diplomacy work in a just and unembittered manner. Adding their voices to the denunciation of Germany's sole responsibility were two politicians who had both written histories of the outbreak of the war; Churchill, in three volumes of *The World Crisis*, stressed as Lowes Dickinson had done, the anarchic nature of pre-war politics, ascribing much responsibility for the war to 'the mechanical processes of mobilization and the outburst of national fervour and excitement'. He felt that the Austrian ultimatum to Serbia had 'fired the train which led to a mine loaded by the vice and virtue of half a century' and that 'the flame ate remorselessly along the fuse'.[8] As one of the Cabinet Ministers who had opposed hanging the Kaiser, Churchill re-affirmed his belief that the Kaiser was in the grip of circumstances beyond his control – that what he had wanted was 'a great Diplomatic triumph without a shot fired'; that all he wished 'was to feel like Napoleon, and be like him without having had to fight his battles'.[9] But it was Lloyd George who delivered the most decisive blow to the war guilt clause. In his *War Memoirs*, published in 1933, and written with full access to the documents of his premiership and the Peace Treaties, he fell severely upon Grey – 'a pilot whose hand trembled in the palsy of apprehension, unable to grip the levers and manipulate them with a firm and clear purpose' – and was convinced that had Grey 'warned Germany in time of the point at which Britain would declare war . . . the issue would have been different'.[10] Lloyd George's conclusion reinforced the growing belief that war between Britain and Germany had been a mistake, that Germany ought in no way to suffer because of old-fashioned feelings that she had been responsible, and that between the two nations there was no traditional or historical reason why they should not co-operate and combine constructively for the benefit of each other, and of Europe, for, he wrote:

I am convinced after a careful perusal of all the documents available on all sides that the Kaiser never had the remotest idea that he was plunging – or being plunged – into a European war. . . . He was not anticipating a costly war but a cheap diplomatic triumph. . . .
The negotiations were botched by everybody engaged in directing them. It is incredible that so momentous an issue should have been handled in so unbusinesslike and casual a manner. When a collision seemed inevitable, engine drivers and signalmen lost their heads and pulled the wrong levers. . . . Had it been a matter of a railway strike, the two sides would have conferred before proceeding to extremities. War ought to have been, and could have been averted.[11]

Appeasement in the 1920s and 1930s was an attitude of mind based upon both the realization of the horrors of war, and upon a reluctance to lay the responsibility for those horrors at Germany's door. From these two premises, it was possible to find both a moral and an intellectual justification for seeking close Anglo-German co-operation, and for trying to use such co-operation as the basis for a viable European settlement.

Among those who sought such co-operation was Lord Lothian who, as Philip Kerr, was one of Lloyd George's assistants during the war, and had given Lloyd George important help in drafting the Treaty of Versailles.

Lothian became more and more convinced during the 1920s that the Treaty, and in particular, Article 231, was the obstacle which prevented an Anglo-German rapprochement. As the political chaos in Germany intensified, and as the Nazi movement gained adherents, and denounced the Versailles 'Diktat', Lothian's conviction was strengthened. By 1935 he was writing, to politicians and the press, letters like the following one to the *Manchester Guardian:* 'National Socialism in its brutal aspects both at home and abroad, is in considerable measure due to the fact that her neighbours were not able to make peaceful revisions in the treaties as war passions died down.'[12]

Lothian was puzzled by the War Guilt clause; how could something, which in the retrospect of a decade was clearly the source of bitterness and misunderstanding, have been inserted into the strictly economic part of the Treaty. When he was asked by a friend about the origin of the clause he decided to make inquiries for himself, and contacted a civil servant who had been at the Paris Peace Conference and had, presumably, kept some of the records with him. The civil servant consulted his files. It appeared that the clause had had its origin before the end of the war. The Supreme War Council, meeting under the leadership of Clemenceau and Lloyd George at Versailles on 4 November 1918, had drafted a note to President Wilson, explaining to him the need for reparations from Germany. The note began: 'They (the Allied Governments) understand that compensation will be made by Germany for all damage caused to the civilian population of the Allies by the invasion by Germany of Allied territory. . . .'[13]

As Germany had never denied invading Belgium, Luxembourg, or France, this clause was a fair one: a statement of acknowledged fact. But someone at the meeting pointed out that as the clause stood, while Germany would have to pay for damage done from the Channel to the Vosges, there was nothing in this wording to enable any economic compensation to go to the non-continental allies, the USA, India, Australia, Canada, or even Britain, and that certainly the Dominions, who had played such a large part, not only in providing men but also materials, would resent their exclusion from money payments. The clause would therefore need re-drafting. The new draft cut out 'the invasion by Germany of Allied territory' and replaced it by 'the aggression of Germany'. Aggression was a word that could cover a much wider sphere: it could be claimed that every aspect of war costs was involved. But it was also a condemnatory word. Invasion had been admitted; aggression had not. The justification in German eyes for the invasion was self-defence; aggression was a word pregnant with moral disapproval, allowing of no subtle interpretation; spelling, all too clearly, guilt.

Lothian was surprised to learn of the change in the draft, with all that it entailed, and asked the civil servant whose idea the word 'aggression' had been. The civil servant again consulted his files, and replied: 'the alteration was made by you. It is in your handwriting.'

Lothian's memory, once jogged, was restored, and a year later, in 1931, writing to a South African historian, he explained precisely how the clause had come to be written: a clause to whose revision he was now both politically and personally committed.

I remember very distinctly discussing with L. G. the interpretation to be put upon the question of 'restoration' or 'reparations'. His view was – 'We must make it clear that we cannot charge Germany with the costs of the war. . . . She could not possibly pay it. But she must pay ample compensation for damage and that compensation must be equitably distributed among the Allies and not given entirely to France and Belgium. Devastated areas is only one item in war loss. Great Britain has probably spent more money on the war and incurred greater indirect losses in, for instance, shipping and trade, than France. She must have her fair share of the compensation.'

He then instructed me to prepare a form of words. . . . I did so. . . . I remember thinking, after the draft had been taken by L.G., that it did not cover adequately the point that compensation was due to all the Allies. . . . I therefore revised it to read 'damage to the civilian population of the allies by the aggression of Germany by land, air and sea.'[14]

Thus was written the clause which most aggravated Anglo-German relations between the wars, made the task of appeasement with Germany so difficult, and made the Germans feel that, whatever concessions Britain made, whatever gestures of friendship she volunteered, in reality her policy was dictated by an explicit belief in German guilt.

CHAPTER 4

The Elusive Peace

For four years all English aspirations concentrated on victory. Peace meant the ending of hostilities, and a chance to rest from the mutual slaughter. Yet there were always those who saw that peace would bring problems of its own, which would not be solved merely by the euphoria of victory. Anyone who felt that the coming of war had been a blunder, a mistake which careful diplomacy could have avoided, hoped for a lenient peace treaty with Germany. If Germany were only an 'accidental' enemy it would clearly be wrong to perpetuate the bitterness of war in a punitive treaty. It would be equally wrong, if it was for Belgium's defence alone that Britain had gone to war, to demand from Germany anything more than the restoration of Belgian independence and a renewed pledge that this independence would be respected.

But as the war progressed, and as the propaganda justifying Britain's part in it grew, a new attitude developed towards peace terms. They became in the public mind the means whereby every grievance could be aired and every national advantage ensured. In particular, Germany's overseas empire began to appear as a possible 'prize' for victory. It was an empire whose government was no worse than that of other European powers, nor had its acquisition brought it into conflict with the British Empire; yet as the hope of spoliation became grafted upon the hope of peace, its retention under German sovereignty was to be impossible. Equally impossible, it was hoped, would be a revival of German militarism which, the Government asserted, had encouraged war, and provoked it. To crush militarism, Germany would have to be disarmed, and the allies would have to ensure, if necessary by military occupation, that no German armies, and no German armaments, should be built up again. Under the stimulus of war patriotism a further item was added to the growing list of potential prizes:

Germany must be made to pay for the damage done, not only in the battle zones, but also in the homes from which the soldiers had come. The mounting popular aspirations were encouraged and spurred on by Horatio Bottomley, on public platforms where he called for volunteers, and in the pages of *John Bull*, where he poured scorn upon any sympathy shown towards the 'Germhuns', as he called them. When the wife of an interned German was given 12s 6d a week public assistance for herself and her four children, Bottomley wrote:

> On the whole we must be one of the nicest countries in the world for the Germhuns to live in. Somehow he can always rely upon our tender feelings towards the Deutscher in distress. Even in time of war, when he is an alien enemy in our midst, if he is naked we clothe him, if he is hungry we feed him, and if he is athirst we give him drink, bless his dear heart.[1]

Bottomley fanned the flames of anti-Germanism. He denounced civil servants with German-sounding names or German relatives; he published weekly lists of people who changed their German-sounding names into English ones; he wanted all captured German sailors to be hanged, or, even better he said, to be left to drown; he suggested the use of poison gas before the Germans had begun to use it; he wanted all German citizens in England to be arrested and all naturalized Germans to wear a distinctive badge. Nor did he seek a rapprochement after the war: Germany must pay and Germany must suffer, for there was no place for Germans in any civilized community. Therefore, advised Bottomley, when the war ends:

> If by chance you should discover one day in a restaurant that you are being served by a German waiter, you will throw the soup in his foul face; if you find yourself sitting at the side of a German clerk, you will spill the inkpot over his vile head.[2]

These were crude attempts to stimulate anti-German feeling, yet they were effective. Those who sought an Anglo-German rapprochement after the war were always liable to the popular taunt of 'pro-German'. The accusation of 'pro-Germanism' was a gremlin which dogged the footsteps of appeasement for twenty years. There were always those who regarded any attempt to create good relations with Germany as a betrayal of all that had been sacrificed in the war. Much of the effort of those who did wish to draw closer to Germany was spent fighting this feeling. Bottomley was not alone in his outspokenness. In 1917, when the question of German reparations was being widely discussed, Rudyard Kipling added his influential voice to the mounting throng:

> These were our children who died for our lands: they were
> dear in our sight.
> We have only the memory left of their home-treasured
> sayings and laughter.
> The price of our loss shall be paid to our hands, not
> another's hereafter.
> Neither the Alien nor Priest shall decide on it. That is our
> right.
> *But who shall return us the children?*
> That flesh we had nursed from the first in all clearness was
> given
> To corruption unveiled and assailed by the malice of heaven
> By the heart-shaking jests of Decay where it lolled on the
> wires—
> To be blanched or gay-painted by fumes – to be cindered
> by fires—
> To be senselessly tossed and retossed in stale mutilation.
> From crater to crater. For this we shall take expiation.
> *But who shall return us the children?*[3]

Bottomley quoted part of this poem in the House of Commons in 1919, when he opposed Lloyd George's suggestion that Britain should send help to those Germans in danger of starvation.[4] The intensity of war-time anti-Germanism spurred on those who feared a peace treaty based upon such crude feelings. G. Lowes Dickinson, believing that the origin of the war sprang from international rivalries and fears, and feeling that although Germany's behaviour was 'monstrous' it was nevertheless 'not unique', deplored a peace designed primarily to crush Germany. In his pamphlet *After the War*, published in 1915, he cast doubt upon both the usefulness and the morality of disarming or partitioning Germany:

A nation has never been crushed by anything short of annihilation. Look at Ireland! Look at Italy! Look at the Balkan States! You may weaken Germany, yes; you may cripple her for a time. . . . What of it? She will rise from humiliation stronger for the reverse. We can no more crush her than she can crush us. And the attempt to do so can only lead to a new war.[5]

Lowes Dickinson was sceptical about the efficacy of frontier changes. He pointed out accurately that although the war might result in the establishment of an independent Poland, that in itself would not save the Jews in the new state from Polish domination, while any increase in the size of Serbia would bring non-Serbs under Serb sovereignty. It was clear to Lowes Dickinson that self-determination was not the panacea some believed it to be. He also feared that after the war Britain would forget that it was pledged not to annex any German territory, and would take the German colonies, thus standing in his view 'self-convicted of hypocrisy'. He urged a post-war 'League of Peace' which could employ first moral, then economic and finally military pressure against any power which sought to gain its ends by force or the threat of force. To make such a League effective, he wrote, Germany must be a member; and for Germany to accept membership and co-operate in the peaceful settlement of disputes, 'everything possible should be done, in the event of a victory by the Allies, not to alienate Germany from the European system'.

Between 1915 and 1918 hundreds of pamphlets and articles took up Lowes Dickinson's plea. In 1917 H. G. Wells, in a pamphlet *A Reasonable Man's Peace*, declared that the war only continued because the Germans were afraid of what would happen to them when it was over. No nation, he wrote, had the confidence or the vision to declare reasonable peace terms; to offer a compromise that would repair the damage done and create no new damage. Instead of discussing peace, politicians talked only of how to win the war – of air offensives and knock-out blows:

They seem to be incapable even of thinking how the war may be brought to an end. They seem incapable of that plain-speaking to the world audience which alone can bring about a peace. They keep on with the tricks and feints of a departed age, with bureau politics.

Both on the side of the Allies and on the side of the Germans the declarations of public policy remain childishly vague and disingenuous, childishly 'diplomatic'. They chatter like happy imbeciles while civilization bleeds to death.[6]

Wells feared Allied avariciousness in imperial affairs. He felt that they would try to exclude Germany from Africa altogether, while denying Germany commercial rights elsewhere. For a lasting peace, he wrote, Germany should be allowed 'a fair share in the control and trade of a pooled and neutralized Central Africa', and this should be stated plainly at once. Wells wanted the popular idea of a permanent economic alliance, to prevent the economic reconstruction of Germany, to be denounced, and in its place a plan put forward for European economic co-operation, based on the internationalization of commercial treaties, inter-state shipping, and transport rates. By refusing to make an open commitment to internationalization the Allies would leave Germany 'no choice but a war of desperation'; by failing to scotch the rumours of territorial designs and of punitive economic proposals, the Allies were unifying the German people and prolonging the war.

This feeling of allied incompetence and duplicity gave an added impetus to those who feared a peace treaty which would seek to crush Germany. Norman Angell argued in favour of moderation almost monthly in his magazine *War and Peace*, and when his pen rested others took up the plea with equal vigour. The efforts of such publicists were greatly helped by President Wilson's growing conviction that Europe must be given specific points around which peace should be made, and in particular by his address to Congress on 8 January 1918, in which he enumerated fourteen points which in his opinion would ensure a fair place for all nations, and would provide, in his words, 'the moral climax of this, the culminating and final war for human liberty'. The most important assertion explicit in six of the points and implicit in others, was that frontiers should follow 'clearly recognizable lines of nationality'. It was Wilson's conviction that the war had its roots 'in the disregard of the rights of small nations and of nationalities which lacked the union and the force to make good their claim to determine their own allegiances', and that, while Germany must restore and respect these rights, so the Allies must renounce all annexations and all punitive damages. Addressing Congress on 11 February 1918, Wilson said:

Peoples are not to be handed about from one sovereignty to another by an international conference or an understanding between rivals and antagonists. National aspirations must be respected; peoples may now be dominated and governed only by their own consent. 'Self-determination' is not a mere phrase. It is an imperative principle of action, which statesmen will henceforth ignore at their peril.[7]

This speech encouraged the opponents of a harsh peace. It came therefore as a disruptive shock to conciliatory opinion when, three months later, the new Bolshevik régime in Russia published the secret treaties of the war, revealing the many territorial changes, none based upon self-determination, to which Britain was already committed. This shock was reinforced by contrasting the secret treaties with the first of Wilson's fourteen points: 'Open covenants of peace, openly arrived at, after which there shall be no private international understandings of any kind, but diplomacy shall proceed always frankly and in the public view.' While not condemning treaties previously entered into, this point cast an aura of moral disapproval upon them; and, in as much as they were at variance with the idea of self-determination, upon which the peace was now to be based, they would presumably either have to be renounced, or else cause deep dissension between Britain and America at the peace conference. The texts of the Secret Treaties were first published in English in April 1918, by the Union of Democratic Control.[8] Among them was the Treaty of London of April 1915, by which Italy, in return for becoming an ally, was to receive much of the Dalmatian Coast, a prospective share in the partition of Turkey and the chance of colonial territory in Africa. German territory was also involved in the secret documents, in one of which, dated February 1917, the Russians gave their support to France for an 'autonomous and neutral State' to be set up on the left bank of the Rhine, and including Cologne, Bonn, Mainz, and Coblenz.

These revelations were a blow to those who hoped for a moderate peace, for they showed how far considerations of territorial gain had already entered into Allied calculations. But in April 1918 it was difficult to win much support for such indignation. The Germans had broken the Allied line in March, in a last attempt to break the stalemate of trench warfare, and had pushed towards Paris. They were halted before Amiens at the end of March, but attacked again further south, and again advanced. British losses were extremely high. It now seemed that Britain might be defeated in France, and peace-through-victory speculation dwindled. It was not until the middle of July, after a series of battles crippling both sides, that the Allies were able to take the offensive. On 8 August a major Allied attack was launched which caught the Germans by surprise; and on that same day the Kaiser declared:

'We are at the limits of our endurance. The War must be brought to an end.' Of the ensuing month, when the Germans were driven back, eastwards across the old line of trenches, and towards the Belgian border, Lloyd George later wrote:

Starved, decimated, despairing, the German soldiers fought on, making us pay a heavy price for every mile we wrested from them. Throughout the whole War the Germans had shown themselves doughty fighters, but there was nothing finer in their record than the pluck with which they continued to withstand us in the hour of their defeat. They could not but know that they were beaten. At home their families were starving. . . . Let us do honour to a brave people with whom we have had but one deadly quarrel.[9]

By the last week in September it was clear that the Allies had won the war. The question of peacemaking, which had been submerged by the sudden severity and uncertainty of the conflict for nearly six months, reappeared. The problem was a pressing one, particularly for Britain. The Government had not repudiated the secret treaties, nor had it given up hope of gaining German colonial territory. Wilson's Fourteen Points were being put forward by America as the only acceptable basis of any peace negotiations. It was now very much in Germany's interest to accept them, for they would provide important territorial safeguards, and on 4 October, Prince Max von Baden, the German Chancellor, informed Wilson that his Government accepted the Fourteen Points 'as a basis for peace negotiations'. For nearly a month notes and telegrams passed between the warring nations. Armistice terms were discussed, and President Wilson announced that the abdication of the Kaiser was an essential condition of peace. The final, decisive blow, was the surrender of Germany's Allies, Austria–Hungary, Turkey, and Bulgaria.

Before the Germans had accepted the Armistice terms there was a prolonged crisis of opinion in the British Cabinet. On 13 October members of the Cabinet were surprised to hear from Lloyd George, at a private meeting of Ministers in the country, that he was disturbed by the thought of making peace, on the basis of the Fourteen Points, by negotiation rather than conquest. He asked his colleagues whether

. . . the actualde feat of Germany, and giving to the German people a real taste of war, was not more important, from the point of view of the peace of the world, than a surrender at the present time, when the German armies were still on foreign territory.[10]

This desire to continue the war, presumably to a point of unconditional surrender, shocked the Cabinet, who were becoming alarmed at the mutinous state of some of the soldiers, and the fear that, if they did enter Germany, they would be 'contaminated' by the Bolshevik ideas which had become so strong in Germany that revolution seemed imminent. Two of the Prime Minister's Conservative colleagues, Balfour and Milner, were strongly opposed to continuing the war now that a chance of arranging a cease-fire had arisen. Lloyd George continued to press for a more decisive and dramatic ending to the war. He feared that the British public might feel cheated if the victory to which they had so long looked forward, and which in April had suddenly seemed to be slipping away from them was, at the moment their armies approached the German borders, somehow watered down and whittled away. But he had an even more basic fear:

If peace were made now the Allies would not have occupied a yard of German soil. . . . In twenty years' time the Germans would say that they had made this mistake and that mistake, and that by better preparation and organization they would be able to bring about victory next time. . . .

In a short time the Germans would say that these miserable democrats had taken charge and had become panic-stricken, and the military party would get into power again.[10]

Thus, in a manner both prophetic and almost telepathic, Lloyd George reflected, in cabal with his colleagues, the same feelings that were troubling the mind of Adolf Hitler, a wounded corporal in a German military hospital. It was by exploiting those exact sentiments, by claiming that the brave, indestructible German army had been forced to surrender by the treachery of 'cowardly democrats', that Hitler first attracted attention and support.

But Lloyd George's doubts were soon dispelled. The war had gone on too long, and had brought despair and damage to too many homes, for a chance of peace to be neglected. And as the French armistice terms became known, it became clear that Germany would have to make a heavy sacrifice in order to obtain a cease-fire. Wilson's Fourteen Points might later be produced to guide a peace conference, but it was the armistice terms which were to come into force at the end of the war. By these, Germany was to evacuate France, Belgium, Luxembourg, and Alsace-Lorraine; hand over to the Allies large quantities of military stores; allow the Allies to occupy Germany west of the Rhine, together with all important bridgeheads across the Rhine; surrender all ships and submarines; and promise to pay 'reparation for damage done' – a phrase admitting of the widest, and wildest, interpretation.

The British Government approved of these terms. But they raised doubts in the minds of some observers as to how far Germany was to be allowed to recover her dignity, and to avoid also a crippling economic burden which would harm all Europe by the dislocation and unrest which it could cause. Lord Milner, possibly to influence public opinion, or at least to show Lloyd George that he held his views tenaciously, gave an interview to the *Evening Standard*, which was published on its front page on 17 October. According to the report, which Milner had approved before publication:

He is inclined to think that if the Allies ... attempt to dictate to Germany certain drastic changes in their own Government both as regards constitution and personnel, the resistance of the German armies and people, already waning, may be stiffened.[11]

Milner opposed the imposition of a crippling armistice on Germany. Although he wanted Germany defeated in the West, he had no objection to Germany being the dominant power in the East. He had little sympathy with self-determination, and thought the emergence of Poland, Czechoslovakia, and Yugoslavia in eastern Europe would only disrupt further an area where Germany, if paramount, could exercise a decisive influence for stability. Above all he feared the spread of Bolshevism in Germany if Wilson insisted upon a republican form of Government. Once the Kaiser abdicated, Milner felt that it was only a question of time before Bolshevism triumphed, and, once Germany went over to revolution, it might not be long before England too were shaken by social unrest. This argument influenced Lloyd George, and probably made him withdraw from his unconditional surrender stance of 13 October, for, by 10 November, he was warning his colleagues that British troops in Germany might catch 'the virus of Bolshevism', and listening to Churchill's even more outspoken plea that 'we might have to build up the German Army, as it was important to get Germany on her legs again' to check the spread of Bolshevism.[12]

On the day after Milner's *Evening Standard* interview, Balfour told the Cabinet that he thought the territorial changes which France and America proposed were unrealistic. If there were a plebiscite in Alsace-Lorraine, he doubted whether the majority of voters would opt for France; while Wilson's insistence upon a Polish outlet to the sea would, he thought, by cutting off East Prussia from the rest of Germany, be most unwise.[12] General Smuts, a member of the Imperial War Cabinet, raised further alarms about the effect of self-determination in two memoranda on 23 and 24 October; alarms which again influenced Lloyd George:

There is a serious danger that the bad, but more or less orderly, political pre-War system of Europe may give place to a wild disorder of jarring and warring state fragments. . . . With the creation of an 'independent' Poland, there will be a chain of these discordant fragments right across Europe from Finland in the north to Turkey in the South. No League of Nations could hope to prevent a wild war-dance of these so-called free nations in future.[13]

The public did not know of the doubts in the minds of its leaders. The impending defeat of Germany was too exciting, too precious a prospect to be marred by scepticism. Yet the Cabinet had begun to see that the peace would inaugurate disputes, no less bitter and ultimately perhaps no less bloody, than those which had in the past four years brought such havoc and destruction. The minds of many politicians were already breaking out of the anti-German mould, viewing French objectives with suspicion and American idealism with scorn. There was a growing irritation in the corridors of power that British common sense and realism were being eclipsed by the extremes of French anguish and American utopianism. When George V warned Balfour of the dangers of Austria and Germany uniting, he received an answer which showed how far British official thinking had ceased being influenced by the views which still troubled the minds of the British people and their sovereign:

I do not see that we can really oppose the union of the Germans of Austria with the rest of the Germanic peoples – provided it is clearly desired by the inhabitants themselves. To do so would violate one of the cardinal principles for which the Allies have been fighting – the right of self-determination. Nor am I clear that such a union would be politically disadvantageous. It would greatly increase the strength of South Germany as opposed to the North and the leadership might pass from the hands of Prussia. . . .

If Germany got the German Austrian Provinces and lost what she ought to lose to the Poles, the French, and the Danes, her net gain would, (I believe), be insignificant.[14]

Written on 11 November 1918, the day on which the armistice was declared, while vast crowds moved excitedly through London, these words were conciliatory and sensible, undistorted by the emotions of the hour and unclouded by the elation of victory. But, as Lloyd George wrote twelve years later, the war 'had poisoned the mind of mankind with suspicions, resentments, misunderstandings and fear';[15] and these neither the imperturbable calm of the Foreign Secretary nor the magnanimity of his colleagues could allay. The moderation and common sense with which the British Government approached the Peace Conference were shared neither by its public opinion nor by its allies.

CHAPTER 5

Appeasement:
The Essential Prospect

Germany surrendered in November 1918 and signed the Treaty of Peace at Versailles in June 1919. During those seven months all Europe was in turmoil: the influenza epidemic reached its climax, and killed in all over forty million people, a heavier toll than the war itself; demobilization created a vast unemployment problem; the breakdown of trade and communications brought famine conditions to much of Germany, Austria, and the Ukraine; communist revolutions broke out in Hungary and Germany; and frontiers were fixed without agreement by nations who had created themselves, not been created by the Allies, at the moment when Germany and Austria-Hungary collapsed. The chaos created by these uncontrollable circumstances provided a background of fear, anger, and bewilderment to the Peace Conference. None of its decisions could be made without taking the *status quo* into account. Yet the *status quo* was continually shifting; Europe had no shape, the new nations knew no precedents, the defeated nations were not listened to, and the victors were not united. All was a quicksand into which long cherished ambitions, subtle compromise, firm resolve, and the call for caution could sink, and be lost without trace.

Lloyd George's position was an uncomfortable one. He feared that Europe's future would be blighted if the new republican Germany were saddled with debts which it could not pay and with a loss of territory which it could not accept. He shied away from the French insistence upon a severe treaty. But he knew that the French attitude was explicable, even justifiable; that France had since 1870 been taught to dream of revenge, and that now the dream was on the point of realization. He realized that France had lost more soldiers than Britain, and that most of the devastation of the war in the west had been on French territory – that it was French towns that had been shelled and French villages razed to the ground. But he feared the consequences of a punitive peace.

It was not against French demands alone that Lloyd George had to fight. Many Englishmen, in the elation of victory, while their sense of loss was still acute, spoke of vengeance. Three days after the Armistice it was announced that a General Election would be held at the end of December, before the Peace Conference met. This gave all demagogues a platform. Anti-Germanism became the fever of the moment. To speak in favour of moderation seemed an invitation to electoral defeat. The Government's growing sense of the urgency of calm tempers and broad compromises found no echo in an electorate which, knowing so few of the facts, could not form an objective view of what was needed. Nor might the facts, as weighed by the cautious mind of Balfour or the prophetic insight of Lloyd George, have made much impact on the public mind. As Churchill wrote:

The Prime Minister and his principal colleagues were astonished and to some extent overborne by the passions they encountered in the constituencies. The brave people whom nothing had daunted had suffered too much. Their unpent feelings were lashed by the popular press into fury. The crippled and mutilated soldiers darkened the streets. The returned prisoners told the hard tale of bonds and privation. Every cottage had its empty chair. Hatred of the beaten foe, thirst for his just punishment, rushed up from the heart of deeply injured millions. All who had done the least in the conflict were as might be expected the foremost in detailing the penalties of the vanquished. . . . In my own constituency of Dundee, respectable, orthodox, life-long Liberals demanded the sternest punishment for the broken enemy. All over the country the most bitter were the women, of whom seven millions were for the first time to vote. In this uprush and turmoil state policy and national dignity were speedily engulfed.[1]

Churchill and Lloyd George both tried to resist, and even to abate popular prejudice. But neither Churchill, who could hold a cabinet spellbound while giving one of his magnificent historical and philosophical disquisitions, nor Lloyd George, whose persuasive powers were such that he was said to be able to charm a bird from a tree, could make any impact upon the public resolve to take its revenge. One Cabinet Minister told a delighted London audience that 'we would squeeze the German lemon till the pips squeaked'. This was what the populace wished to hear. When Churchill told a Dundee audience that the limit of reparations would be about £2,000 million the local papers 'gibbered with strident claims' and he received a telegram from a Chamber of Commerce: 'Haven't you left out a nought on your indemnity figure?'[2] In a letter to his electors Churchill made it clear that there would be a limit to what Germany could pay, and that to demand a specific sum before seeing if it were feasible, and enforcing its payment, would result in a valueless treaty. These moderate opinions received little publicity. The press, both in England and abroad, took up the cries of the extremist orators. When George Barnes, the only Labour Member of the War Cabinet, said, 'the Kaiser has been mentioned ... I am for hanging the Kaiser', that was headline news; when Churchill said, 'we must be very careful to stand firm upon those great principles for which we have fought',[3] it was ignored. Most dramatic, most damaging of all, while addressing a large meeting at Bristol, and worn out by many days and nights of hectic electioneering, Lloyd George declared: 'They must pay to the uttermost farthing, and we shall search their pockets for it.' This was neither his belief nor his policy; it was the result of exhaustion and exhilaration. Yet it was this shrill, irresponsible cry that Britain, Europe, and America heard. Public opinion could not know that at that very moment, preparatory to the Peace Conference, Lloyd George had obtained the approval of the Imperial War Cabinet to a limitrope formula which he wished at the time to make, and later did make his guide in the discussions with France on which he was about to embark. The formula outlined British policy as: 'To endeavour to secure from Germany the greatest possible indemnity she can pay, consistently with the economic well-being of the British Empire and the peace of the world, and without involving an Army of Occupation in Germany for its collection.'[4]

At the Peace Conference Lloyd George was handicapped by the moods and utterances of the General Election: the anti-German moods, continuing fierce, meant that in any moderation he urged he had to keep one eye on his own public opinion, which when it felt that he was exercising undue leniency could, and did, protest; while the bravado of the Election speeches, vivid in French minds, meant that when Clemenceau urged severity he could always refer

to Lloyd George's public statements as support for his own conten-
tions. Although Lloyd George tried, throughout the negotiations,
to control the evolution of the Treaty, he began from a position of
weakness from which he was unable fully to recover, and which
obstructed many of his efforts to obtain a viable peace.

At Paris Lloyd George was the leading advocate of moderation.
He sought to act as if he were above national antagonisms. He
tried to be the arbiter of conflicting passions. But the House of
Commons would not let him forget in what tone the election had
been fought. When it became clear the reparations were being
calculated on the basis of what Germany 'could' pay, rather than
on what she 'ought' to pay, 370 Coalition Conservatives sent a
petulant telegram, reminding him of what they and the electorate
expected, and ending:

Although we have the utmost confidence in your intention to fulfil
your pledges to the country, may we, as we have to meet innumerable
inquiries from our constituents, have your renewed assurance that you
have in no way departed from your original intention?[5]

Within a week of receiving this challenge Lloyd George returned
to London, and on 16 April 1919 rebuked the House of Commons
for its impatience. He reminded MPs that he was having to settle
the fate of five continents in Paris; that ten new states had to be
brought into existence; that territorial, military, and economic
questions had all to be decided upon, and that 'you are not going
to solve these problems by telegram'. He reminded them that,
even if mistakes were made, the League of Nations, which was
being set up as part of the Treaties, would be able to make the
necessary adjustments later. He made it clear to his critics that if
they insisted upon terms which the League were ultimately to
judge unduly severe, those terms would be modified. For an hour
Lloyd George cajoled, threatened, appealed to, and won over his
listeners:

. . . and when enormous issues are depending upon it, you require
calm deliberation. I ask for it for the rest of the journey. The journey is
not at an end. It is full of perils, perils for this country, perils for all
lands, perils for the people throughout the world. I beg, at any rate,
that the men who are doing their best should be left in peace to do it, or
that other men should be sent there. . . .

We want a stern peace, because the occasion demands it. But its severity must be designed, not to gratify vengeance, but to vindicate justice. . . .

[It is the duty of] statesmen in every land, of the Parliaments upon whose will those statesmen depend, of those who guide and direct the public opinion which is the making of all – not to soil this triumph of right by indulging in the angry passions of the moment, but to consecrate the sacrifice of millions to the permanent redemption of the human race from the scourge and agony of war.[6]

Lloyd George returned to Paris. But although he appeared to have convinced the House of Commons that leniency was needed, he was unable to convince the French. They made some concessions, abandoning their hopes of a separate Rhineland State and of a Polish annexation of Danzig, but in general French desires were met. The Treaty as finally published had a vindictive tone about it. Lloyd George's published views were different: indeed, it was the publication of his innermost thoughts that had led to the parliamentary telegram. Together with Philip Kerr, Lloyd George had spent a week-end at Fontainebleau, trying to work out the broad principles upon which peace ought to be based. In the memorandum which Lloyd George wrote at Fontainebleau, he declared that his concern was to create a peace for all time, not for a mere thirty years. A short peace might be possible by punitive measures against Germany. But unless the Germans were placated, they would go Bolshevik, and Russian Bolshevism would then have the advantage 'of the organizing gift of the most successful organizers of national resources in the world'. The initial shock of war would pass, and then, according to Lloyd George:

The maintenance of peace will depend upon there being no causes of exasperation constantly stirring up either the spirit of patriotism, of justice, or of fairplay, to achieve redress. . . . Our Peace ought to be dictated by men who act in the spirit of judges sitting in a cause which does not personally engage their emotion or interests, and not in a spirit of a savage vendetta, which is not satisfied without mutilation and the infliction of pain and humiliation.[7]

This was utopian. Yet Lloyd George was convinced that he was right. He went on to criticize all clauses which might prove 'a constant source of irritation', and suggested that the sooner reparations disappeared the better. He deprecated putting Germans under alien rule, fearing that by doing so 'we shall strew Europe with Alsace-Lorraines'. He emphasized that the Germans were 'proud, intelligent, with great traditions', but that those under whose rule they would be placed by the Treaty were 'races whom they regard as their inferiors, and some of whom, undoubtedly for the time being, merit that designation'. These arguments fell upon stony ground: the French could not understand Lloyd George's sudden conversion to what they could only describe as imbecilic pro-Germanism. Clemenceau replied icily to the Fontainebleau Memorandum that 'if the British are so anxious to appease Germany they should look . . . overseas . . . and make colonial, naval, or commercial concessions'.[8] Lloyd George was particularly angered by Clemenceau's remark that the British were 'a maritime people who have not known invasion', and countered angrily that 'What France really cares for is that the Danzig Germans should be handed over to the Poles.'[9] These bitter exchanges were symptomatic of a growing rift in Anglo-French relations. For Clemenceau, the Treaty was perhaps the best chance that France would have of designing effective protection against a Germany that was already almost twice as populous as France, and must therefore be shown by deliberate, harsh action that it would not pay to think of revenge. For Lloyd George, the Treaty was an opportunity to arbitrate for Europe without rancour, and to create a Continent whose future problems could be adjusted without malice. Britain, by supporting the League of Nations, would be willing to help in the process of adjustment. Clearly it was the Treaty that would first need to be altered: Lloyd George did not fear that. For him the Treaty was not a sacred instrument but a pliable one. It was obvious from his comments while it was being drafted that he would not be content to see it become the fixed rule of the new Europe. On his return from Fontainebleau he opposed strenuously, but in vain, the transfer to Poland of areas predominantly German. His protest was a forceful one, yet it was not forceful enough to break the French desire for the maximum reduction of German territory. Wisely and perceptively, Lloyd George wrote:

I am strongly averse to transferring more Germans from German rule to the rule of some other nation than can possibly be helped. I cannot conceive any greater cause of future war than that the German people, who have certainly proved themselves one of the most vigorous and powerful nations in the world, should be surrounded by a number of small states, many of them consisting of people who have never viously set up a stable government for themselves, but each of them containing large masses of Germans clamouring for reunion with their native land. . . . [These proposals] must, in my judgement, lead sooner or later to a new war in Eastern Europe.[10]

Lloyd George reiterated this theme on every relevant occasion. But whereas the French could add the voice of Czechs and Poles, who would benefit by French plans, to their own, Lloyd George could not call in the Germans to support his view. They were not invited to the discussions. The detailed delineation of their frontiers, the distribution of their border people among neighbouring sovereignties, and the loss of their colonies and overseas trade concessions were all discussed and agreed upon without their participation. Lloyd George was their only champion among the heads of state: even Wilson, from whose idealism so much had been expected, seemed for the most part to have become Clemenceau's tool, just as, twenty-seven years later, Roosevelt succumbed to Stalin's blandishments at Yalta, leaving Churchill isolated and outvoiced.

Lloyd George's subordinates in general supported his actions. Balfour and Milner played important parts in drafting various clauses, and among the more junior officials J. M. Keynes and Harold Nicolson both waxed indignant at what they regarded as French folly and British weakness. Harold Nicolson wrote optimistically to his father early in June:

I have every hope that Lloyd George, who is fighting like a Welsh terrier, will succeed in the face of everybody in introducing some modification in the terms imposed upon Germany. Now that we see them as a whole we realize that they are much too stiff. They are not stern merely but actually *punitive*, and they abound with what Smuts calls 'pin pricks' as well as dagger thrusts . . . the real crime is the reparation and indemnity chapter, which is immoral and senseless. There is not a single person among the younger people here who is not unhappy and disappointed at the terms. The only people who approve are the old fire-eaters.[11]

Yet Lloyd George failed: the 'old fire-eaters' were too strong for him. His economic advisers were divided, and only the younger ones seemed disposed towards moderation. Keynes, one of the Treasury representatives at the Conference, resigned over this issue. His resignation made no impact either upon the course of

c

the discussions, or upon the British public. Yet another unknown civil servant had obeyed the dictates of conscience, and lapsed into oblivion. Writing to Austen Chamberlain, Keynes explained his action:

> We have presented a Draft Treaty to the Germans which contains in it much that is unjust and much more that is inexpedient. . . . It is now right and necessary to discuss it with the Germans and to be ready to make substantial concessions. If this policy is not pursued, the consequences will be disastrous in the extreme. . . .
> The Prime Minister is leading us all into a morass of destruction. The settlement which he is proposing for Europe disrupts it economically and must depopulate it by millions of persons. The New States we are setting up cannot survive in such surroundings. Nor can the peace be kept or the League of Nations live. How can you expect me to assist at this tragic farce any longer, seeking to lay the foundation, as a Frenchman puts it, 'd'une guerre juste et durable'.[12]

These doubts were exaggerated; but the arguments used to counter them were equally unbalanced. When the Germans read the clauses on reparations they argued as Keynes had done that European economic chaos would result and that, in seeking to cripple Germany, the Allies would simultaneously destroy themselves. Lloyd George sought the opinion of Lord Cunliffe on these criticisms. Cunliffe was a former Governor of the Bank of England, and had worked closely with Lloyd George at the beginning of the war. Cunliffe wrote in reply:

> It is unfortunately only too manifest to anyone connected with business that the demands of the Allies have fallen far short of the German capacity to pay, and I am more than ever convinced that Germany can and will pay the whole of what is demanded, and without nearly as much interference in her economic life as she so richly merits.[13]

Cunliffe's views prevailed over those of Keynes. Once the Treaty was signed the doubters had nothing to look back on but a sense of frustration and, in Keynes's case, a sense of grievance. It was the Cunliffes, Kiplings, and Bottomleys who had reason to be satisfied. Not only the 'war-guilt' clause, but the tone of all the clauses, revealed the spirit of retribution. The war was far too recent, France too wounded, Paris too emotional a conference centre, the virulence of the British electorate too vivid, for the result to be otherwise. For Lloyd George it was a bad treaty; not the one he had wished to sign, but the one whose execution could lead Europe back to war with little delay.

On 29 June 1919 Lloyd George returned from Paris. He was met at Victoria Station by the King, and they drove in the royal carriage to Buckingham Palace. 'History,' wrote Churchill, 'will not overlook the significance of this act'.[14] Lloyd George, author of the People's Budget, enemy of the Peers, architect of unemployment insurance, and now 'the man who won the war' had reached the climax of his career. At his death twenty-six years later Lord Beaverbrook could recall the opinion of the multitude at that euphoric moment:

Lloyd George was the idol of the nation, the Premier under whose aegis Germany was overthrown and the Empire saved. . . . He dictated to Europe; he flung out great dynasties with a gesture; he parcelled out the frontiers of races; everything was in his hands, and his hands showed that they had the power to use everything.[15]

Reality was otherwise. Lloyd George, the acclaimed master of both war and peace, had persevered, but he could not prevail. His dominant personality had been eclipsed by that of Clemenceau. His brilliance in discussion had been matched by the tenacity of his allies. His vision of what could be and ought to be done had been clouded by less enlightened and more urgent counsels. With his flair, amounting to genius, for seeing what lay in the field beyond, he sensed the frailty of what had been accomplished. But he could not convince his colleagues that his forebodings were justified. The moment of his public triumph was exactly the moment of his private disappointment. He had stumbled and indeed fallen; but the public saw only the figure of a man standing proudly in the moment of universal acclaim, hair flowing, moustache voluminous, and eyes a-twinkle. Again it was Beaverbrook, Lloyd George's Minister of Information in 1918, who caught the man and the mood:

In the day of our dire need, when the blast of the terrible one was against the wall, a strange figure sprang into the arena to do battle. It was clad in a jewelled breastplate set in a vesture of rags and tatters. It faltered in its walk, and yet leapt with a wonderful swiftness. The sword looked as fragile as a rapier and yet smote with the impact of a battle-axe. As it was held on high, so was the hope of Britain. And when the swordsman stumbled, anxiety filled the breasts of the multitude.[16]

Yet at Paris, Lloyd George's powers had been severely curtailed. The result was a Treaty of which many Englishmen disapproved. British thinking on Europe and on foreign affairs soon began to concentrate on the terms and interpretations of the Treaty. Men argued that where clauses were punitive, they should be removed; where demands were incapable of fulfilment, they should be modified; where frontiers created national animosities, they should be re-drawn; and that only by drastic Treaty modification could European peace be secured. The alternative was an aggrieved and disturbed Germany, whose population, industry, resources, and determination would surely win by force the 'justice' that had been denied in defeat. Germany no longer appeared as the sinner, but as the victim. The dispute over responsibility for the war continued unresolved, but no one could dispute the authorship of the Treaty; the Allies had put themselves in the dock, and with a poor defence. H. A. L. Fisher, Lloyd George's Minister of Education, saw one way out of the difficulty. Writing to Gilbert Murray from Paris during the Conference he doubted whether a permanent settlement could be reached, for he saw the strength of French fears and the territorial greed of the new nations. But he hoped that if a treaty of some sort were signed there would be 'an appeasement, and by degrees readjustments and modifications can be introduced which will give Europe a prospect of stability'.[17] Fisher regarded appeasement as a necessary corrective to the Treaty. It provided a hope that the injustices of the Treaty would disappear peacefully. It also gave Britain a part to play. By becoming the leading advocate of appeasement, Britain could redress the balance of injustice. The British sense of fair play could operate on Germany's behalf. The British desire for a quiet life, undisturbed by European alarms and cross-channel excursions, could be satisfied. Appeasement was the balm for a guilty conscience.

The public first heard of appeasement through the *Manchester Guardian*. Its editor, C. P. Scott, was a nonconformist and a liberal; he had been a stout opponent of the Boer War; he criticized British support for France during the Agadir crisis; and in July 1914 he tried to urge upon Lloyd George the folly of Britain supporting France and Russia. Immediately after the war he denounced the election campaign as 'reckless and vulgar', and in a personal talk with President Wilson, assured him that it represented a mood that would soon pass. Scott was determined to help alter the mood

EUROPE after the Peace Treaties, 1919-1937

Miles
0   100   200

Ceded by Germany 1919
Saar: League of Nations trusteeship 1919-1935
Ruhr: occupied by France 1920 and 1923
Danzig: Free City 1919-1939
Austria-Hungary until 1918
Former territory of Imperial Russia
Frontiers of 1919

through his paper, which, from November 1918, was the foremost advocate of Anglo-German co-operation.[18] On the day after the Armistice he wrote in his leading article that as a result of the Kaiser's abdication Germany was 'most wonderful of all – freed from Prussian dominance'; and a week later he rejoiced that 'a militarist and autocratic Germany' having disappeared, it would be easier than had been thought earlier to set up a scheme to prevent future war. Commenting on the Peace Treaty, he was alarmed that East Prussia had been separated from Germany, seeing in this 'a source of deep and, we fear, permanent unrest . . . in the heart of Europe'. Of Danzig's position, cut off from Germany as a Free City, he wrote:

You cannot with impunity violate national self-consciousness or place people of a higher civilization under those of a lower, the implacable adherents of one religion (protestantism) under the fanatical professors of another (catholicism). . . . Poland is assured of the permanent hostility of her mighty neighbour.[19]

Scott was depressed by the Treaty. It seemed to him to contain too many potential causes of national strife, and too many violations of Wilsonian principles, to be of value in settling Europe's problems. It would be wrong, he wrote, to deprive Germany entirely of her sense of pride and self respect: 'our task in Europe is not to destroy but to build. Even a diminished Germany will still be the greatest State in Europe.' Scott's conclusion was the epitome of appeasement. Germany, he wrote, was not in a position to resist the harsh terms:

But a wise policy will treat her no longer as an enemy to be feared and destroyed, but as a part of the Europe of which we ourselves form an integral part, and which for many a long year will need all our help and all our care to save it from ruin. . . . For us the fundamental question is whether we desire a peace of appeasement or a peace of violence.[20]

These were not cries in a wilderness; not mere tokens of liberal dissent or political sensitivity. Appeasement was not a mood confined to well-meaning but powerless publicists; not merely the flitting thoughts of marginal men dabbling in public affairs. Every Prime Minister between the wars accepted this policy and pursued it. Appeasement was the corner-stone of inter-war foreign policy. For twenty years it dominated all arguments and blessed or bedevilled all policies. Lloyd George cautiously, Ramsay MacDonald enthusiastically, Stanley Baldwin doggedly and Neville Chamberlain defiantly pursued it throughout their premierships. Their contemporary reputations depended upon its immediate effects; their subsequent stature rested upon its long term success or failure.

CHAPTER 6

Versailles:
The Nagging Doubt

The Treaty of Versailles has had few defenders. From the moment that it was signed, until virtually the outbreak of the second world war, it was the object of sustained and wide-ranging criticism. Nor were its enemies drawn solely from the crowded salons of arm-chair critics; some of its more effective assailants had actually been at the Paris Peace Conference, and had contributed to its discussions and decisions. Politicians, diplomats, and civil servants added their authoritative, politically influential voices to those of polemical pamphleteers and academic historians.

The Treaty began at a disadvantage: for some time before the German surrender potential peace terms were everywhere under discussion, and by June 1919 there cannot have been a single person of keen intelligence who did not have his own version of the ideal Treaty clearly formed in his mind. All the problems with which the negotiators had to deal, and upon which they reached their final decisions within five months, had been exercised both privately and publicly for almost five years. It is not therefore surprising that the Treaty contained almost no uncontroversial clauses, or that where a clause was criticized its critics were themselves often divided as to why it was wrong, or what changes would improve it.

Appeasement and the Treaty were linked inextricably. Those who considered the Treaty adequate, or not severe enough, wanted Germany to be made to comply with all its demands. Such men denied the need for either sympathy or revision, and felt no sense of responsibility for the emergence of an embittered, revision-searching Germany. Robert Vansittart, a member of the British Delegation, wrote in retrospect:

Few frontiers are ideal, few doctrines wholly palatable, few restrictions universally acclaimed, but the *ensemble* had much more to respect than to condemn. . . . Yet our delegation was smitten by meaculpism. There are always Britons who nibble the fruits of victory with the guilty conscience of Adam.[1]

Those whose consciences were troubled felt increasingly certain, as Europe passed from one catastrophe to another and seemed to be hurrying towards collapse, that the Treaty was to blame, and that therefore it ought to be radically revised. In this context, revision could only mean revision in Germany's favour. It was thought that if Germany could be appeased by revision, Europe might yet avoid the chaos, economic and political, to which adherence to the Treaty was felt to be leading. The worse one considered the Treaty to be, the more urgently one felt obliged to call for its revision.

In his book *What Is Coming?*, published in 1916, H. G. Wells had made a series of shrewd prophesies about the post-war world, and had outlined the nature and needs of peace. Victories and conquests, he suggested, would be less significant than economic recuperation and social reconstruction. Boundaries would be less vexatious than finance. 'Very jaded and anaemic nations will sit about the table on which the new map of Europe will be drawn';[2] and uppermost in their minds would be social and economic problems. Wells saw the war ending without a clear victory for either side, but in exhaustion for both. He argued that the prime need of any post-war settlement would be to eliminate all potential causes of a second holocaust: 'Men who cannot be swayed by the love of order and creation may be swayed by the thought of death and destruction.' Unless this were so the world would descend into barbarism. Both the need and the danger were clear, Wells wrote, and to him the god of war spoke in unambiguous words:

Get your houses in order. If you squabble among yourselves, waste time, litigate, muddle, snatch profits, and shirk obligations, I will certainly come down upon you again. I have taken all your men between eighteen and fifty, and killed and maimed such as I pleased; millions of them. I have wasted your substance – contemptuously. Now, mark you, you have multitudes of male children between the ages of nine and nineteen running about among you. Delightful and beloved boys. And behind them come millions of delightful babies. . . . Go on muddling, each for himself and his parish and his family and none for all the world, go on in the old way, stick to your 'rights', stick to your 'claims' each of you, make no concessions and no sacrifices, obstruct, waste, squabble, and presently I will come back again and take all that fresh harvest of life I have spared, all those millions that are now sweet children and dear little boys and youths, and I will squeeze it into red pulp between my hands, I will mix it with the mud of trenches and feast on it before your eyes, even more damnably than I have done with your grown-up sons and young men. And I have taken most of your superfluities already; next time I will take your barest necessities.[3]

This, the lurid panorama of a Goya, was an accurate forecast. Yet Wells was convinced that it could be averted. Revolted by his own portrayal of the world as it would be, if men tried to settle the peace by traditional, narrowly-selfish criteria, he moved on to a view of Europe as it ought to be, and in his opinion could be, if common sense were the basis of the Treaty.

Wells's criticism of a Treaty that in 1916 existed only in his own imagination was both perceptive and prophetic. He felt convinced that the German monarchy would collapse at the end of the war, and be replaced by a republican government. Against the Kaiser he was willing to impose a severe peace; against a republic he felt that similar severity would be a major mistake. Republican Germany, he wrote, should not only be forgiven, but should receive 'a warm welcome back to the comity of nations'. He was convinced that it would be wrong to put any Germans under alien rule. He thought that even Strasbourg and parts of Alsace might properly remain inside Germany, and that it would be folly to set up a detached buffer state in the Rhineland. Nor, he wrote, should the victors seek to weaken German commercial power: 'Let but Germany cure herself of her Hohenzollern taint, and the world will grudge her wealth and economic pre-eminence as little as it grudges wealth and economic pre-eminence to the United States.'[4] Wells was also worried about the emergent nations, realizing the power of their propaganda and the magnetism of their cause, but fearing their impact on the post-war world. He doubted whether nations long submerged inside the Central European empires could easily establish viable governments. He urged the establishment of confederations, all larger than single states, and none based on nationality alone. The Swiss model appealed to him. He envisaged a United States of Eastern Europe as best combining national aspirations and economic feasibility. But he feared the result of frontiers based upon nationality alone: 'An entirely independent

Poland will be a feverish field of international intrigue – intrigue to which the fatal Polish temperament lends itself all too readily; it may be a battlefield again within five-and-twenty years.'[5]

Wells deprecated a peace based upon the belief that the Germans were a militaristic people, and should therefore be so crushed as to prevent any possibility of a revival of German power. He pointed out that German socialists had always opposed the expansionist utterances of the Kaiser and von Tirpitz. These Germans, he wrote, should be recognized as having no profound quarrel with Britain. People should give up all talk of 'wicked Germans':

Elderly Protestant ladies used to look under the bed and in the cupboard every night for a Jesuit, just as nowadays they look for a German spy, and as no doubt old German ladies look for Sir Edward Grey. . . .
There are indeed very grave grounds for the German complaint that Germany has been the victim of alien flattery and alien precedents. And what after all is the Prussian dream of world empire but an imitative response to the British empire and the adventure of Napoleon?[6]

Once the German monarchy had fallen, according to Wells, there would be no reason why German bombast and militarism should not rapidly disappear, and all the nations of Europe, their war passions dying down, work together to build a better world, based upon multi-national economic organization and freed from the shackles of dynastic ambition. 'Amid these realities,' he wrote, 'the great qualities of the Germans mark them for a distinguished and important rôle.'[7]

Such was the vision; but reality did not follow the same reasoning. Even when Lloyd George took up what were essentially Wells's points, and gave them the stamp of official thinking in the Fontainebleau Memorandum, they failed to mould the new Europe. Everything that Wells and Lloyd George regarded as carrying the seeds of future war found a place in the Treaty of Versailles. Both men wished the victors to discuss the details of the Treaty at length with the vanquished; but no such discussions took place.

Even though the Kaiser had abdicated and a republic been established, the Germans were not considered responsible enough to help determine their own destiny. The French view of an imposed peace prevailed.

By the terms of the Treaty of Versailles, many Germans were

separated from Germany, and became minorities under alien rule; Austria was forbidden to unite with Germany; all German over-seas commercial concessions obtained before the war by negotiated treaties were abrogated; every German colony was taken away; Germany was forbidden to have an air force; the German economy had to adjust itself to reparations payments to the allies; and Germany was excluded for the time being from the League of Nations. This was not the peace that either Wells or Lloyd George had envisaged. The Fontainebleau Memorandum contained a devastating criticism of the final Treaty:

> You may strip Germany of her colonies, reduce her armaments to a mere police force and her navy to that of a fifth rate power; all the same in the end if she feels that she has been unjustly treated ... she will find means of exacting retribution from her conquerors.... Injustice, arrogance, displayed in the hour of triumph will never be forgotten or forgiven.

Lloyd George and his advisers were not alone in fearing the consequences of the Treaty, even before it was signed. Lord Esher, a member of the Committee of Imperial Defence, wrote on the day after the armistice that war would come again if any attempt were made 'to crush the soul of eighty millions of German people',[8] and while the Conference was sitting he told Sir Douglas Haig that:

> The Conference is, by this time, a hotbed of intrigue.... The moment you gathered together all those elements composed of men who have individual axes to grind in a city like Paris steeped in the old traditions, it followed that old methods would prevail ... intrigue, and the grouping of powers according to their pure material interests. The result will be a series of compromises and the sowing of the seed of fresh war hereafter.[9]

Before the Treaty was signed some optimism as to its final form still prevailed. It seemed incredible to many observers that Lloyd George's persistent efforts to modify the Treaty should fail. His prowess at negotiation was well known; his determination to avoid a peace based on might rather than morality was manifest. How could his wishes be overruled? H. A. L. Fisher wrote to Gilbert Murray from Paris in April 1919, a week after Lloyd George had handed the Fontainebleau Memorandum to the French:

> I think that everyone here takes the commonsense view that an irre-

dentist Germany would be of all Evil legacies to Europe, the worst, but we are not sole arbiters of the situation. Still I hope that our undoubted weight in international affairs may be sufficient to prevent an unprincipled Peace.[10]

Two months later the Treaty was signed, and even those who felt uneasy at its terms were glad that five months of argument and uncertainty were ended. Even those who saw in the 440 articles ample cause for future conflict felt the need for a brief moment of relief, if not of rejoicing. Two Germans, albeit unknown ones, had at least signed the Treaty, even if their objections had been ignored. The danger of Germany refusing to sign, and of the Allies having to renew the war, was thus averted. That, at least, was a reason for satisfaction. A Treaty existed, proof that the war was finally over, and that it had been won. Now those who found the Treaty unjust could devise in their minds many means of remedying the injustices or of hoping that, by some miracle, its faults would not prove as disruptive of European peace as they then appeared to be.

Austen Chamberlain, Lloyd George's Chancellor of the Exchequer, felt that a democratic Germany would renounce militarism. He echoed Wells in his belief that 'no democracy can or will make aggressive war its year-long study and business'. But his mind was not set entirely at rest. He knew that even in a democracy war 'may easily enough flare up in sudden passion', and he sensed that the Germans might well seek action in the east against Poland, for whom they had such strong 'racial' dislike. Austen Chamberlain also saw what a strain the blunt facts of demography would impose: 'But think of Germany with its 60 or 70 millions of people and France with its dwindling 40! I shudder!'[11] Others shuddered with him, seeing in a bad peace a stark invitation to revenge, and realizing the impossibility of keeping Germany weak for all time. Asquith, after a luncheon with Foch, wrote to a friend: 'I thought he talked a lot of nonsense about Germany sinking never to rise again'[12]; and Bertrand Russell wrote caustically to Gilbert Murray:

I am going this afternoon to see your Trojan Women at the Old Vic. Nowadays we no longer cohabit with the vanquished women: we cause them and their children to die of hunger. It does not seem to me a very marked improvement. Do you know of any instance in history where more suffering has been inflicted on the vanquished ?[13]

Doubts grew as to the wisdom of the Treaty, and as to the possibility of revising it; doubts which were strengthened as 1919 drew to an end. Esher feared that despite the sacrifice of 'the best blood and sinew of our race', the hope of a war to end all war had been dashed by the Treaty, and that 'others must hereafter arise destined to that same old Moloch of aimless war'.[14] It seemed clear to him that none of the Wilsonian phrases or principles – self-determination, open diplomacy, the League of Nations – had been translated 'into the faintest semblance of reality'. Yet only a year had passed since the armistice, when Lloyd George had told the House of Commons that he hoped all war had come to an end, and Asquith had predicted that the world was entering on a new chapter in international history 'in which war will be recognized as an absolute anachronism never to be repeated'.[15]

The private doubts of public men were limited in their effects to a small circle of friends. Only in the Fontainebleau Memorandum did such doubts have a moment of national publicity. Then they returned to the obscurity of private correspondence, or to the unabsorbed chatter of the dinner table. But J. M. Keynes, the Treasury official who had resigned rather than accept any further responsibility for the Treaty, was preparing a denunciation of the Treaty, strongly encouraged to do so by Smuts. 'The battle is lost,' Keynes wrote to Lloyd George in June 1919; but six months later he published *The Economic Consequences of the Peace*, and battle was joined once more. Keynes was not content to criticize. He also offered advice on how Europe ought to be organized. He castigated the Treaty, and pointed the way to sanity. His book shocked Britain to the core. Its message swiftly embedded itself in the British conscience, as deeply and indestructibly as 'Calais' upon the heart of Mary Tudor. Meaculpism was born. Doubt flourished; German guilt faded; British guilt spread.

Keynes described the atmosphere in Paris as one of 'levity, blindness, insolence'.[17] While hourly reports of hunger and chaos came from Central and Eastern Europe, he wrote, the Big Four 'fulfilled their destinies in empty and arid intrigue'. He pointed out that most of the proposals were first put forward by Clemenceau, who made them extreme knowing they would be moderated, and could even, by agreeing to alterations, then pose as a moderate himself. Yet, wrote Keynes, over points where British or American interests were not directly involved, 'their criticism grew slack, and some provisions were thus passed which the French themselves did not take very seriously'. Keynes was indignant that Germany had not been allowed to propose substantial modifications. He was severe on Clemenceau, whose aim, he said, was to crush Germany by a Carthaginian peace and to destroy her economic system; not to negotiate with Germany or to conciliate Germany, but to dictate to Germany. Keynes decried such a policy:

This is the policy of an old man, whose most vivid impressions and most lively imagination are of the past and not of the future. He sees the issue in terms of France and Germany, not of humanity and of European civilization struggling forwards towards a new order. The war has bitten into his consciousness somewhat differently from ours, and he neither expects nor hopes that we are at the threshold of a new age.

From Clemenceau, Keynes passed to Wilson, and sought to show how Wilson was so weak and inexperienced that he allowed his principles to be side-stepped, and committed himself to clauses which even Lloyd George rejected as too harsh. 'The blind and deaf Don Quixote,' wrote Keynes of the President, 'was entering a cavern where the swift and glittering blade was in the hands of the adversary.' He had, said Keynes, 'no proposals in detail'; his mind was 'slow and unadaptable', his ideas were 'nebulous and incomplete'. These were severe judgements on a man whose claim to represent idealism, and whose presence at Versailles, had persuaded many Englishmen that the Treaty must therefore be a just one. But Keynes refused to prop up these comforting illusions. He did not spare any individual, or any aspect of the Treaty, from his fury. He despised Wilson for abandoning his principles while pretending to uphold them, thereby encouraging 'the weaving of that web of sophistry and Jesuitical exegesis that was finally to clothe with insincerity the language and substance of the whole Treaty'. It was Wilson, Keynes wrote, who had been pushed by French casuistry into refusing to allow Austria and Germany to unite; into separating Danzig from Germany; and into placing Germany's rivers under foreign control. Lloyd George's desire for compromise came too late; for, as Keynes explained:

After all, it was harder to de-bamboozle this old Presbyterian than it had been to bamboozle him; for the former involved his belief in and respect for himself.

Thus in the last act the President stood for stubbornness and a refusal of conciliation.

Keynes examined every aspect of the Treaty, emphasizing its severity. He showed how every possible attempt had been made to hamper German post-war recovery. He deplored the refusal of the Allies, both at Paris and on the many Commissions set up to execute the Treaty, to allow the Germans an effective voice. 'Little has been overlooked,' he concluded, 'which might impoverish Germany now or obstruct her development in future.'

Keynes reserved his most caustic comments for the reparations clauses. It was wrong to leave the final amount open, he wrote. It was brutal in the extreme to suggest some £20,000 million as a feasible total. Keynes, like Churchill during the 1918 election campaign, considered £2,000 million a more sensible figure. Keynes thought the Churchillian figure 'wise and just', and not at all impossible for Germany to pay. But more than that would be criminal folly. Keynes examined the details of the reparations claims, and judged them unjustifiable. He pointed out that Germany had lost her colonies, her overseas trade concessions, her foreign property, her fleet, three-quarters of her iron-ore, a third of her territory, and two million soldiers killed in the war; that she was hampered by 'Revolution at home and Bolshevism on her borders'; and that as a result 'we have no adequate knowledge of Germany's capacity to pay'. To enforce payment might lead to poverty, starvation, and revolution; to insist upon Treaty fulfilment would strengthen all hatreds and sharpen all nationalism. 'If we aim deliberately at the impoverishment of Europe,' Keynes wrote, 'vengeance, I dare predict, will not limp.'

Keynes's book caused a revolution in British thought. Views held until then only by a minority became widespread. Soon, few educated people could be found to defend the Treaty; many to decry it. Lord Robert Cecil, formerly Minister of Blockade, wrote to Gilbert Murray that he had read Keynes, and that 'I am quite clear that we shall have to begin a campaign for the revision of the Treaty as soon as possible'. Despite a little exaggeration, wrote Cecil, the book was 'an extraordinarily brilliant and effective statement of what is substantially a true criticism of the Treaty'.[18]

Keynes destroyed British faith in Versailles. He opened the floodgates of criticism. For the next twenty years the Treaty was assailed by means of his arguments. Every clause came under scrutiny; many were found to be faulty. The British public discovered that it had put its signature to what appeared to have been 'exposed' as an instrument of injustice. A feeling of guilt came to pervade all discussion. The German Republic began to receive sympathy in all its difficulties, and a hand outstretched to help it. Keynes made appeasement public property. His writing became the handbook of reconciliation. His warnings became the spur and incentive to all advocates of 'peaceful change'. The historian W. H. Dawson, the politician Lord Birkenhead, the diplomat Harold Nicolson all dipped their fluent and persuasive pens in the Keynsian ink. Their books confirmed the Keynsian analysis. Birkenhead, in *Turning Points in History*, insisted in 1929, that above all the status of Danzig needed revision, its position being 'a very real danger to the peace of Europe'.[19] Dawson, in *Germany Under The Treaty*, detailed in 1932 ten major territorial changes, including Memel, Danzig, and the Sudetenland, where he felt revision of the Treaty in Germany's favour was essential if European peace were to be preserved. Harold Nicolson's *Peacemaking 1919*, published in 1933, effectively clarified and reiterated the Keynsian picture. He considered that at Paris Lloyd George had been 'at the mercy of a jingo Commons and a jingo Press'; that the territorial settlements of the Treaty 'were based on mere adjustments and compromises between the claims of rival states' with provinces and people treated 'as pawns and chattels in a game'; that throughout the Conference 'the nerves of Paris jangled in the air'; and that when it was over many of its participants were filled with 'a mood of durable disbelief – a conviction that human nature can, like a glacier, move but an inch or two in every thousand years'.[20] Nicolson agreed with Churchill's description of Versailles as 'a turbulent collision of embarrassed demagogues',[21] and concluded in Keynsian vein:

We did not realize what we were doing. We did not realize how far we were drifting from our original basis. We were exhausted and overworked. We kept on mumbling our old formulas in the hope that they still bore some relation to our actions. . . . In the dust of controversy, in the rattle of time-pressure, we lost all contact with our guiding stars. . . . We still desired ardently to maintain our principles intact: it was only in the after-vacancy that we realized that they remained for us only in the form of empty words.[22]

German-Speaking Peoples 1919-1939

German speaking peoples
(from Austrian map 1920)

Thus, for thirteen years, Keynes's message was constantly and powerfully reinforced. Few were the voices raised in protest, many the disciples seeking expiation in some form or other of pro-Germanism. All the phrases of the 1920s – peaceful change, treaty revision, bringing Germany back to her rightful place in Europe, obtaining equality for the former foe, appeasement – gained impetus from the Keynsian flood. Morality and appeasement seemed to go together. Keynes's fierce words dominated the thought of the inter-war years:

The policy of reducing Germany to servitude for a generation, of degrading the lives of millions of human beings, and of depriving a whole nation of happiness should be abhorrent and detestable – abhorrent and detestable, even if it were possible, even if it enriched ourselves, even if it did not sow the decay of the whole civilized life of Europe. Some preach it in the name of Justice. In the great events of man's history, in the unwinding of the complex fates of nations, Justice is not so simple. And if it were, nations are not authorized, by religion or by natural morals, to visit on the children of their enemies the misdoings of parents or of rulers.[23]

Walpole, Burke, and Fox were the Patriarchs of appeasement. Lloyd George was its Moses and Keynes its Isaiah. The Fontainebleau Memorandum was the Tablets of Stone, thrust forward by Lloyd George and rejected by Clemenceau. *The Economic Consequences of the Peace* was a warning and an exhortation that could not easily or lightly be ignored.

CHAPTER 7

The First Appeasement

Lloyd George did not allow the disappointments of the Versailles Treaty to depress him unduly. Although he was somewhat deflated by his difficulties in obtaining all the modifications which he had wished, he was determined to exert a moderating influence upon those carrying out the Treaty. Between January 1920 and December 1922 there were twenty-three international conferences, most of which he attended, and where his voice was raised continually in favour of appeasement. The French resented his attitude and made every possible effort to challenge it. Two years of intensive and acrimonious debate created strong anti-French feeling in British official circles, and also made it quite easy for the German Government to appeal effectively to Britain for protection against the 'ferocity' of French policy.

Although the Peace Treaty with Germany was signed in June 1919, its final form needed much further negotiation. The precise amount of reparations had still to be fixed, and the German 'war criminals' had yet to be brought to trial. Both these tasks required the help of American arbitration to prevent them from becoming the cause of violent and prolonged Anglo-French friction. But in November 1919 the United States' Senate refused to ratify the Treaty. America rejected responsibility in the finalization and execution of a settlement which President Wilson had done so much to shape. His policy of supervising European developments and soothing European tempers was, literally overnight, abandoned in favour of isolation. The shock of America's withdrawal was a severe one, and threw an immense burden upon Britain and France, both of whom had built up hopes, often conflicting and at times somewhat naïve, of winning Wilson to their particular point of view, and of using his support to turn the balance of opinion decisively in their favour.

Harold Nicolson wrote shrewdly on this problem in retrospect:

The whole Treaty has been constructed on the assumption that the United States would be not merely a contracting but an actively execut- ant party. France has been persuaded to abandon her claim to a buffer state between herself and Germany in return for a guarantee of armed support from the United States. The whole Reparation settlement was dependent for its execution on the presence on the Reparation Com- mission of a representative of the main creditor of Europe. The whole Treaty had been deliberately, and ingenuously, framed by Mr Wilson himself to render American co-operation essential.[1]

With this co-operation lost, Lloyd George became, unwittingly, the sole non-German spokesman for the German view. Partly because of continual examples of French extremism and partly by reason of his own lack of vindictiveness, he emerged as the only European statesman willing to examine each allied proposal in the light of pragmatism rather than of passion.

Within a week of the ratification of the Versailles Treaty on 10 January 1920, the first inter-allied conference, at Paris, came to an inconclusive end. It had as one of its purposes the drawing up of a list of German 'war criminals' whom the allied powers would ask Germany to make available for trial, presumably by arresting them. It was agreed that Britain, France, Belgium, and Italy would draw up lists of those whom they considered culpable. But no standards of culpability were laid down. No difference was specified between necessary actions as a result of obeying orders, and actions flagrantly violating the rules of war. When the French list was shown to Lloyd George he was furious to find on it the names of Bethmann-Hollweg, the Imperial Chancellor from 1909– 17, and of Hindenburg and Ludendorff, Germany's two national heroes, probably the only two leaders who had emerged from the war with credit in German eyes. Lloyd George felt that the trial of these three would so antagonize the German public as to drive them into total refusal to carry out any further Treaty demands, including reparations payments. The Cabinet agreed with Lloyd George, and sent the Lord Chancellor, Lord Birkenhead, to Paris on 6 February 1920 to put their views as forcibly as possible. Birkenhead spoke to Millerand in no uncertain terms:

... in the history of war, so far as I am aware, no such demand has ever been made. . . . We know full well that the Germans have signed an undertaking which they seem to be attempting to evade. But although from the legal point of view the Germans are bound by their signature, we have to consider the situation that exists in Germany today and the actual power of the German Government to control the situation. . . . Time has now passed – considerable time – since the Treaty of Peace, or those articles of it – were considered. The passage of time has itself produced, both in our country and in Germany, changes of which we feel bound to take cognizance, and which urge that these matters be reconsidered.[2]

The French did not take kindly to the concept of reconsideration, which, in their view, could only result in changes favourable to Germany, and in a greater leniency than they were willing to countenance. Millerand pressed for a literal and exact fulfilment of the terms of the Treaty. When the French list was finally published, against Lloyd George's wish, it roused much anger in Germany, and some scorn in Britain. A week later Millerand was in London for the second of the myriad conferences upon which the European statesmen were now, at great personal inconvenience, embarked. Within ten minutes of the opening of discussions, Lloyd George raised the question of the list of criminals. He was convinced, he said, that

. . . to demand the surrender and prosecution of Hindenburg before a tribunal of his enemies was to ask something which no nation could agree to, however crushed and defeated it might be. . . . To demand Hindenburg was a political mistake of the first magnitude. . . . If the Germans said they would not give up Hindenburg, what would be the position ? Would any country go to war for that reason ? Would Italy, Great Britain, or France go to war in order to force the surrender of Hindenburg ? It was incredible. . . .

He hoped therefore that his colleagues would not press for the handing over of men in these categories [who were merely carrying out the war]. It meant a new war, in which the British Government would not engage, and against which the common sense of the world would protest, and the Allies would be humiliated.[3]

Millerand replied that once the Allies began to compromise, the Germans would assume that they could by vigorous protest obtain modifications in every aspect of the Treaty. The Belgian Prime Minister, Delacroix, insisted that allied unity was essential, and that it would be dangerous to give the Germans any hint of allied disagreement. He was willing to see the lists modified, provided this could appear as a unanimous inter-allied decision. Lloyd George gladly accepted modification, but went on to point out that the decision did not rest entirely upon the personal wishes of those at the Conference, but rather that:

Everything depended upon the Allied Governments having public opinion behind them. It was no use their trying to enforce anything if they were not fortified by this public opinion. He was sure public opinion generally would not stand Marshal Hindenburg and General Ludendorff being surrendered for trial, as this would be repugnant to the ordinary citizen.[3]

Lloyd George was successful. The trials were abandoned. Appeasement won its first triumph. But his arguments were misleading. Public opinion in Britain was indeed turning away from its initial support of a punitive peace, but hardly to the extent of finding judicial trials 'repugnant'. Lloyd George posed as the man responding to a public mood; in reality he sought to control and modify that mood. He saw clearly what he hoped would happen in Europe in the coming decade. The public could not be expected to have such a clear vision. In using the argument of a non-vindictive public, Lloyd George was casting his own hopes for the future of Europe into the mould of a non-existent situation. The desire for appeasement did not yet command a majority of English opinion. It was not as a reaction to Versailles that appeasement gained its main adherents. The harsh peace had created the mood, but it had not ensured its universal acceptance. The public mind in 1920 was still clouded by doubts and hesitations. The idea of a working partnership with Germany had not yet found a wide or enthusiastic audience. It was a fear of French recalcitrance, fear of France forcing Germany to arms again, that confirmed the public in its views, and strengthened them. French 'folly' was the fertilizer which turned appeasement from a feeble offshoot into a frantic bloom.

In March 1920 a Communist revolution broke out in the Ruhr. The German Government asked the Allies if it could move troops into the Ruhr to suppress the uprising. Fear of German communism was a consistent theme in British foreign policy. The Cabinet were well aware of the dangers of bolshevism on the Rhine. Not only were the doctrines of communism abhorrent to the rulers of the non-Bolshevik world, they were also doctrines which denied the validity of former war debts and treaty obligations. Bolshevik Germany would repudiate Versailles and not pay reparations, just as Bolshevik Russia had repudiated Tsarist debts and denounced all Tsarist treaties. It was therefore necessary, in Lloyd George's view, to give the German Government every encouragement to stifle revolutionary movements, even if this involved the use of German troops commanded by German officers and using weapons which ought under the Treaty of Versailles to have been surrendered already to the Allies. He approved of the German Government's promptness in preparing to act.

The French had no such sympathies. Any manifestation of German strength was anathema to them. They wanted to be the arbiters of domestic German politics, and in particular of all events whose focal point was the Rhine. Having failed at Versailles to obtain a separate Rhineland State, they were nevertheless determined to impose the solutions which they preferred upon this area. They therefore refused to allow the German Government to move its troops. But allied dissension, together with the urgency of the situation, gave Germany both the encouragement and incentive to action. On 3 April 1920 eighteen thousand German troops moved into the Ruhr. Three days later, without consulting Britain, France occupied five Rhineland towns, including Frankfurt and Darmstadt.

That same morning the French Ambassador in London, Paul Cambon, saw Andrew Bonar Law, a member of the Cabinet and leader of the Conservative Party, to explain the French action.[4] He described the German movement of troops as 'a grave violation of the treaty, and a serious menace to France'. Bonar Law was not impressed. He pointed out to Cambon that this was probably the first time since the war had begun in 1914 that one ally had acted against the known wishes of another, without consultation. This created grave difficulties, as the British Government now found themselves, in Bonar Law's words, '. . . in the embarrassing position of having either to declare to the world that the unity of the alliance was broken, or to express approval of, and assume responsibility for, a policy which they held to be wrong and dangerous.'

Two days later the Cabinet discussed the French action. Curzon was asked to communicate their collective disapproval to the French Government. He rebuked Cambon for a French announcement that their action followed consultation with Britain, a statement which implied that Britain had approved.[5] He pointed out that Millerand had failed to inform him of the course of his negotiations with the Germans. Such methods, he insisted, were incompatible with the mutual understanding and common action 'upon which the stability of the Alliance and the security of Europe alike depended'. In a defiant mood, a crowd at Frankfurt had provoked some French troops, who opened fire and killed some eight people. Curzon made use of the incident to stress even further British disapproval:

I also pointed out to the Ambassador – holding in my hand the newspaper which recorded the unfortunate collision which had taken place in Frankfort . . . that this was precisely the kind of incident which we had anticipated from the appearance of French forces in the areas in question. I did not remind him, as I might have done, that the situation had doubtless been aggravated by the fact that the large majority of these forces appeared to be black.[5]

Here was a cause for complaint that was to re-occur during the second French occupation of the Ruhr in 1923. The use of Moroccan troops was regarded by many Englishmen as perfidy. Lloyd George considered it a political blunder which would accentuate Anglo-French hostility. The coloured troops were thought by Britons and Germans alike to be particularly vicious and insensitive. In the public mind they were associated with stories of violent assault and rape. The British public's suspicions of France were confirmed and strengthened by this use of 'savage' troops, an action seen by some as a deliberate French policy intended to frighten the local inhabitants.

The British Cabinet were encouraged in their opposition to France when they discovered that the Italians and Japanese shared their views. British anger was turned, not primarily against the French action as such, but against all unilateral action. The British Government's hope was for peaceful change, which they thought was best obtained by co-operation and consultation. Powers acting alone could only disrupt the European harmony which peaceful change was expected to bring about. As Curzon pointed out in an urgent telegram to the British Ambassador in Paris, Lord Derby, which Derby was instructed to read to Millerand 'without delay':

... as time goes on no power may be able to enforce the terms of the Treaty single-handed against a resuscitated Germany.

In these circumstances, His Majesty's Government wish to make it clear that so long as the French Government persist in taking independent action, they must themselves bear the whole responsibility.[6]

The French withdrew from the Ruhr, but the *Entente* was broken. No longer would French fears act as a check upon British action. No longer would the concept of allied solidarity stand in the way of a policy of Anglo-German reconciliation. The French occupation of the Ruhr seemed to confirm British suspicions of French irresponsibility, and made the need for an Anglo-German rapprochement appear more urgent. It seemed necessary to show Germany that she would be allowed to become an equal member of the European community; and this would clearly have to be done before French extremism further disturbed and embittered the European scene. For six years, when Englishmen talked of atrocities, they had meant atrocities attributed to German soldiers in Belgium. In 1920 the word gained a further association. In the public mind it became linked with stories of French atrocities in the Ruhr, perpetrated by coloured soldiers. This was considered a challenge, not only to the moral code, but also to racial unity. The thought of African troops as the instruments of a vindictive French policy went against the grain of English ideas of decency. Slowly, almost imperceptibly, and yet by very definite gradations, the balance of sympathy was tilting towards Germany.

The remaining five Conferences of 1920 were a constant source of Anglo-French friction. At San Remo in April Lloyd George argued in favour of opening negotiations with Germany in order to fix a lump sum for reparations; but the French wanted to be able to increase the amount as Germany recovered economically.[7] At Lympne in June Lloyd George tried to cast the net of appeasement over Russia, pleading eloquently in favour of allied mediation in the Russo-Polish war; but the French spoke enthusiastically of sending military help to Poland.[8] At Lympne in August the French pressed for action against Russia, whose forces had then almost reached Warsaw, and against whom the armies of the newly independent Poland seemed incapable of much further resistance. Lloyd George explained his difficulty with stark clarity:

He did not wish the working classes to be able to say ... that he missed any chance of making peace. If they could say so with truth, it would rot the navy, and it would rot the working classes and lead to the triumph of Bolshevism in England.[9]

The French were insistent, however, that the Bolshevik armies should be halted, and preferred to try to halt them on the Vistula than on the Rhine. Lloyd George then proposed a blockade of Russia, not by Britain and France alone, but 'partly by securing the co-operation of the members of the League of Nations, and also of the United States and Germany'. This was not what Millerand wanted. Not only did he suspect that any action in which League nations had to co-operate would never materialize, but he was alarmed by Lloyd George's inclusion of Germany in the draft. Nothing would induce him to co-operate with Germany against Russia, for German help would clearly throw a burden of obligation upon France which would weaken her ability to push Germany to the utmost limit of her capacity to pay reparations. Millerand told Lloyd George that: 'He would prefer that the word [Germany] should disappear at once, otherwise he would have to enter a formal protest at the end of the document.' Lloyd George agreed to alter the draft. But the British view of Germany had clearly changed from one of overt but distant sympathy to one of searching for means of working together.

Appeasement was never a mere sentimental attitude; it had many practical applications. The French took particular offence at an article on the subject of German help which had appeared in the *Evening News* on 28 July 1920, just before the Conference met. The author of the article, Winston Churchill, was Secretary of State for War and Air. He feared the imminent destruction of Poland, and the Russian armies poised on the German frontier:

It will be open to the Germans either to sink their own civilization in the general Bolshevist welter and spread the reign of chaos far and wide throughout the Continent; or, on the other hand, by a supreme effort of sobriety, of firmness, of self-restraint, and of courage – undertaken, as most great exploits have to be, under conditions of peculiar difficulty and discouragement – to build a dyke of peaceful, lawful, patient strength, and virtue against the flood of red barbarism flowing from the East, and thus safeguard her own interests and the interests of her principal antagonists in the West.

If the Germans were able to render such a service, not by reckless military adventure or with ulterior motives, they would unquestionably have taken a giant step upon that path of self-redemption which would lead them surely and swiftly as the years pass by to their own great place in the councils of Christendom, and would have rendered easier the sincere co-operation between Britain, France, and Germany on which the very salvation of Europe depends.[10]

Events in Europe seemed to conspire against France, and to shorten beyond Germany's wildest hopes the period when she would be approached once again as a potential ally rather than as a beaten foe. In September Lord Robert Cecil, Britain's most energetic supporter of the League of Nations, said that if Germany applied for admission to the League in 1921 he would support her request, and thought it would succeed.[11] In October the British Government decided that if Germany were unable to pay reparations at the scheduled time, Britain would not exercise her right under the Treaty of Versailles to seize the property of German nationals in England.[12]

This brazen decision was taken by the British Cabinet without consultation with France. It caused an immediate and justifiable outcry in France. Austen Chamberlain, the Chancellor of the Exchequer, explained in the House of Commons that the threat of seizing German assets had already resulted in much German money staying out of England.[13] As London was the financial centre of the world, he felt that no obstacle should be placed in the way of its further expansion. It was clearly bad business to drive out even German money. The French were not mollified by this explanation. But when the French Chargé d'Affaires called on Lord Curzon to protest, Curzon repeated Chamberlain's statement, and proceeded to give copious examples of French hostility to Britain as shown in the Paris press. Curzon deplored the constant and shrill attacks on 'British honour, British good faith, and British policy' and ended by warning the Chargé d'Affaires that:

Phlegmatic as the British people were, a time might come when they would say that, though they were convinced of the immense importance of friendship between France and this country, they were being asked to pay almost too high a price for it, if they were to continue to be subjected to incessant abuse.[14]

As 1920 drew to a close this warning was repeated in different forms on a variety of occasions. No amount of diplomatic tact was able to join the fragments of the *Entente* together. When, in November 1920, H. A. L. Fisher proposed in the League Assembly at Geneva that the League Council should at once invite all the League nations not to increase their armaments over a period of two years, prior to arranging for a general disarmament, it was France that took the lead in quashing the proposal. Among the powers France persuaded to support them were Poland and Rumania. France was looking eastwards, not northwards, for her security. Fisher wrote to his wife that 'the French were very foolish not to let so harmless a resolution through.'[15] But France felt that her only security against German recovery was to keep, and even to increase the level of her armaments, and to find eastern allies equally conscious of the importance of large armies and burgeoning armaments. The League became as much a scene of Anglo-French discord as were the inter-allied conferences. Quarrels arose on every issue, not solely through an inability to agree on technical points, but rather through differences of national outlook and tradition. Whether over the means of controlling the illegal international drug traffic, or halting the white slave trade, of protecting the Armenians from Turkish violence, or keeping Danzig out of exclusive Polish control, Anglo-French interests always seemed to clash.

The final breach of the year arose over reparations. In June 1920 the total amount payable by Germany had been reduced from £24,000 million, the sum decided upon in 1918 by the Hughes-Cunliffe Committee, to £13,450 million. It was decided, on a British initiative, to open discussions with the Germans on how this amount should be paid. A conference was arranged, to be held in Brussels in December. Lord D'Abernon, the British Ambassador in Berlin, wrote forcefully to Curzon early in November, warning him that the German economic situation was precarious and that the value of the Mark was in danger of collapsing. 'It is in my judgement important,' he wrote, 'to keep the discussion at Brussels off the more or less Byzantine question of Germany's duty, and to confine it to the practical question of Germany's ability.'[16] Lord Hardinge, who had succeeded Derby as Ambassador in Paris, warned the French Minister for Foreign Affairs, M. Leygues, at the beginning of December, that 'it was generally realized in England that it would be absolutely impossible to carry out the intention, at one time proclaimed by both the French and

British Governments, to extract from Germany payment of the whole cost of the war.'[17]

The Brussels Conference upheld the British view. While not fixing a final limit to German payments, as Lloyd George wanted, it did arrange a much more moderate scale of payments than that demanded by France. Germany was to pay £150 million a year for five years, after which the question would be reviewed. But the French refused to accept the opinion of financial experts, and, despite protests from Lloyd George, France obtained in May 1921 German acceptance under duress to a total sum of £6,600 million. The British disapproved, not primarily because of the size of the sum, which was the lowest yet agreed on, but mainly because the French had threatened to occupy the Ruhr again if the Germans refused to accept it. The Germans, however, gave way. But British irritation at the hectoring methods France had used remained.

On the Reparations Commission set up at Versailles, which was intended to have an American representative as a moderating influence, the British representative, Sir John Bradbury, was in a minority. He could always be outvoted by his French and Belgian colleagues. It was a galling position for Britain, and one in which the fundamental difference between the British and French positions was constantly forced into the open. Yet because of the composition of the Commission the British view could not prevail.

It was not French harshness alone which made the diplomacy of 1920 so acrimonious, and pushed Britain towards Germany. Equally harmful to the *Entente*, neither Lloyd George nor Curzon was temperamentally sympathetic to French fears. Both wanted to dictate to Europe. Neither wished to defer either to his own colleagues, or to other nations. Neither was easily persuaded to modify his opinions. Lloyd George was tenacious, and appeared impervious to the most vigorous of arguments; Curzon was volatile, and, having accepted a compromise, could veer back unexpectedly to his original position without qualms. Neither provided the moderating influence needed at the succession of conferences. Although both were the exponents of moderation, both presented their case with little chance of gaining adherents.

The alienation of France from Britain was a spur to appeasement. If Britain wished to have some influence over European affairs, she needed a power other than France with whom she could co-operate, and whose goodwill could be exerted on Britain's behalf. Germany was the obvious choice. By 1921 an Anglo-German rapprochement was becoming both possible and desirable. The danger of communism in Germany, either by internal revolution or Russian invasion, was receding. The Weimar Republic seemed capable of making parliamentary democracy work. The disarmament carried out under the terms of the Versailles Treaty prevented, or seemed to prevent, the rise of militarism. The Kaiser was securely in exile in Holland. Many hoped that British friendship would encourage Germany to persevere with her new form of Government, and to feel that the sacrifices made after the armistice had not been entirely in vain. Germany should be pleased at having gained Britain's respect, sympathy, and friendship. Britain's willingness to contemplate Anglo-German co-operation was part of the tradition of British foreign policy. Britain, from a position of strength, could make concessions without fear of weakening herself, or of being deceived. In Burke's words: 'Peace implies reconciliation; and where there has been a material dispute, reconciliation does in a manner always imply concessions on the one part or the other. . . . The superior power may offer peace with honour and with safety'.[18]

Lloyd George and his Government were clearly the superior power. Birkenhead, Bonar Law, Austen Chamberlain, Curzon, Churchill, and Lloyd George himself had all shown themselves interested in 'peace with honour'. Recognizing the weaknesses and even faults in the Versailles Treaty, they wished to create a post-war world in which the prevailing spirit of international relations would be that of Lloyd George's Fontainebleau Memorandum. The Germans had only once been Britain's enemy in war: there seemed no need to regard Anglo-German conflict as a fixed part of European affairs. France had been the traditional enemy from medieval times to the Napoleonic Wars. Germany had often provided cause for British respect and emulation. Lloyd George himself had drawn inspiration from German social legislation, and based much of his own radical programme upon it.

Appeasement in 1920 was a shrewd policy, designed to end the division of Europe into the warring camps of 1914. It was also a cautious policy, aimed at dissociating Britain from French hostility to all aspects of German recovery. It was a policy which depended for its success upon European economic co-operation, and upon the revision of all clauses in the Versailles Treaty whose alteration could be shown to be conducive or even essential to European peace. It was a practical policy, one of whose aims was to stimulate trade and recreate the flourishing and confident business activity of the pre-war years. Lloyd George was the first active appeaser. But his success was limited to a single year, 1920. And it was seriously hampered by French intransigence.

CHAPTER 8

No Victor, No Vanquished

In 1920 Lloyd George had led the way towards the appeasement of Germany. But the general mood in Britain was more anti-French than pro-German, and any overtly sympathetic policy towards Germany might have been resented. French actions in 1921 increased anti-French feeling. It became clear that France would never let Germany forget her defeat, or agree to reducing German reparations indebtedness. Part of the reason for French obduracy was the feeling that Britain could no longer be relied on to support France. As Philip Kerr wrote to Lord Curzon in February 1921: 'The French public and the French press now know that opposition to their point of view comes not merely from the FO or the PM but has deep roots in British public opinion.'[1]

In 1921 two moderating influences withdrew from Lloyd George's Government: Milner, the Colonial Secretary, resigned because he was weary of public life and Bonar Law retired because of illness. Lloyd George consulted Curzon less and less. Churchill and Birkenhead were his two principal colleagues, and if he took advice, it tended more and more to be theirs. Neither was regarded by the public as a man of peace, and this attitude, which was in many ways a shallow one, created a general sense of insecurity in the public mind. Many feared that Churchill sought further war with Russia, and that both in domestic and foreign affairs he was not a man of measured judgement. Members of Parliament sensed the danger of social unrest in the prevailing anti-socialist policy of the Government, a policy based upon a deep reluctance to consider socialists as responsible politicians or mature citizens. Leopold Amery, a Junior Minister, felt this strongly. He wrote in retrospect that 'nothing would have been more short-sighted politically than a purely negative policy', and at the time pressed for more effective social legislation, and a more sympathetic approach to Labour aspirations.[2] He found that his fears of impending social upheaval were shared by the most junior member of the Cabinet, Stanley Baldwin, who also had doubts about the wisdom of Lloyd George's leadership. Both at home and abroad Britain seemed ready for a return to unspectacular, cautious, soothing government. But a European settlement seemed as remote as domestic calm. France remained, in British eyes, the principal disturber of peace, Asquith writing in May 1921: 'Lloyd George has been fighting the French pretty hard, and they nearly came to rupture . . . There is no doubt that the French are becoming increasingly unpopular here – especially in the City'.[3]

Philip Kerr's solution was to persuade America to put pressure on France in favour of a more lenient reparations policy. Britain's relations with America were improving. At the Washington Naval Conference, which began in November 1921, Britain, Japan, and the United States worked out an agreement to limit naval armaments in the Pacific. The Pacific thus became the first area in which all disputes would be settled peacefully, all national rivalries halted before they reached the point of war, and all alliances with military implications abandoned. Britain ended her alliance with Japan. The extension of naval defences at Hong Kong and in the Philippines was halted. Battleship building was severely restricted. In February 1922, with the ending of the Conference, a major act of faith, one of whose articles seemed to be a belief in perpetual peace, if only in the Pacific, was completed.

Within two months of the signature of the Washington Naval Agreement, Lloyd George returned to Europe. In his view, the time had come for a comprehensive settlement. Nearly four years had passed since the end of the war. The European turmoil could not go on for ever. The world crisis had to be brought to an end. Churchill described the 'universal gloom' of 1922:

No peace had been made acceptable to Germany or given security to France. Central and Southern Europe had broken into intensely nationalistic fragments sundered from each other by enmities and jealousies. . . . The United States in 1922 had shaken the dust of the Old World off her feet and dwelt in opulent, exacting, and strongly arming seclusion beyond the ocean. . . . The League of Nations, not yet reinforced by Germany . . . raised a frail and unsure bulwark against strong seas and sullen clouds. . . . England, bowed by debt and taxation, could only plod forward under her load.[4]

In going to the Cannes Conference in January and to the Genoa Conference in April 1922, Lloyd George hoped to turn this 'plod' into a more purposeful and productive pace. He hoped to obtain a final reparations settlement by persuading France to reduce by at least a half the £6,600 million upon which the last conference had agreed, and which was increasingly regarded in England as a grossly exaggerated demand. He hoped also to end Russian isolation, and in return for British recognition of Russia to persuade the Communist Government to play a 'normal' part in international affairs. Above all, he wanted America to abandon her war-debts, thereby freeing Britain and France from their heavy indebtedness. If America were to give up her French debts, France would not feel so acutely the need to collect such high reparations from Germany. The emotional desire might remain, but the practical necessity would to a large extent have disappeared. But the Cannes Conference, at which Lloyd George declared he would begin to remedy 'the paralysis of the European system', collapsed with Briand's resignation. Lloyd George was not deterred. Just before setting off for Genoa he wrote to Lord Beaverbrook:

I mean to go wherever the policy of European pacification leads me. There is nothing else worth fighting for at the present moment. Office is certainly not worth a struggle apart from what you can accomplish through it. It is the policy that matters and not the premiership.[5]

But European pacification was not uppermost in other minds. National advantage, interpreted narrowly, still dominated most European political thinking. The wider needs were ignored.

Lloyd George's aspirations were not altruistic; he was no idealist seeking to impose impractical solutions merely because they seemed morally right. For him, European appeasement had a sound economic basis. Only by mutual co-operation and a weaving together, at least into a European pattern, of economies limited since 1918 by a closed nationalism, could the world economic situation improve. Reparations, the most obvious barrier to a relaxed economic atmosphere, had to be reduced. Trade must also be freed from the restrictions imposed by the need of the victor states to pay back in full their heavy American loans. But Lloyd George's attempt to return to the relaxed, free trade atmosphere of before 1914 did not work. Every European nation, weakened economically by the war, sought financial protection by collecting debts and imposing high tariffs. European economic nationalism was rising. It resulted in isolation as total, and as damaging, as the political isolation of the United States.

The Genoa Conference was a failure. All Lloyd George's hopes were dashed to the ground and broken beyond repair. America, upon whose co-operation and magnanimity he had depended, refused to attend the Conference. The post-Wilsonian politicians sought no part in European appeasement. Isolation was the policy to which their electorate had responded with enthusiasm, and it limited their actions for nearly twenty years. In 1922 America was not even prepared to intervene to ameliorate European economic chaos. It turned its back utterly on European political disruption.

France also hampered Lloyd George's plans. Barthou, the French Foreign Minister, wanted neither Germany nor Russia to have an equal status with France or Britain at the conference table. France still clung to the Versailles division between allied and enemy powers, hoping, by perpetuating it, to secure some permanent political advantage. But by 1922 this dichotomy no longer represented any real division between the States themselves. Germany was disarmed, republican, democratic, and on the verge of bankruptcy. It was, in Lloyd George's opinion, unrealistic to repeat *ad nauseam* that she was an enemy. It was also dangerous to perpetuate a humiliating division beyond its useful span. To tell Germany on every possible occasion that, as an enemy in the past, she must accept inferiority in the future, was a humiliation which could only create deep resentment among Germans of all classes and all political parties. Lloyd George pressed Barthou to allow the conference table to be free from the rancours of 1918:

At this Conference we meet as equals. There is no victor, no vanquished: we are here on equal terms to do our utmost to rehabilitate Europe. Is Germany, a nation of 63 million people, and Russia, with 120 million people, to be left standing on the doorstep until we call them in? That is not equality, and such a thing as you suggest cannot be tolerated for one moment.[6]

Lloyd George's appeal came too late. Germany and Russia, brought together to receive favours from Britain or insults from France, found on the Italian Riviera a congenial climate, and without warning met separately at Rapallo to sign the draft terms of a Treaty whereby all Russo-German debts were cancelled and the

Germans recognized the Bolshevik Government as the *de jure* Government of Russia. This was a shock for Lloyd George, who had hoped to supervise such reconciliation himself, and to make it a part of a wider agreement. Nor was he able to persuade Barthou to make concessions in the German reparations demand. Wickham Steed, the editor of *The Times*, published an account of what claimed to be an interview between Lloyd George and Barthou. Faced with public indignation, fomented by the press, Lloyd George denied it. But in substance it was accurate. Steed reported that Lloyd George told Barthou that:

Great Britain considered herself henceforth free to seek and cultivate other friendships. His advisers had long been urging him to make an agreement with Germany, even at the cost of abandoning British claims to reparations. France had made her choice between British friendship and Belgian friendship. She had opted for Belgium, although the help she had received from Belgium was not comparable to the help she had received from Great Britain . . . .

British opinion was hostile to France, and his advisers, especially Lord Birkenhead, the Lord Chancellor of England, had been constantly advising him to break with France. Letters from all parts of the country gave him the same advice.[7]

No doubt this was an attempt to bully France into concessions by threats. If so, it failed. The Genoa Conference resulted in no practical advance in the appeasement of Europe.

Lloyd George put his problems succinctly in a letter to Frances Stevenson, one of his secretaries: 'The Russians difficult – hesitating – with their judgement warped in doctrine. The French selfish – Germans impotent – the Italians willing but feeble – the little countries cowed. *The Times* devilish!'[8] He hoped optimistically that the French were somewhat afraid of him, or rather of the fact that he had 'a certain hold on Liberal opinion throughout the world'; but a month of negotiations ended in disappointment. Asquith told the House of Commons that the results were 'depressingly, even distressingly, meagre'.[9] But for Lloyd George no single setback could obscure the final objective. In his farewell speech to the Conference he pointed out that the process of reconciliation had begun before Genoa and would continue after it:

At Cannes we threw out the lifeline. We have not yet drawn it in, as I thought we might; neither has it been snapped; neither has it been let go;

it is still there. We would like to draw all the distressed, all the hungry, all the suffering in the East of Europe back to life, with all the help that the accumulated energy and skill of other lands can give.[10]

The lifeline was not grasped: only Britain continued to believe in the appeasement of Germany. Lloyd George was strongly encouraged in his policy by Lord D'Abernon, the British Ambassador to Germany, who from the moment of his arrival in Berlin in 1920 had insisted in his dispatches that close and constructive Anglo-German co-operation was essential for European peace. He was convinced that only Britain could provide what he called 'a safety curtain' between France and Germany, and that while Britain had much to fear from irate French action, there was little danger from Germany. D'Abernon wrote in November 1921:

The attitude assumed in certain circles that Germany, through survival or revival of her old military organization and equipment, is today, or will be in the immediate future, a grave military danger to the peace of the world, is a Rip van Winkle conception, totally inapplicable to present circumstances. The military hegemony of the Continent today is with France. It is very necessary to recall the fact – so often forgotten in current controversy – that the balance of military power has entirely shifted since 1914.[11]

In June 1922 Lloyd George told D'Abernon that he was anxious to bring Germany into the League of Nations. 'It was essential,' he said, 'that the world should learn to treat Germany again as an equal.'[12] In his dealings with the German Government D'Abernon made it clear that Lloyd George's sympathies were also his own. When Lord Robert Cecil pressed Poincaré to allow Germany into the League, Poincaré showed extreme hostility, and Cecil allowed the question to drop. D'Abernon commented:

This is another instance of our perpetual failing; having formed a right conclusion and formulated a sensible policy, we put it forward. Poincaré says 'No' – and our people drop the discussion instantly. No resistance: no argument. The same thing has occurred ten times. Lloyd George is the best fighter – the most vigorous – the most skilful.[13]

But Lloyd George seemed unable nevertheless to conduct British foreign policy into any practical form of appeasement acceptable to France.

In July 1922 the German Government, feeling that it was economically impossible for Germany to go on paying reparations, appealed for a two year moratorium on all payments. The British Government sympathized with their plight and supported their proposal. But before it was discussed at the international conference being arranged in London in early August, the Cabinet debated a more fundamental solution, involving a radical revision of the whole economic section of the Versailles Treaty. Both Lloyd George and Balfour felt strongly that the complex web of international indebtedness was weakening every European economy and keeping national tempers high. Until both war-debts and reparations were a thing of the past, appeasement would fail. But Europe could not wait for these debts to be paid: forty years might pass and Britain still owe the United States large sums; sixty years might not see the end of German reparations. The Cabinet therefore worked out a daring scheme. All war-debts should be voluntarily abandoned, whatever their origin. Britain owed America £850 million. At the same time, Britain was owed by others, in war-debts and reparations, £3,400 million. The British Government proposed to cancel both amounts, and asked all other Governments to do likewise. This proposal was published on 1 August 1922. A week later the London Conference on Reparations opened. France was represented by Briand's successor, Raymond Poincaré, the man who had played a large part in bringing both the Cannes and Genoa Conferences to grief.

The London Conference was no more constructive than its predecessors. Poincaré welcomed the idea of cancelling inter-allied debts, but deprecated any tampering with reparations. He also refused to agree to a moratorium unless France were given as security all German revenues from mines and forests, twenty-six per cent of the output of all factories, and full control of German currency exchange and export licences. To this Lloyd George could not agree. He pointed out to Poincaré that it meant re-writing the Treaty of Versailles. He urged Poincaré to accept the opinion of the experts on the Reparation Commission that a moratorium was essential if the German economy were to avoid utter ruin. Turning dramatically to the delegates Lloyd George declared:

M. Poincaré says that he cannot trust the Reparation Commission to do what he wants, so he would brush it aside, and act without Germany having been declared in default. He wishes to go straight into Germany and get his own reparations. If he likes to break the Treaty, he must do it alone. I stand by the Treaty.[14]

A week of argument brought no solution. Neither the cancellation of all Allied debts nor a moratorium for Germany were agreed upon. After four years of good intentions and hectic diplomacy Germany was still the European pariah. France remained the stubborn opponent of reconciliation. Lloyd George had given as his aim 'dreams that are realizable'.[15] Yet with all his charm, all his persuasive powers, all his energy, and all his determination, appeasement was still as much a dream in 1922 as it had been in 1918. Nor could another seventeen years of equally tenacious activity by his successors bring those dreams much nearer to reality.

As a political philosophy appeasement had everything in its favour. It was Christian to love one's neighbour, and sound business to encourage his prosperity. It was common sense to seek an end to war passions, and courageous to try to build a working partnership upon the foundations of such reconciliation. But as a practical policy appeasement was confronted throughout the interwar years by serious obstacles: the resentment of old allies, the suspicion of potential friends, and the reluctance of former enemies. Appeasement was the fight against a *status quo* based upon greed, prejudice, and fear. But even its supporters could not guarantee that, however vigorously policymakers struck out at the *status quo*, they could remove the traumas upon which the *status quo* was based, or create a new order in which new greed, new prejudice, and new fears would not be equally active, and even more destructive.

CHAPTER 9

Cry Havoc

Despite his dedication to appeasement for nearly four years, the public did not regard Lloyd George as a man committed to reconciliation with Britain's former enemies. Partly as a result of press hostility, particularly in *The Times* and the *Daily Mail*, his image was that of a sharp operator with few scruples as to how he got his way, and no ideals to guide or inspire him. The failure of the London Conference in August 1922 was portrayed in the press as the personal failure of a vain, aggressive demagogue, whose sole aim was to remain in power, whatever the cost to the nation at home or abroad. The man who had made pacification his goal did not inspire the public with confidence in his moderate intentions. Even the ending of Civil War in Ireland, and the settlement of the Irish question by negotiations, won him few laurels. His reputation was at its lowest ebb. The honours scandal had made him appear financially dishonest, and stirred memories of the Marconi Affair in which he had been involved ten years before. Among his colleagues some, like Baldwin, disliked what they considered irregularities in his private life; others, like Curzon, began to wonder whether they could possibly have any political future in Lloyd George's coalition government. Back-benchers dreamed of a restoration of the Conservative Party as an independent political force. Seventeen years had passed since Balfour's last Conservative administration. The Lloyd George coalition, held together by loyalty to the Prime Minister and reliance upon his patronage, seemed to a growing number of Conservatives to be a heavy weight, dragging their Party into disunion and oblivion.

Lloyd George had championed appeasement in Europe. But in Asia he pursued a different policy. He did not seek with Turkey the reconciliation he had sought with Germany. He supported Greek expansionist aspirations in Anatolia, and strongly encouraged the Greeks in their desire to control the Turkish mainland around Smyrna. He was so enthusiastic about the Greek cause that one of his pronouncements was used by the Greek Army in an Order of the Day. He appeared to believe that the Greeks were in every way superior to the Turks, and that militarily they would easily prevail.

Fighting between Greeks and Turks continued in Turkey for over a year until, on 18 August 1922, the Greek Army broke in disarray, and the Turks drove them back into Smyrna itself, and into the sea. Flushed with victory, the Turkish forces turned towards the Dardanelles, and to·the town of Chanak, which was under French, Italian, and British control. In September, Turkish troops approached the line held by the erstwhile allies. War seemed inevitable. Lloyd George and his colleagues were determined not to withdraw. At a Cabinet meeting on 15 September Churchill, Birkenhead, Balfour and Austen Chamberlain strongly supported Lloyd George in his demand for an immediate Turkish withdrawal. They refused to accept the national 'humiliation' which withdrawal from Chanak would involve.

Lloyd George was convinced that he could destroy the Turkish initiative. He urged Curzon to seek support in the Balkans in order to resist any Turkish move across the Dardanelles. 'The country would be behind us,' he wrote to Curzon, 'in any steps we took to keep the Turk out of Europe. The Slavs and Rumanians would gladly supply troops.[1] Lloyd George was confident of support, not only from the British public and the Balkans, but also from the Dominions. Imperial troops had played an important part in the Great War. They would certainly be most welcome in any further conflict. Both Churchill and Birkenhead, who for over a year had opposed Lloyd George's anti-Turk policy and urged reconciliation with Turkey, now, confronted by an emergency, became the Prime Minister's most ardent supporters.[2] Britain was in danger. The Empire must be called in to ensure a swift Turkish surrender.

Churchill drafted the telegram which was intended to fire the Dominions with crusading zeal:

Secret. Following for your Prime Minister from the Prime Minister. Begins. Decision taken by Cabinet today to resist aggression upon Europe by the Turks. . . . Not only does the Freedom of the Straits for which such immense sacrifices were made in the war involve vital imperial and world wide interests, but we cannot forget that there are twenty thousand British and Anzac graves in the Gallipoli peninsula.³

The telegram claimed that France and Italy would act with Britain. It gave a strong hint that military help would be forthcoming from Greece, Rumania, and the new Serb-Croat-Slovene State (later called Yugoslavia). It requested an immediate promise of Dominion troops. Before any answers could come, a Press Communique was issued from 10 Downing Street. It stated that the French, Italian, and Dominion Governments were all supporting Britain. This announcement was issued late on the evening of Saturday, 16 September. It was published in the Canadian and Australian papers on Sunday. Yet the original telegraphic request for support was still being decoded, and only reached the respective Prime Ministers *after* they had read in the newspapers that they had already promised support. All Lloyd George's hopes for a united front collapsed. Only Newfoundland and New Zealand offered to send troops. France and Italy then withdrew their soldiers from Chanak. The Canadian Prime Minister, Mackenzie King, refused to commit himself. Smuts, the South African Prime Minister, was silent. The Australian Prime Minister, Billy Hughes, telegraphed:

We are a peace-loving democracy. We have been through a dreadful ordeal in which we hope that you and the world will agree we played our part worthily. In a good cause, we are prepared to venture our all; in a bad one, not a single man.⁴

This was also the view of the British public. Lloyd George had gone too far. He was preparing for war without popular support. Even the King sent a warning note in the slim disguise of approval:

While congratulating you and the Government upon the prompt and complete measures that have been taken to deal with this grave emergency, the King is sure that you all are as averse as he is to a renewal of war and that everything will be done to avoid such a calamity. . . .⁵

Lloyd George continued to prepare for war. He proposed in Cabinet an ultimatum demanding an immediate Turkish withdrawal. Curzon and Baldwin opposed such an extreme step. But it was taken despite their doubts. Both argued in favour of negotiations instead of threats, of appeasement instead of war. But the ultimatum was finally sent to General Sir Charles Harington, the

British Commander-in-Chief at the Straits. It went no further. Encouraged by the British High Commissioner at Constantinople, Sir Horace Rumbold, Harington decided to ignore it. Instead, they asked the Turks to open negotiations.[6] On October 3 the Turks agreed. Eight days later a settlement was reached, the troops withdrew on both sides of the zone, and war was averted. The appeasement of a General and a diplomat paid handsome dividends.

Although the danger of immediate hostilities was over as soon as Harington and Rumbold began negotiations on October 3, the impact of the policy had yet to be felt fully. Lloyd George had clearly abandoned the political philosophy of appeasement in favour of what was later to be called 'brinkmanship'. He had been prepared to resort to war as an instrument of policy. The public shuddered at the thought of a new war. The press was quickly infected by the public mood. Lord Beaverbrook, owner of the *Daily Express* and friend of Lloyd George, decided to become, in his phrase, an 'agitator for peace'. He urged Bonar Law to come out publicly against Lloyd George's 'dangerous' policy. In Beaverbrook's judgement, which was a sound one:

The people by this time were against war. The Government had failed completely in their efforts to stir up a war spirit. . . . It is possible that if the Cabinet had persisted, some headway would have been made in the direction of securing public approval but, as soon as Bonar Law raised the standard of peace, around which people could rally, the whole enterprise was at an end. Some Ministers might still wish to go to war. They could unfurl the banners and beat the drums. But the nation would not march.[7]

Bonar Law's 'standard of peace' was a letter to *The Times*, published on October 7. Beaverbrook ensured that it was given simultaneous prominence and even greater editorial support in the *Daily Express*. While not condemning Lloyd George's decision to force the Turkish advance to a halt, Bonar Law asked whether Britain was to go on acting in this way, without obtaining the co-operation of the Empire, the allied powers, or the United States. Repetitions of this sort of crisis would throw an unfair burden upon the British people: 'We cannot act alone as the policeman of the world. The financial and social condition of this country makes that impossible.'

Bonar Law's letter became the clarion call to revolt against what the public saw as an adventurous, dangerous foreign policy. It led to a political revolt of Conservatives anxious to end the coalition and reconstitute their party. Having accepted Lloyd George's premiership willingly in 1916, they now regarded themselves as shackled to an erratic adventurer: now they looked to Bonar Law, the Leader of the Conservative Party since 1911, to lead them from tempest to tranquillity.

Lloyd George tried to answer the charge that he was endangering world peace. Replying at Manchester on 14 October to his critics, Liberal and Conservative alike, he said:

Mr. Asquith has asked why we did not emulate the patient, forbearing policy which Lord Grey displayed in 1914 towards the Germans, instead of indulging in the amateur tactics of Downing Street today? Well, the old patient and forbearing policy of 1914 ended in the most disastrous war which this world has ever seen. The amateur diplomacy of 1922, has at any rate, brought peace.[8]

This was true; but the Conservative rebels found that their criticisms of Lloyd George's war fever gained wide and rapid support. Leopold Amery among Junior Ministers, Sir Samuel Hoare, and Edward Wood, later Lord Halifax, from among influential backbenchers, Stanley Baldwin from the Cabinet itself – he was President of the Board of Trade – all urged Lloyd George's removal on the grounds that he had endangered peace both in domestic politics and in foreign affairs. On 18 October 1922 Conservative MPs meeting at the Carlton Club voted by 187 to 87 to leave the Coalition.[9] Stanley Baldwin had appealed to them to challenge the 'dynamic force' of the Prime Minister; Bonar Law had supported him. That afternoon Lloyd George resigned. At six o'clock in the evening Bonar Law agreed to form a Government. By raising up the spectre of war Lloyd George had spurred on his enemies to combine against him. Peace was the only policy the British people seemed willing to endorse. Fear of war dominated and oppressed the public mind.

The 1922 election gave the Conservative Party its electoral mandate. Bonar Law remained Prime Minister, with Stanley Baldwin as his Chancellor of the Exchequer. The election was fought and won on Bonar Law's slogan, 'Tranquillity'. In vain Lloyd George attacked this slogan and all that it implied. 'It is not a policy,' he said, 'it is a yawn.' But the public wanted a chance to yawn. The Turkish war alarms had caused sleepless nights and restless days. Bonar Law and Baldwin represented the new mood in British politics. Both were cautious, colourless men. Both spoke without clamour, without bravado. Both appeared self-effacing and insignificant. And yet the very policy of reconciliation which Lloyd George had tried to ease forward for four years now became not only the policy but the passion of the nation.

After 1922, those who were thought to favour war instead of negotiations became the object of much derision. Churchill, in particular, was singled out for adverse comment. He was made the prototype of the 'warmonger', whose views ought to be listened to no longer. He had actually been defeated in the 1922 election, after twenty-two years as an MP. His support for lenient peace terms in 1919, his hostility to high reparations and his belief that war was ugly, degrading, and utterly wasteful were all either unknown or ignored. Only his desire to crush Bolshevism by force, and his alleged keenness to shoot strikers, were repeated by critics again and again. By maligning Churchill, his enemies denounced all bellicose moods. Churchill's unpopularity was a sign that appeasement was in the ascendent. Among those who set upon Churchill was H. G. Wells, who described him as a fifteen year old 'who ought to be kept out of mischief in some sort of institution where he can play *kriegspiel* for the rest of his existence without endangering human life'.[10] In his novel, *Men Like Gods*, Wells enlarged on this unjust yet popular theme. Of Churchill, who is thinly disguised in the novel as Rupert Catskill, Secretary of State for War, Wells wrote:

I sometimes think it would have been better for all of us if Rupert had taken to writing romances instead of living them. . . . He has lived most romantically. He has fought bravely in wars. He has been a prisoner and escaped wonderfully from prison. *His violent imaginations have caused the deaths of thousands of people.*[11]

Such crude hostility was not confined to novels. When Churchill tried to return to Parliament in 1924, these accusations were hurled at him from the soap-boxes. In his election address the Independent Labour Party candidate, Fenner Brockway, encouraged by Clifford Allen, described Churchill as 'a public danger and a menace to the peace of the world', claiming that:

Of all politicians Mr Churchill has shown himself most unfit for the responsibility of government. His forte is to be a disturber of peace, whether at home or abroad. He is a political adventurer, with a genius for mischievous irresponsibility. He is militant to the finger-tips.[12]

Lloyd George and Chanak were never forgotten. Churchill became a man to be feared for his alleged eagerness to make war wherever possible. Bonar Law and Baldwin became the guardians of the quiet life. For sixteen years this quiet life was sought and buttressed by the pursuit of appeasement in Europe. Two of those who had voted against Lloyd George at the Carlton Club, Samuel Hoare and Edward Wood (Lord Halifax), were both later Foreign Secretary, and each supported Baldwin and Neville Chamberlain in the search for an effective appeasement policy. Ironically, both had signed the telegram urging Lloyd George to be severe at Versailles. Thus were the swords of patriots beaten into parliamentary ploughshares.

CHAPTER 10

The Crisis with France

For ten years appeasement was the guiding philosophy of British foreign policy. From 1919 to 1929 successive British governments sought to influence European affairs in favour of an amelioration of tempers and an acceptance of discussions and negotiations as the best means of ensuring peaceful change. That any change was necessary, France tended to deny. But British official opinion doubted whether a secure Europe could be based upon the Treaties of 1919, and had strong hopes of obtaining serious revision of those aspects of the Treaties that seemed to contain the seeds of future conflict. For ten years those hopes propelled policy forward. Under the aegis of Lord Curzon, Ramsay MacDonald, and Austen Chamberlain important progress was made each year. Appeasement seemed not only morally justifiable, as being clearly preferable to rearmament, temper, and war, but also politically acceptable and diplomatically feasible.

The basis of appeasement was the acceptance of independent national states, each based as nearly as possible upon the Wilsonian principle of self-determination. With the disintegration in 1918 of the Russian, Turkish, German, and Habsburg Empires, the final stage had been reached in a process that had begun in Europe during the Napoleonic wars – the evolution of strictly national as opposed to dynastic or strategic frontiers. Post-1918 diplomacy was geared to securing the final rectifications of frontiers still not conforming to this principle. Such frontiers were few. Most of them were the result of Versailles boundaries which had been drawn to the disadvantage of Germany. Thus there were German-speaking people outside, but contiguous to the German frontier in Poland and Czechoslovakia, as well as Germans in Austria who had been forbidden union with Germany under Article 80 of the Treaty of Versailles. Even this clause was not irrevocable. According to the Treaty it could be altered 'with the consent of the Council of the League of Nations'. Although France was unlikely to make such consent possible, the principle of making territorial adjustments was specifically and officially acknowledged.

National 'inequalities' other than those of frontiers were also part of the Versailles Treaty, and were equally prone to the egalitarian touch of appeasement. The disarmament of Germany, while France remained rearmed, was a German grievance which could be met either by disarming France or allowing Germany to rearm. Both alternatives were considered by British policy-makers, and when the first proved impossible to secure, the second became logically difficult to resist.

A further 'inequality' was the exclusion of Germany from the League of Nations. British policy worked for Germany's inclusion, and looked forward to a time when the difference between 'Allied' and 'Enemy' powers, as embodied in the Versailles Treaty, would disappear, and cease to disturb and irritate Franco-German co-operation. In pursuing an appeasement policy, the British Government sought to mediate between France and Germany. It was the policy of the 'honest broker'. Its aim was to allay mutual suspicions. It depended for its success upon both France and Germany realizing that it was a 'neutral' policy, designed to provide both countries with adequate security, under British patronage, and thereby to make rearmament, military alliances, and war-plans unnecessary. The weakness of the policy was that France often felt that it was intended only to weaken her, and Germany that its aim was to keep her weak.

The policy of appeasement, as practised between 1919–29, was wholly in Britain's interest. It was in no sense intended as an altruistic policy. British policy makers reasoned that the basis of European peace was a flourishing economic situation, unhampered by political bickerings, which, by ensuring general European prosperity, would also promote mutual understanding. Only by success in this policy could Britain avoid becoming involved once again in a war rising out of European national ambitions and frustrations: a war which might well prove even more destructive of human life and social order than the 1914–18 war had been.

Early in 1920 J. W. Headlam-Morley, Historical Adviser to the Foreign Office, who had been with the British Delegation at Versailles, raised the question of British post-war policy in a series of Foreign Office minutes and letters. He pointed out that the uncertainty as to what amount would be demanded in reparations was causing anxiety in Germany and hampering German economic recovery. He deprecated the tendency to shrug off all responsibility for German economic distress by saying that 'they have brought their misfortune on themselves by the war'. Germany, he pointed out, was suffering as much from the uncertainties and severities of the peace as from the cost and carnage of the war. He stressed the difference between British policy and the French hope of enforcing the Treaty to the letter, even to the extent of trying ultimately to separate the left bank of the Rhine from Germany. This, he wrote, was stated by Curzon in the House of Lords as being the policy of supporting the revision of the Treaty. Headlam-Morley urged the need for 'a serious inquiry as to what is meant by the revision of the Treaty'.[1] His opinions were judged premature and mistaken by his superiors. Lord Hardinge, the Permanent Under-Secretary of State at the Foreign Office, noted unenthusiastically that 'the present moment seems hardly the best chosen to start an inquiry', and Curzon replied tersely that 'When I spoke of revising the Treaty, I did not contemplate an immediate or even an early formal, official, authoritative Allied revision'[2]. Curzon suggested that revision, if it were to come, should come through the League of Nations, and he foresaw an increasing number of appeals, presumably from Germany, Austria, and Hungary, to the League. But Curzon's view was unrealistic. In the League Council, revision could easily be forestalled by France and its friends. If British policy were to favour Treaty revision, it could not expect results by standing at the side-line and offering occasional cheers. Revision would need active British participation. It called for a clear view of precisely which changes Britain would support, and what sort of pressure she would be prepared to exert, particularly against France.

Headlam-Morley continued to press for a more specific examination of British policy. He criticized the existing attitude towards Germany as designed only to produce 'temporary palliatives' aimed at warding off immediate chaos. He wanted a long-term approach, based upon the search for European economic recovery and the 'permanent restoration' of some measure of co-operation between the allied and enemy powers. American help, he pointed out, would eventually be needed to restore European financial stability: did British policy make it likely that American help would be forthcoming when it was most needed? Headlam-Morley felt that

... they will be very reluctant to give help to a Europe which comes merely as a beggar; they will be inclined to inquire whether the help they give will be part of an organized scheme and whether it may not really be made futile by the continuance of the political animosities which prevent the different nations, enemy and allied, working together in the common task of restoration.[3]

Headlam-Morley's appeal for a more specific statement of policy was taken up by another member of the Foreign Office, S. P. Waterlow, who, in a minute four days later was even more precise in his suggestions. He realized that the question of reparations and war debts stood in the way of any form of appeasement:

... it is impossible for H M Government to have a distinctly British policy towards Germany, which would act as a check on the short-sighted policy of the French, until the Cabinet have decided the question ... of our allies' [war] debts to us. If the Cabinet agree to let the French off their debt to us, we shall then, and only then, be in a position to insist upon and initiate a reasonable European policy. Otherwise our hands will be tied by bitterness about indemnities.[4]

War debts remained. France refused to give up reparations in return. Britain could hardly announce a unilateral abandonment of the money owed to her by France. Compromise involved mutual concessions. The French, safeguarded by the Treaty, and willing to try to extort reparations by force if necessary, saw no advantage in debt-cancellation, only much danger. For France, the existence of unpaid reparations seemed to provide a powerful means of preventing German economic recovery.

Headlam-Morley reiterated his plea for a revision a month later, urging that greater powers be given to Boundary Commissions to advise on frontiers differing from those basically laid down at Versailles. He pointed out in a Foreign Office memorandum that at the Conference 'the work was done entirely from maps and volumes of statistics, and none of those who did it had any real local knowledge'. He had himself taken part in deciding where frontier lines should go, 'and instantly felt how very unsatisfactory the conditions of our work were'.[5] But Headlam-Morley's suggestion for even quite limited revision met with a stern rebuff from

Sir Eyre Crowe, the Foreign Office official whose anti-German suspicions were said to have been a major influence on Sir Edward Grey before 1914, and who was regarded in revisionist circles as the man responsible for preventing the Foreign Office taking the lead in a policy of Anglo-German rapprochement. Crowe minuted on Headlam-Morley's memorandum:

> I am most reluctant to recommend the issue of any instructions which would clearly contemplate modifications of the frontiers as described in the treaty.
>
> The treaty is being assailed from every side and proposals for revising it fill the air to such an extent that I believe an impression is being widely created not only here but in Germany that nothing in the treaty is really sacred. Against this growing tendency to weaken the foundations, I think the only effective remedy is to stand up for the maintenance of the treaty. If modifications are ultimately necessary, they will impose themselves. We need not proclaim that we are looking out for opportunity to bring them about.[6]

Under Crowe's influence, this attitude prevailed inside the Foreign Office itself, even if it failed to affect successive Foreign Secretaries, or convince Lord D'Abernon in Berlin. The difficulty of those who opposed treaty revision was to justify the extreme attitude of France, whose rigid policy towards Germany alienated many of those who had been previously well-disposed towards her. As irritation with France grew, sympathy with Germany grew also. In 1921 French policy came under severe criticism when the Plebiscite in Silesia, whose result was not as favourable to Poland as France had hoped, was manoeuvred through the Council of the League to produce a compromise solution much to Poland's advantage. This appeared to many to be misuse by France of her powerful position inside the League.

Philip Kerr wrote to Lord D'Abernon from London that: 'The Silesia decision provoked great discontent here. Nobody believes it will work, and it throws discredit on the League of Nations that it could have adopted a procedure which could lead to such a result.'[7]

D'Abernon was equally upset, feeling that the decision was 'deplorable', for it certainly gave the Germans the impression that Britain could not use her influence in Germany's interest against French intransigence. D'Abernon replied to Kerr:

> It has put us back tremendously in Germany. For the last six months we were really masters of the situation here – a fact of immense Euro-

pean importance. Now we have lost our position. . . . Of course this is temporary, but it is disappointing to fall back after so great an improvement.[8]

In 1922 Keynes fired another salvo from his already effective gun in the form of a second book, *A Revision of the Treaty*. He gave Lloyd George some grudging credit for protecting Europe 'from as many of the evil consequences of his own Treaty, as it lay in his power to prevent . . . preserving the peace, though not the prosperity, of Europe, seldom expressing the truth, yet often acting under its influence'; and he rejoiced that reparations were beginning to crumble. He deplored the Silesian decision, whereby the plebiscite area was divided between Poland and Germany, as the judgement of a Solomon – 'Divide ye the living child in twain' – without Solomon's wisdom. Instead of a flourishing economic unit covering all Silesia, the result of the manipulation of the plebiscite was an invitation to economic and political chaos:

> The Wilsonian dogma, which exalts and dignifies the divisions of race and nationality above the bonds of trade and culture, is deeply embedded in the conception of the League. . . . It yields us the paradox that the first experiment in international government should exert its influence in the direction of intensifying nationalism.[9]

Keynes felt strongly that France had nothing to fear from Germany 'except what she may herself provoke'.[10]

Despite the gradual reduction of the reparations demand, France continued throughout 1921 and 1922 to use the threat of occupation in order to seek payments, irrespective of German economic difficulties. Keynes denied the legality of France's action. He pointed out that there was no provision in the Treaty for French troops to move across to the eastern bank of the Rhine if Germany failed to pay on time. He also stressed the fact that any occupation, to fulfil the terms of the Treaty, had to be agreed upon by all the Allies, and that there was no justification for 'isolated action by a single Ally'.[11] There was yet another cause, he wrote, for deep dissatisfaction at French action:

> It is *obligatory* on the Council of the League, under Article 17, to invite Germany, in the event of a dispute between Germany and the Allies, to accept the obligation of membership in the League for the purposes of such dispute, and to institute immediately an inquiry into the circumstances of the dispute.[12]

This, Keynes pointed out, had not been done. Nor did it seem likely that it would be done in future. France clearly intended to act towards Germany as severely as possible. She did not propose to heed British warnings, or to believe that British interests would ever lead to an Anglo-German rapprochement.

Anti-French feeling was mounting in England. Coloured troops in the Ruhr, the Silesian plebiscite, the constant French threats to occupy the Rhineland, these all strained Anglo-French relations to breaking point. When, in December 1922, Germany failed to make her full payment of timber to France, Poincaré announced that France would occupy the Ruhr once more. Bonar Law protested. At a Conference in London he proposed a reduction in Germany's overall liability from £6,600 million to £2,500 million. His proposal was rejected. At the Paris Conference in January he opposed with equal earnestness the occupation of the Ruhr. Poincaré ignored him. French troops were ordered into the Ruhr. Sir John Bradbury had already made it clear that he regarded the German default as 'almost microscopic'. When the Ruhr occupation began on 11 January 1923 British public opinion began to move firmly against France. Curzon wrote in March that 'public opinion here is getting more restive and will not stand benevolent neutrality *ad infinitum*'. Asquith's daughter, Lady Violet Bonham-Carter, gave Lady D'Abernon a graphic description of conditions in the French-occupied zone:

Everything the French touch they paralyse. Chimneys are ceasing to smoke – railways are stopping – coke-ovens, which take a month to light, damping down. They are terrified out of their wits and, though armed with machine-guns, tanks and every sort of ridiculous implement of war complain that the schoolchildren attack them – and they cover the walls with placards ordering civilians to walk in single file in the middle of the street with their hands *turned outwards* so that the palms are clearly visible. . . . A more futile and frivolously dangerous adventure one cannot imagine. . . . In England the French would have been torn to bits by the women alone long before this.[13]

Lord D'Abernon was equally angered by the French action. He felt that it had been a mistake to disarm Germany at Versailles without obtaining general disarmament, for the existing French military predominance made France feel that her best security lay in maintaining and exercising her power. D'Abernon wanted Britain to take the initiative in proposing 'some guarantee to

Germany against aggression', as well as a guarantee 'making France really secure'. He considered that France's action in the Ruhr 'has shown that the real danger of military violence at the present moment is infinitely greater from France than from Germany'.[14] The German policy of passive resistance continued all summer. The Ruhr was silent. Britain tried to encourage Franco-German discussions, but failed. French instransigence to end the occupation was seen in Britain as an attempt to bring about the permanent detachment of the Rhineland from Germany. In July Curzon informed France that the British Government was 'resolutely against any modification of the German-French frontier'.[15] On 11 August he sent a strongly worded note to France, in which he stressed the illegality of the Ruhr occupation, and declared that no further reparations should be taken from Germany until her finances were restored and her currency stabilized.

Curzon's hostility to France now reached its climax. Although it never made him consciously pro-German, all its manifestations concerned Franco-German relations, and resulted in advantage to Germany. When the French Government demanded the surrender of the German Crown Prince in November 1923, Curzon not only refused to allow Britain to be associated with this demand, but intimated at once that if it were persisted in, Britain would withdraw from all inter-allied committees. The threat succeeded.

A month later the French announced that 'an autonomous Government of the Palatinate' had been established in the Rhineland, which France supported. Curzon at once declared publicly that Britain would not recognize the new régime, describing it in the House of Lords as 'this hasty and upstart simulacrum of a Government'. Robert Clive, the British Consul-General at Munich, was sent to make an on-the-spot report. Poincaré's refusal to accept Clive's mission was ignored.

Clive's report was received by Curzon on 20 January 1924 and presented to Parliament on the following day. It stated unequivocally that the majority of the inhabitants of the Palatinate were strongly opposed to autonomy, that anti-French feeling there was fierce, and that the new régime could neither have come into existence nor survived without the support of the French army of occupation.[16] Curzon's decision to publicize the Clive Report made it impossible for the French position to be maintained. The last French hope of detaching some part of western Germany from the whole was gone. In challenging and breaking French policy, Curzon had preserved German unity. He had shown how little was left of the *Entente Cordiale*, and made it clear that if Britain felt Germany was being improperly treated, British pressure could be brought to bear to redress the balance.

The publication of the Clive Report was Curzon's last official act. A day later Ramsay MacDonald became Prime Minister of Britain's first Labour Government and Curzon's career as Foreign Secretary was over. Towards France his relations had always been disturbed; towards Germany he sought to take a broad view, tempering justice with generosity. He belonged to a generation for which, over a period of almost twenty years, war with Germany had seemed an impossibility, something unnatural. Although he had written almost hysterical letters to Lloyd George demanding the trial of the Kaiser in July 1919, this mood of temper and triumph had passed quickly away. He was never vindictive towards Germany. If at times he appeared to Germans aloof, remote, and unemotional, he also appeared in similar guise to his fellow countrymen.

Curzon left the Foreign Office in January 1924, but Lord D'Abernon remained in Berlin. Continuity of foreign policy was thereby assured, despite the radical political change in England. The new German Foreign Secretary, Gustav Stresemann, worked closely and constructively with D'Abernon, who wrote of him:

> Once reassured as to the essential good faith of English policy; once convinced that we were not seeking to hold Germany down in a subordinate position, but to secure Peace in Europe on a durable basis, his whole attitude became one of cordial co-operation.[17]

This Anglo-German co-operation led to two monuments of European appeasement, the Dawes Plan, and the Locarno Agreements, both of which seemed to augur well, not only for peaceful change of a profound sort, but also for a future working partnership of Britain, Germany, and France. The French occupation of the Ruhr, and French 'obstinacy' over reparations, by seeming to threaten chaos and renewed war in Europe, stimulated British activity in favour of appeasement. Two successive British Prime Ministers, the Conservative Stanley Baldwin and the Socialist Ramsay MacDonald, accepted the need for an active, ameliorative British policy. Between them they constructed what, to all but the most cynical observer, was clearly the foundation of lasting peace in Europe.

CHAPTER II

The New Leader

Ramsay MacDonald became Prime Minister in January 1924 and fell from power nine months later. Although he was Prime Minister again from 1929–35, it was during his first brief tenure of office that he made his greatest mark upon foreign affairs. During these nine months he acted as his own Foreign Secretary, having rejected the view canvassed by the UDC that E. D. Morel should have the post.[1] MacDonald had his own strong views on foreign policy. He did not intend to defer to the wishes or prejudices of others. E. D. Morel's dislike of France, a dislike widely shared by the left-wing of the Labour Party, could only have increased the Anglo-French friction which Curzon had built up, and made overall European appeasement impossible. MacDonald sought negotiation, not recrimination in Europe. He announced boldly in the House of Commons that 'France has nothing to fear from any policy that we may pursue'.[2] Nor did Germany. MacDonald aimed at removing fear as a factor in European diplomacy.

In some ways MacDonald's policies were part of the British socialist tradition. Germany before 1914, with Europe's largest parliamentary socialist party, had been an object of admiration; France, a country denounced for its alliance with totalitarian Russia. Post-war Germany seemed equally attractive, once the initial Labour enthusiasm for Bolshevik Russia had begun to fade. Germany, republican now as well as strongly socialist, seemed an obvious partner in European reconstruction. Perhaps Labour sympathy for the underdog played its part. Certainly Labour publicists made every effort to sympathize with German problems and to praise German achievements. In his book *After the Peace*, published in 1920, Brailsford described post-war Germany as 'half-starved, pitiably tame' and needing, not military occupation,

105

punishment or recrimination, but sympathy and support:

> One does not save civilization by drawing maps. One saves it by food and fuel, by the work which restores sanity to the artisan, hope to the mother, and health to the child. [The Peace Treaties] seemed designed to perpetuate the economic death of half a continent.[3]

But MacDonald's desire for good Anglo-German relations did not spring from sympathy alone. In 1914 he had opposed war with Germany, although the Labour Party officially supported the war. MacDonald resigned the leadership, and for four years was isolated from his own followers. Frequently they abused him. While anti-German hysteria affected people of all political parties, MacDonald remained calm. He believed that if the war was not to be the prelude of repeated conflict, someone must keep alive 'the mental temper of peace' so that after the war he would have both the moral stature and intellectual preparation for building a fair post-war world personally unfettered by the legacy of four years of hate and fear.[4] Writing in the *Socialist Review* of October 1915 MacDonald stressed the danger of militarism as an attitude of mind:

> Militarism rests on fear, and fear exists because the peoples do not come close enough together. . . .
> If German militarism is to be crushed so that it is no longer to be a European menace, Germany must not be given, as an inheritance from this war, the spirit of revenge.

Nine years later, when he became Prime Minister, Germany was in no way free from the spirit of revenge which MacDonald feared would blight the peace. Defeat, hunger, the Treaty of Versailles, the two French occupations of the Ruhr all kept alive in Germany a spirit of sullen discontent. MacDonald felt that a British initiative could redress the balance; that if Germany were treated as an equal, and given proof that the final reparations figure could be fixed by negotiation, the spirit of revenge would begin to waver.

A serious obstacle threatened to destroy MacDonald's hope. Anti-French feeling had mounted inside the Labour Party to gargantuan proportions. Since the Armistice, France had replaced Germany as the nation to be abused, maligned, cursed, ridiculed, and reviled.[5] But European appeasement needed French co-operation, and no French Government could survive at election time

which made concessions to a hostile British Labour Government.
MacDonald himself had not entirely escaped from the prevailing
mood. Having alienated himself from his Party because of his
hostility to the war, he could hardly hold his renewed leadership by
unpopular professions of sympathy for France. Even in the House
of Commons he had accused France of wanting to crush Germany,
not for her own security, but in order ultimately to dominate
Europe.⁶ This was the Labour theme. France was the scheming
villain; Germany the innocent victim; Britain, like St George,
should be the protector of innocence. The occupation of the Ruhr
seemed a clear proof of French wickedness. 'More certainly, and
much more swiftly than Bismarck's folly,' wrote Brailsford, 'this
wickedness of M. Poincaré will make its inevitable war.'⁷ A Labour
MP, Oswald Mosley, was Chairman of the British Bureau for
Ruhr Information, which published a weekly bulletin of conditions
in the occupied zone, laying great emphasis on French 'wickedness':

For the last two months the population of the Palatinate have oscil-
lated between hope and despair. Mr Clive's visit inspired hope, which
died away after his departure, when those who had given evidence were
penalized, and terrorism was renewed.⁸

The Bulletin stressed every aspect of the occupation unfavourable
to France – the iniquities of hasty billeting, the French failure to
meet the urgent need for medical facilities among the civilian
population, the reduction of pensions for war widows, and the
removal from school of 880 German schoolboys to make way for
thirteen French students who did not wish to mix with the
'enemy'. Such stories kept anti-French feeling in the Labour
Party at fever pitch. The *New Leader*, under Brailsford's editorship,
produced weekly diatribes against France. In the week that
MacDonald became Prime Minister Norman Angell wrote in the
New Leader:

There is something comic about the suggestion that France, more
powerful relatively than any State in Europe since the days of Napoleon,
with enormous air, sea and under-sea armaments, with a round dozen
of satellite States and the vast reserves of savage Africa to draw upon,
should tremble at the thought of Germany – disarmed, helpless, hope-
less, paralysed, starving; more comic still when the France which fears
the vengeance of Germany commits daily acts which would inflame the
vengeance of any people under the sun.

But anti-French feeling, so easy to rouse, and equally easy to sustain, did not lend itself to promoting European appeasement. MacDonald, from the outset of his premiership, sought to influence France by sympathy. On 21 February 1924 he wrote a conciliatory letter to Poincaré, pointing out the reasons for their divergent views, and asking for a general discussion on the future of reparations, without renewing 'the old wearisome round of controversy and altercation on points that may be important but are not fundamental'.[9] Poincaré responded cautiously. The hostility of the Left towards France had been so virulent that he was caught unawares. Two days before the French elections in May 1924, MacDonald invited him to talks at Chequers. His desire for appeasement thus cut away the shackles of Party prejudice. When Poincaré lost the elections, and Edouard Herriot, the Radical Socialist leader, became Prime Minister, MacDonald at once repeated his invitation. Herriot came to England. The Labour Party took more readily to the idea of co-operation with a socialist than it had done with his predecessor. Norman Angell, for example, was on friendly terms with Herriot; indeed, he appears to have persuaded Angell that France must have guarantees against German aggression before giving up the securities in the Treaty, which, while not lending themselves to European pacification, did enable France to keep Germany weak. Angell later wrote that at this time he 'acquired a strong conviction that all real prospect of effective collective defence in Europe depended first of all upon agreement between France and Britain as the nucleus of the police power of the League'; and thus seems to have accepted MacDonald's view.[10]

In April 1924 the Dawes Report was issued. It provided MacDonald with his opportunity to take the initiative in European affairs. The report stressed that reparations could not continue to be paid unless the German currency were stabilized. This should be done, the report advised, by a foreign loan to Germany. Even then, it said, the rate of reparations payments should be slowed down. Above all, the German economy must be made secure. Reparations could only be paid against a background of relative and increasing prosperity. German industry must be allowed to recover and to prosper. In order to make the Dawes Report more than a mere utopian hope, the United States agreed to put an American representative on the Reparation Commission, and to encourage American businessmen and investors to subscribe to the German loan. The return of America to Europe made inter-European co-operation easier. America's abrupt and unexpected withdrawal in 1919 had thrown each country back upon its own national devices. Renewed American participation, even if limited to economic affairs, took the edge off European fears.

MacDonald was quick to exploit the possibilities of Herriot's premiership and the Dawes Report. On 16 July 1924 he opened a Conference in London at which the French, Belgian, and Italian Prime Ministers were present. For three weeks they discussed the problem of reparations and security. They agreed that the Dawes Report should be accepted as the new basis for reparations, and that sanctions should only be imposed if Germany wilfully defaulted, and were declared to have done so by an Arbitral Tribunal. The Prime Ministers also agreed that before sanctions were applied, the interests of those who had subscribed to the German loan should be taken into account. This would clearly involve America, which would presumably be reluctant to impose sanctions which could only damage the German economy, and thereby reduce the chances of the loan being repaid. These moderate decisions having been reached, and a repetition of arbitrary Ruhr-style occupations having been averted, the Germans were then invited to join the Conference. They came; their delegation being led by Wilhelm Marx, the Chancellor, Gustav Stresemann, and Hans Luther, the Finance Minister. The negotiations were made smoother by the presence of American 'observers', Frank Kellogg, the US Ambassador in London, Logan, the American representative on the Reparation Commission, and Owen D. Young, the chief author of the Dawes Report. Discussions continued for over three weeks, under MacDonald's chairmanship. He was determined not to allow a repetition of Versailles – a conference of victors at which the 'enemy' interests would be ignored. He had already, before becoming Prime Minister, made it clear in a pamphlet, *The Foreign Policy of the Labour Party*, that he was opposed to the League of Nations becoming a mere committee of the allied powers 'with other nations invited to look on and give an appearance of respectable authority to what the victors decide'. He was determined to avoid this at the London Conference, where both the sincerity and efficacy of his policy were on trial. Speaking during the Conference he declared:

I should like to impress upon the German people, if I might, that . . . we have created a system of arbitration, of examination, of revision, which will enable both them and us to observe the working of the Dawes plan; to watch projects that may be doubtful in their effects and to come together in a sincere desire to rectify mistakes as soon as mistakes are discovered.[11]

D'Abernon, from Berlin, gathered favourable reports on the progress of the Conference. Although the first day had apparently been marked by 'wrangling between the Allies, followed by wrangling with the Germans', the atmosphere rapidly improved:

Herriot has impressed everybody by his goodwill, and his desire to find a possible arrangement.

The Germans have been well treated, and received with courtesy. . . .

Ramsay MacDonald appears to have shown tact and skill and to have done his best to reduce the period of delay in the evacuation of the Ruhr. Time after time . . . [he] has surmounted or turned extreme difficulties. His power of work is astounding everyone.[12]

MacDonald's party were divided as to the wisdom of his work. E. D. Morel was hostile. Writing in the *New Leader* at the end of July he urged that Britain should not seek a compromise over the amount of reparations to be paid, but should abandon reparations altogether. He felt that the Conference was based upon the acceptance of the Versailles Treaty, which he considered a mere repetition of the pre-war alliance systems, pivoted upon the manipulation of the balance of power, and therefore not a viable base for European reconstruction. He claimed that MacDonald's policy was spreading 'the dry-rot of suspicion and disillusion' in Labour ranks because:

Everyone is aware that so long as an unamended Versailles Treaty continues to be the public law of Europe, Europe will not know Peace. We have been told so by our leaders for five years, and we knew it without their telling us. Principles proclaimed for years cannot be abandoned in a night.[13]

But Morel's fulminations did not go unchallenged. In the same issue of the *New Leader* Norman Angell defended the idea of the Conference, feeling that it represented the first attempt since the war to break away from the pattern imposed by the Treaty. He urged that the Germans 'must be completely free to state their views and difficulties', but he accepted the continuation of the

Reparation Commission, and advised Labour supporters to have faith in MacDonald.

Angell's optimism was not ill-founded. The Conference ended in August, the loan was floated, and Franco-German confidence seemed partially restored. The French agreed to evacuate the Ruhr within twelve months. The Germans accepted the continuation of reparations at a reduced rate. The 'enemy' had been treated as an equal, listened to, compromised with, and appeased for the first time since the war had ended. The conference table had proved a proper place for adjustments in the post-war settlement. Once the principle of 'peaceful change' had been accepted, once Germany had been treated as a partner and not as a pariah, the way was open to more wide-ranging modifications to the Europe of Versailles. There seemed no longer any reason why appeasement should fail. As MacDonald told the Conference in his concluding speech:

> We are now offering Europe the first really negotiated agreement since the war; every party here represented is morally bound to do its best to carry it out, because it is not the result of an ultimatum. . . .
> This agreement may be regarded as the first Peace Treaty, because we sign it with a feeling that we have turned our backs on the terrible years of war and war mentality.[14]

Appeasement became the monopoly of no political party. Stanley Baldwin, who succeeded MacDonald as Prime Minister in November 1924, had no desire to return to the frictions of the pre-MacDonald era. He considered himself the purveyor of tranquillity in 1924, just as he had done at the time of the fall of Lloyd George two years before. Curzon, who strained Anglo-French relations so badly in 1923, was not brought back to the Foreign Office. Instead, Baldwin chose Austen Chamberlain as Foreign Secretary. But Chamberlain was at first reluctant to open negotiations with Germany on the question of security. At the Guildhall Banquet in November he spoke of Britain's desire to have 'a more intimate friendship' with its former Allies than with others. To D'Abernon's proposal for discussions which might lead to a series of guarantees for Germany's western frontier Chamberlain wrote that 'these overtures were premature'.[15]

But men and events moved more swiftly than Austen Chamberlain could determine. From Berlin, D'Abernon was an indefatigable advocate of Anglo-German co-operation. In

November he was in London, working out the terms of an Anglo-German commercial treaty with the Treasury, and obtaining the support of the new Chancellor of the Exchequer, Churchill. By this Treaty, Germany benefited from a reciprocal tariff agreement. D'Abernon was elated by this success, which the British press applauded as a step leading to 'the blotting out of war mentality'. He continued to press for a political agreement which would provide both France and Germany with territorial security, and which would base this security upon an instrument quite separate from the Versailles Treaty.

Austen Chamberlain's interest in a tripartite agreement grew only slowly. He had never had much patience with Curzon's hostile attitude towards France. 'It seems to me,' he wrote in 1923, 'that we are becoming the scold of Europe. We run about shaking our fists in people's faces, screaming that this must be altered or that must stop.'[16] D'Abernon's proposals seemed a sensible means of enabling Britain to play a less governess-like part in Europe. On 9 February 1925, D'Abernon wrote from Berlin to the King, urging negotiations with Germany, and stressing that if Germany were treated 'with a certain degree of confidence' France might find security in a British-sponsored agreement. The King wrote immediately to Chamberlain. 'Now,' he said, 'is a unique, but perhaps only a passing, moment, and one not to be lost to expedite the work of peace.'[17] Chamberlain replied to the King explaining some of the difficulties, but also outlining the more optimistic possibilities:

The French are very fearful and therefore often unwise and aggravating, and the Germans seem to be singularly obtuse to their own interests and the effect of what they say and do upon French opinion.

I regard it as the first task of statesmanship to set to work to make the new position of Germany tolerable to the German people in the hope that, as they regain prosperity under it, they may in time become reconciled to it and unwilling to put their fortunes again to the desperate hazard of war. I am working not for today or tomorrow but for some date like 1950 or 1960 when German strength will have returned and when the prospect of war will again cloud the horizon unless the risks of war are still too great to be rashly incurred and the actual conditions too tolerable to be jeopardized on a gambler's throw. . . . I believe that the key to the solution is to be found in allaying French fears, and that unless we find means to do this we may be confronted with a complete breakdown of our friendly relations with France and an exacerbation of her attitude towards Germany.[18]

But Chamberlain found it difficult to allay French fears. Nor did he relish the German attitude of somewhat plaintive self-pity. On 20 February D'Abernon's scheme encountered a large obstacle, in the foreboding form of Memorandum prepared in the Foreign Office and circulated to the Cabinet. This memorandum, with whose conclusions Chamberlain had come, with some reluctance, to agree, advocated the rejection of the so-called 'D'Abernon-Stresemann' proposals for a Reciprocal Pact of Guarantee between Germany and her former enemies. It proposed instead a unilateral defensive pact between Britain and France. This proposal, behind which the influence of Eyre Crowe was thought to be paramount, amounted to a return to the *Entente Cordiale* of 1904 in an even more specific and binding form.

The Cabinet met to discuss this proposal on 6 March 1925. Chamberlain tried to persuade his colleagues to abandon the policies previously pursued by Lloyd George, Bonar Law, and Ramsay MacDonald. Those who spoke against him were those who had been most influential, seven years earlier, in persuading Lloyd George to turn towards appeasement – Balfour, Curzon, Birkenhead, and Churchill. Chamberlain gave way. Two days later he was in Paris, explaining to Herriot that Britain could not proceed with the proposals for an Anglo-French alliance. Within a month, support for the 'D'Abernon-Stresemann' plan was spreading rapidly, and the idea of a comprehensive settlement was widely canvassed in European political circles. D'Abernon noted in his diary on April 2 that:

Public opinion in England is growing more favourable to the Pact of Mutual Security. Grey made a most excellent speech at the League of Nations meeting the other night, unreservedly accepting the policy of reciprocal Guarantee. Ramsay MacDonald has also spoken wisely.

Chamberlain became a reluctant advocate of the policy he had previously opposed. After six months of intense diplomatic activity a Treaty was ready. The German and 'Allied' delegates met at Locarno in October. Chamberlain seems still to have been uncertain of the wisdom of the proposals. When the Germans asked for a revocation of the 'War Guilt' clause to be part of the new

E

agreements he was abrupt and firm in his refusal to allow this. D'Abernon did not approve of Chamberlain's action, feeling as he did that 'the first opportunity should be taken to dissociate German liability for reparation from the charge of war guilt'. But despite Chamberlain's doubts, the Pact of Mutual Security was initialled at Locarno on 16 October 1925. The preamble stated that the Treaty 'will contribute greatly to bring about a moral relaxation of tension between nations'. The text contained pledges by Germany, France, and Belgium not to attack each other, and promises by Italy and Britain to help either Germany, France, or Belgium if they were attacked. 'All is well,' D'Abernon noted laconically in his diary, and Chamberlain wrote from Locarno:

Only once did I hesitate and nearly go wrong – when I thought of leaving the first drafting of a Pact to the French . . . it would have been a crucial error.

Briand, large-hearted, generous . . . pledged himself immediately on his return to set to work to give the largest measure of satisfaction to the hopes which the German representatives had left unuttered but which he understood so well and found so natural and so sympathetic.

Briand finding my wife waiting for me in the passage had taken both her hands in his and with tears in his eyes had spoken of my help and support. . . . And next moment Mussolini, the simplest and sincerest of men when he is not posing as the Dictator, had caught her hands in his and was covering them with kisses.[19]

The euphoria continued for some months. If Versailles had come, after six years, to embody in the public mind all that was mistaken and ill-considered in international relations, Locarno was at once portrayed as the final solution of Europe's post-war problems. 'One cannot repeat too often,' wrote D'Abernon, 'that the German view is largely what Allied action makes it; recognize goodwill, show appreciation of German action, and you have a different Germany from that produced by unjustified suspicion and un-restrained criticism.' In his opinion Locarno brought to end 'the war entente against Germany'. At the formal signing of the Treaty in London on 1 December 1925 Stresemann, under the influence of what was already being described as the 'Locarno spirit', tried to raise the question of a Colonial Mandate for Germany. But Chamberlain persuaded him not to press for a solution for so difficult an issue at that moment. No cloud was permitted to cross the azure sky. In London, D'Abernon's friends gave him a dinner to celebrate his own part of the triumph. The guests were all advocates of European pacification – Balfour and Asquith, both former Prime Ministers, Churchill, Keynes, Geoffrey Dawson, Editor of *The Times*, and Philip Kerr. All hoped that Locarno would launch an era of untroubled peace. As D'Abernon had written to Kerr in October, 'the advantages of the Pact both to Germany and France are such that they must prevail against prejudice and ignorance.'[20] But how could a Treaty accomplish so much? Was it not as much the outcome of exhaustion and weariness, a truce or pause, while both sides searched for new allies and new strength before attempting once more to maintain, or to overthrow the *status quo* by force? Austen Chamberlain, architect against his will of the edifice now thought to be so firm, felt confidence in his handiwork. Speaking in the Commons on 18 November 1925 he said:

... the agreements made at Locarno, valuable as they are in themselves – and I beg the House not to under-rate their intrinsic value – are yet more valuable for the spirit which produced them. ... We regard Locarno, not as the end of the work of appeasement and reconciliation, but as its beginning. ...

But such optimism was not universal. Too much violence had fallen upon Europe, too many national hatreds had been engendered, too fierce a desire for dominance or for revenge had entered the souls of nations whose life-blood had been drained so effusively away, for the spirit of peace to be created by signatures on a piece of paper. Ramsay MacDonald summed up this mood in a private letter during the course of the negotiations:

We can make pacts and agreements by the thousand on matters which of themselves are of very little importance from the point of view of possible causes of war, and which on the outbreak of war would be dealt with by no nation in accordance with agreements. ...
The problem of security is mainly psychological, and as a matter of fact, it is met only to a very small degree by coming to agreements of a military nature regarding it. It is in fact the dramatic form of a deep-seated suspicion that no country is really safe from the machinations of others.[21]

MacDonald was right; appeasement was not a simple question of conferences and treaties. It was an attitude of mind. As such it could not be imposed arbitrarily upon people who had learned through experience not to believe in peace for all time, or even for their own time. Fear of other countries, aspirations for one's own, and a belief in the essentially selfish and brutal base of human behaviour, made appeasement seem an unrealistic policy. There were arguments in its favour as an attempted policy: supreme among them the memories of the Great War and its long drawn-out horrors. But whereas it was quite easy to wish to avoid another war, and to oppose any policy that might lead to war, it was less easy to work out, to support, and to have a faith in a constructive peace policy. It was not easy to accept the idea of a reconciliation with the enemy of less than a decade ago. It was even more difficult to think in terms of enabling that enemy to become once more, not only rich and powerful, but richer and more powerful than any of its neighbours, one's former allies. Yet any policy of constructive appeasement could only end in one way, with Germany the dominant power in Europe. And who could guarantee that, having obtained such dominance, she would continue to regard as her friend and patron the former foe who had set her on her feet again?

CHAPTER 12

Locarny-Blarney

Man does not live by replacing a tyranny based on the rule of short-sighted kings with a tyranny which panders to the sadistic strivings of a mass electorate. Republican democracies could not of themselves bring contentment to Europe. Independence, after many centuries of subjugation, did not automatically produce equilibrium. Before 1914 European diplomacy had been complicated by the problems of unwieldy empires and mounting irredentist feeling. After 1918 a new set of complications replaced the old. Small national states, which had only just come into being, vied with each other in pugnacious self-assertion. Nationhood was not sufficient: Poland hoped to be treated as a 'great power', Lithuania sought redress of grievances over the loss of Vilna, Hungary demanded Treaty revision in Slovakia and Transylvania, Czechoslovakia wanted to ward off the demands of its German-speaking minority for a greater voice in government. Although the new states were based on self-determination, they were discontented. Their political life was disturbed and their electorates volatile. Dictatorship and chauvinism were their inheritance. Against such a background, post-Treaty Europe was unable to make decisive progress towards mutual co-operation.

Ten years of peace was not enough to heal the wounds of four years of war. The material destruction and mental anguish caused during the war found no automatic balm in peace. Recovery was slow, constantly interrupted by frontier disputes, economic setbacks and political upheavals. Arrogant nationalism lay like a blight upon the fields of eastern and central Europe. Social unrest encouraged adventurism. While Britain made a virtue of tranquillity, Europe persisted in escapades. British politicians hoped to persuade the states of Europe that co-operation and compromise were more worthwhile than war; that reconstruction was more sensible than

117

revenge. But the Europe at which such hopes were directed, the Europe which Englishmen hoped to pacify by the logic of their arguments and the sanity of their objectives, that Europe, to which appeasement was aimed, had died at Verdun.

The Locarno Agreements were concise and well-defined. They were also unrealistic. Germany was too conscious of defeat, too eager for Treaty revision, and too anxious to re-establish her position of primacy in Europe, to take seriously a self-denying ordinance only made possible because she was a defeated and disarmed nation. France was too conscious of the German capacity for recovery, too aware of her own numerical inferiority, and too close to the memories of a cruel and as it now seemed unsuccessful war, to put her trust in a German promise made at a time of German weakness. Britain, with all her goodwill, her magnanimity and her persistent search for a stable solution, could not bring France and Germany together on any permanent basis. She could not prevent Germany from continuing to make a great parade of her grievances, or from secretly developing new weapons of war in collaboration with the Soviet Union. Nor could she prevent France seeking security through a series of military alliances with the discontented and ambitious nations of eastern Europe – alliances which, in British as well as German eyes, were a return to the much denounced pre-war policy of 'encirclement'.

Britain's position as a mediator was not fully understood in Europe. The Germans could not believe that, in any serious crisis, Britain would take their side. It seemed to them impossible that the victors should not have retained a binding loyalty to their former allies, or that the passions of war should not still lurk below the surface of all protestations of amity. Germany never understood the full import of appeasement; never realized how seriously successive British governments put their faith for future peace in a Franco-German reconciliation, based upon equality. Nor did France understand the apparent desertion of Britain from the allied cause. While Germans felt that appeasement was an empty concept, Frenchmen felt that it was a betrayal. 'Perfidious Albion' was thought to be incapable of true friendship. Seeking to undermine the 'sanctity' of the Versailles Treaty, publicly hostile to the Ruhr and Rhineland occupations, how could Britain be relied upon in a moment of danger? The revelations by historians in the 1920s that Britain had nearly *not* gone to war on France's behalf confirmed French fears of British duplicity. There was therefore little understanding and much hostility towards Britain when, after Locarno, Baldwin became an advocate of European disarmament and economic co-operation. It seemed clear to many Frenchmen that both disarmament and free trade would give Germany a lasting advantage over France. Had the war been in vain, had Verdun been a futile sacrifice, that Germany would now, under British patronage, be restored to a position of dominance in Europe, thus achieving in defeat the mastery that was denied her on the field of battle?

Austen Chamberlain, who understood these fears, and sympathized with them, allowed Locarno to be his last essay in appeasement, and dampened, in the field of foreign affairs, the growing British ardour for an Anglo-German rapprochement. But the mood of appeasement was taking root, and the British press and politicians continued to speak openly of France as the stumbling block to European contentment, and of Germany as the nation whose cause and interests were compatible with Britain's.

Between 1925 and 1930 the 'Locarno spirit' was taken seriously in Europe. European diplomacy made as its declared aim the extension of the 'spirit' to ensure the elimination of armies, navies, and war itself. All was in vain. The discussions on disarmament in 1927 and 1930 failed to reconcile French and German differences as to the meaning of security. The Three-Power Naval Conference at Geneva in 1927 broke down when Britain and America disagreed over details. And the Kellogg Pact of 1928, outlawing war, while signed by all nations, was believed in by none. Even Britain reserved the right to make war in 'certain regions of the world the welfare and integrity of which constitute a special and vital interest for our peace and safety', thereby showing that for her appeasement was strictly limited to Europe. At the same time France stipulated that if one country violated the 'no-war' pledge, all countries should not remain bound to it, as Kellogg proposed. France thereby assured the viability of her alliances in eastern Europe. If Germany attacked Poland, Czechoslovakia, or Rumania, France would still be able to come to their aid. The spirit of Locarno was thus strictly limited by a narrow view of national self-interest. But appeasement could only be effective if both France and Germany were prepared to recognize more enlightened and harmonious national interests. Britain urged them both to be good Europeans;

but this was a policy which, if examined closely, appeared to them merely a British national interest, not a policy truly in *their* interest. It would leave Britain free from anxiety in Europe, free from the need to become involved in the entanglements of a European alliance system, and free to concentrate upon the growing number of imperial problems that were arising. It was difficult to explain to a French or German politician why he had to abandon what he thought was his national interest in favour of appeasement, while Britain would be furthering her own national interest by this very policy.

Between 1918 and 1925 appeasement in Britain was a policy favoured and pursued in official circles. It probably had little public support, except in so far as it could rely upon the growing anti-French feeling or the general abhorrence of war. There was little actual pro-Germanism. While some sympathized with Germany's position as an under-dog, few were prepared to suggest practical measures such as the return of colonies taken in 1918, or a readjustment of the eastern frontier in Poland's favour. Positive pro-Germanism was a mood confined to a small number of people mostly journalists, writers, and those with philosophical beliefs of an unusual nature. Thus Rolf Gardiner, who in 1928 edited a symposium called *Britain and Germany*, tried to make Anglo-German co-operation the corner-stone of a united Northern Europe. Gardiner made strenuous efforts to foster an Anglo-German cultural rapprochement. In 1922 he took a company of English folk singers to Germany, and in 1927 organized an Anglo-German festival of music, dance, and drama in northern England and Scotland. Gardiner had been much influenced by Charles Sorley's poems, and by Thomas Hardy's denunciation of those who had in his view brought about the situation in which Britain and Germany had gone to war. Gardiner often quoted Hardy's poem *The Pity of It*, written in 1915:

> Whosoever they be
> At root and bottom of this, who flung this flame
> Between kith folk, kin tongued even as are we,
> Sinister, ugly, lurid be their fame;
> May their familiars grow to shun their name,
> And their brood perish everlastingly.

Gardiner sought a philosophic basis for Anglo-German friendship.

He feared that Britain was falling the victim to false values – commercialism and cynicism – and that only by associating with Germany could Britain regain her sense of purpose. He believed that the future of European civilization depended upon the working together of British and German youth, both able to rise above the drabness and materialism of the post-war world:

The new Germans are young, brave, ardent, enthusiastic, alive. The modern British are mature, cautious, over-critical, over-prudent, tired ... for the Germans, the British, the Scandinavians, there may be a common destiny if they chose to make it ... a new unit of quiet strength set between Asia and America.

The Mediterranean peoples have turned aside into the ways of barrenness, seeking those things which moth and rust doth corrupt. The people of France seem to be dying out in regional destinies over which the central authorities in Paris will one day cease to have power. If there is still a cat-like power for anger ... there is no strength and sweetness in their hearts.[1]

Gardiner was able to win a number of supporters, including the historian G. P. Gooch, who wrote in the same symposium that 'neither the British nor the German Government or people desired a world war'. According to Gooch the war came because Europe was divided into hostile camps and 'crowded with armed men'. But this was a return to the well-worn historical arguments about war-guilt; it was a view not seriously challenged at this time. Gardiner's more racist approach had little general support. There was probably less belief in an Anglo-Saxon affinity in 1928 than there had been in 1900, when Joseph Chamberlain had argued on similar grounds in favour of an Anglo-German rapprochement. Gardiner's opinions launched no crusade. Englishmen were growing weary of foreign affairs. Appeasement, to have popular backing, needed the enthusiasm of people deeply committed to it, even if their reasons, like Gardiner's, were unorthodox ones. But Europe roused little enthusiasm after Locarno. A. P. Herbert reflected a widespread mood in his poem *Foreign Policy: or, the Universal Aunt*:[2]

> The foreigner's an alien,
>   He does not rule the waves;
> Give me the good Australian
>   Who cleans his teeth and shaves.

Oh, let the hairy Magyar
  Stew in his horrid juice,
And scrap the Foreign Office,
  For it ain't no kind of use!

Poor old Britannier! Talk about disarm?
It's these here diplomatists that do the greatest harm.
Scrap the Foreign Office! Why d'you want to roam?
Ain't you got enough misfortunes in the home?

The paper's all Croatians
  And Jugo-Slavs and Czechs,
In all these bearded nations
  We're buried to the necks;
But it takes a flood or earthquake
  Or other nasty mess
To get the British Empire
  Into the British Press!

Poor old Britannier! Excuse a little sob;
Ain't your far-flung Empire a whole-time job?
Less of this Locarny-blarney! Why d'you want to roam
Ain't you got enough misfortunes in the home?

The cry of concern for imperial needs was not confined to satirists. Many politicians felt that Britain's prime responsibility was to her Empire, and that if foreign policy were dominated by European problems, imperial interests would suffer. Philip Kerr disliked the Locarno agreements for the very reason that they had been negotiated without Dominion participation. He believed that Britain's strength – and therefore her position to influence even European affairs – depended upon close co-operation between the Dominion and London governments. He deplored a decision which seemed to reproduce one of the worst features of the Chanak crisis. Writing to Lloyd George, Kerr claimed that:

The Locarno Treaties are not treaties of peace so much as understandings to go to war in certain eventualities. This is precisely the one form of Treaty about which it is essential that the Empire should be agreed. . . . Here is Austen Chamberlain making an enormous commitment to go to war, not for a year or two, but for ever, and telling the Dominions that it doesn't really matter whether they agree with it or not.[3]

The years 1925-8 were years of growing British isolation, and of growing official reluctance to take the initiative in any practical scheme of European appeasement. The Dawes Plan and Locarno had been given great publicity as the panaceas for European ills. The time seemed therefore to have come to allow these panaceas to work undisturbed. If Europe remained sick, that could not possibly be Britain's fault. Dawes and Locarno proved British goodwill. Extra effort should not be expended: Europe should be grateful for the attention that had already been paid to her. Stanley Baldwin went annually for his holidays to Aix-les-Bains; but he did not see any need to pass through neighbouring Geneva, where the League of Nations sought to make effective the pacification which Dawes and Locarno were designed to foster, and where his presence would have been interpreted as a sign of British earnestness in seeking a broad-based European settlement.

Yet Baldwin and his Cabinet colleagues did not neglect Europe because they were indolent men. Serious domestic problems dominated their work and demanded their unremitting concentration. Unemployment and the challenge of poverty were powerful claims upon their time. The General Strike of 1926, threatening, as it seemed, to lead the country over the precipice of chaos and civil strife, gripped their attention with fear-induced force. The need of the hour seemed clearly to be social reform. Britain must put her own house in order before seeking to repair European dwellings. Slums must be cleared, employment provided, insurance secured, medical facilities improved, education made more widely available, and poverty treated as a national, not a private, problem. Churchill at the Exchequer tried to revive the flagging economy by the return to the Gold Standard; Neville Chamberlain at the Ministry of Health sought to promote the social legislation which he considered essential if Britain were to survive as a modern state; Baldwin in his public speeches approved this concentration upon domestic problems. Unveiling the War Memorial at his old school, Harrow, in 1926, he said:

Just as at the time of the Renaissance the age devoted itself to intellectual inquiry, so today it is devoting itself to social inquiry. . . .
It may be that the historian [a century or two centuries hence], seeing the events of today in a truer relation and perspective, may be able to write something like this: 'At that time a generation indeed was wiped out, but from their graves sprang the rebirth and a new kindling of the

spirit that raised our country to heights which surpass the dreams of those of her sons who in past ages had sacrificed most and had loved her best'.[4]

Whatever heights were visible in 1926, by 1929 they were obscured. Economic chaos brought misery to all Europe. Tariff barriers, which the League of Nations had proposed to eliminate, were built up with patriotic zeal. Nations sought protection in isolation. Prices rose with the increased tariffs; wages fell with the rise in unemployment. Britain looked for economic security to imperial preference, a decision which increased her isolation from Europe. In Germany the mounting economic distress fed political extremism, and moderate voices were swiftly obliterated by the strident altercations of Communists and Nazis. Economic hardship was an invitation to demagogues everywhere. Dictators ruled in Italy, Poland, Portugal, Spain, and Yugoslavia. Every nation learned to blame its neighbour for the new poverty. Hitler told the Germans that it was the Versailles Treaty that had led directly to unemployment and near-starvation. By the middle of 1931 his followers had become sufficiently emboldened to resort to open violence and shrill anti-semitism. Although his movement's ideas

European Dictatorships before Hitler, 1919-1932

Countries ruled by dictators are shown in black, with dates of beginning of dictatorial rule (and end if before 1932)

were crude and extreme, its chances of electoral victory seemed high. Hitler claimed that he would smash Versailles, restore Germany to her rightful place in the world, and bring dignity as well as prosperity to German people all over Europe. Many Germans found his aims too exciting for them to worry unduly about his methods. Nor did the expansionist undertones in his speeches alarm them. He offered to restore their pride; they did not reckon the price.

CHAPTER 13

The Sargent Chain

The rise of Hitler, and the much publicized growth of extremism in Germany, gave a new impetus to appeasement in Britain. Unless concessions were made to the Weimar Republic, power might soon pass to less democratic and more grasping hands. As Prince Max von Baden, a former Chancellor, wrote to Ramsay MacDonald in 1929, shortly after MacDonald became Prime Minister for the second time:

> I am sure we will have to wait a great many years, and my last words to my countrymen will be a plea for patience, but I feel I must utter the frank warning in this letter – without a hope of the revision of the Versailles Treaty, however distant, Germany will not expect her salvation from pacifism.[1]

But these warnings were not taken seriously at first. Philip Snowden, Chancellor of the Exchequer in the new Labour Government, even tried to reverse British policy towards German reparations. At The Hague Conference in August 1929 he was reluctant to accept American proposals for a further reduction in reparations and for the ending of the Rhineland occupation. As a result of Snowden's stern attitude the final agreement – the Young Plan – was less lenient than the Americans had intended. Britain, instead of taking the lead in appeasement, suddenly and unexpectedly hung back, dragging its heels. Churchill described the scene when Snowden returned from The Hague to London: a man, he wrote,

> ... who was supposed to be stark and stiff in comparison with his predecessor [Churchill] in reclaiming war debts and reparations, was received by rapturous crowds, who saluted him with tremendous cheers as the Iron Chancellor. ...
> I have always held the view that these war debts and reparations have

been a great curse . . . that the sooner we could free ourselves from them and the less we exacted, the better for the whole world.[2]

It was not only economic distress which slowed down the general British desire to satisfy German demands and ameliorate German grievances. Up to 1929 much of the justification for appeasement was the belief that Germany, if treated well, would become a peace-loving democracy. Perhaps, without the terrible disruption which followed the economic collapse, this belief might have been justified. But during the course of 1930 it became clear that all was not well with Germany. In May, Sir Robert Vansittart, the new Permanent Under-Secretary of State for Foreign Affairs, prepared a lengthy memorandum on the state of German opinion and the possible developments of German policy. He felt that there existed distant objectives, on which German policy would concentrate, and to whose attainment every future German Government would be committed. These objectives were, in Vansittart's views, the acquisition of the lost colonies, Anschluss with Austria, rearmament 'so as to obtain at least parity with Poland', and, as a result of the military strength so gained, a drastic modification of the German-Polish frontier.[3] Vansittart described Hitler as a 'half-mad and ridiculously dangerous demagogue'.[4] But Hitler was not yet in power, and Vansittart's fears of a Germany bent on war seemed unduly alarmist to most of his colleagues.

Others were less pessimistic about Germany than Vansittart. J. L. Garvin, Editor of *The Observer*, was certain that Germany would not attack France, but feared that France might attack Germany in the not too distant future.[5] He wrote to Lord Lothian (as Philip Kerr had become) in May 1930:

> What I rely on chiefly is that war by us with Germany can be made just as unthinkable as war between the two English-speaking powers. . . . The whole trouble is, don't you think, that the French Right and Centre do not want merely security proper, but want guarantees for the artificial dominance established for them by the overwhelming power of the Allies and associates in 1919.[6]

But anti-French feeling was difficult to maintain at this time. In May the Rhineland was evacuated by allied troops, a sign that France was not entirely unwilling to contemplate a policy of moderation. But at the same time, German reactions to the evacuation created a bad impression in England. As soon as the allied troops had left the Rhineland, German Ministers began to demand the right to 'undemilitarize' it. This caused alarm in the Foreign Office, where it was felt that the remilitarization of the Rhineland would 'cut at the very roots of Locarno',[7] for at Locarno Germany had agreed to keep the area demilitarized. Sir Horace Rumbold, who had become British Ambassador in Berlin in 1928, doubted whether the German Government would take such a view while Brüning was Chancellor. But he considered the demand for remilitarization, 'only another instance, to my mind, of the German habit of ventilating grievances. No sooner is one grievance redressed than the Germans come forward with another'.[8]

In Rumbold's view the increase of Nazi seats in the Reichstag from 12 to 107 was serious because it was 'undoubtedly calculated to stimulate any Government to pursue a forward foreign policy', and in particular to feel obliged to seek the cancellation even of the reduced reparations demand of the Young Plan.[9] The British Government were in a dilemma as far as their policy towards Brüning's Government was concerned. Under the pressure of Nazi propaganda Brüning appeared to be adopting a revisionist policy. Yet it were surely better to make concessions to Brüning than to refuse him concessions, and thereby give the Nazis a further chance to make electoral propaganda. The Labour Foreign Secretary, Arthur Henderson, explained to Rumbold early in 1931 what the British Government had decided:

The fall of the Brüning Government in the present period of political and economic strain might easily have far-reaching detrimental effects on international relationships. If, therefore, there is a real danger of its not being able to weather the storm to which it is likely to be exposed in the near future, it ought, I consider, to be the policy of His Majesty's Government to give it such support and encouragement as they properly can, in order to fortify its position.[10]

Thus, in 1931, having been neglected by Austen Chamberlain and harassed by Philip Snowden, appeasement came back to prominence and respectability. The unresolved problem was, by what means should appeasement be pursued? Henderson and MacDonald favoured disarmament. Rumbold felt that before either France or Germany would agree to permanent disarmament, German grievances would have to be settled. If they were not, the

Germans would feel that Britain was only trying 'to cauterize the wounds of Europe while poison is still present in those wounds'.[11] He urged the Government to do its utmost to support Brüning by some positive revisionist action. But disarmament was the policy upon which MacDonald had fixed, and this, though a well-meaning attempt to pacify Europe, appealed effectively neither to German aspirations nor to French fears.

In March 1931 the German Government took a sudden initiative, openly proposing an immediate Austro-German Customs Union. The French, fearing that this was but the prelude to a political Anschluss, asked Britain to join them in preventing the Union. But Henderson acted as a mediator, persuading the French not to take drastic action, and the Germans to abandon unilateral talks with Austria and leave all further discussions to the League Council. The provocative, if sensible scheme was abandoned. But European calm dissolved. Two months later the largest Austrian bank, the Viennese Credit-Anstalt, collapsed. Europe was plunged into financial catastrophe. One fact stood out clearly above the chaos: Germany could no longer find the money with which to pay reparations.

From mid-1931 to the end of 1932 appeasement took on an urgent aspect. Germany, economically crippled, lay open to the blandishments of the Nazis. The German Government needed to show its people that Germany could overcome, not only mass unemployment and near starvation, but also the 'indignities' arising from Versailles, of which the pressure used against the Customs Union was a strong reminder. The British Government, and many individual Englishmen, felt that Britain was under an obligation to help the Germans to obtain, not only some measure of economic security, but also redress of territorial grievances. There was some serious talk of giving Germany back Tanganyika. J. L. Hammond, the Labour historian, wrote to a friend in August 1931:

> We seem to be tied up with Germany in finance and some political concession to Germany might avert revolution there. I was talking about it with some dons at Trinity, Cambridge . . . and they suggested that might be easier to give up Togoland. But that would frighten the French I should think. I don't see it happening, though I think that a hundred years hence the failure to give Germany any outlet now will seem a bad, perhaps a fatal, failure of statesmanship.[12]

The search for an active, positive appeasement policy was a difficult one. The almost daily uncertainties caused by the economic crisis did not help speculative thinking. The political and racial extremism of the Nazi Party cast a lurid glow upon all deliberations. Would specific concessions become superfluous as a result of further economic collapse? Would substantial revision of the Treaty merely serve as an incentive to Hitler and his followers for even wilder demands? These questions were unanswerable. Yet some coherent policy had to be evolved. Towards the end of 1931 the economic crisis led to the fall of the Labour Government. MacDonald remained Prime Minister, but at the head of a National Government, primarily Conservative, and with a Liberal, Lord Reading, as Foreign Secretary.

Being 'national', the Government could now speak with greater authority than under the two party system, where a large opposition could challenge and threaten to reverse the policy of the day. Coming into being because of a crisis which affected all Europe, the Government could be expected to seek some swift solution. But the dilemma was a deep one. Certain members of the Foreign Office, anxious to clarify the problems of Britain and Europe, in so far as they could be clarified, were asked by Reading to prepare a memorandum on the 'Changing Conditions in British Foreign Policy'.[13] Two of them, Orme Sargent and Frank Ashton-Gwatkin, had both entered the Foreign Service before 1914, and were men of widely recognized ability. Their contribution was in some ways a depressing one. They doubted the usefulness of attempting to solve the problem of disarmament, or reparations, or frontiers at different moments and in isolated conferences, as was being attempted. They argued that:

We must be prepared for concession and compromise all round. It behoves us to discover not only a means of escape from the present deadlock on the disarmament question, but also a line of policy by which we can solve the far more fundamental political and economic problems from which the whole world is at present suffering. What we must try to do is to assemble and assess all our bargaining counters and utilize them *en bloc* in order to achieve as substantial an advance towards world recovery as possible. On no account ought we to allow them to be frittered away in return for only subsidiary advantages.

Sargent and Ashton-Gwatkin expressed the fear that Britain, by adopting, as appeared imminent, a policy of imperial preference, would thereby make European economic recovery more difficult. They argued that imperial preference would weaken Britain's position as the exponent of a comprehensive European settlement. It was essential, in their view, that Britain should win Europe's confidence by showing France that British policy would not threaten her security, and at the same time by showing Germany that her desire for Treaty revision would be met as fully as possible. The memorandum urged the Government to take a broad view of the situation:

World recovery (the aim of our policy) depends on European recovery; European recovery on German recovery; German recovery on France's consent; France's consent on security (for all time) against attack. The chain is simple to envisage, but so difficult to link together.

It was Vansittart who, perhaps influenced by the arguments of his two officials – whose views covered twenty-one closely argued foolscap pages – tried to devise a workable policy based upon the 'Sargent chain'. Taking the weakest link, which he considered to be the French reluctance to make substantial concessions to Germany, he prepared a memorandum, at the end of 1931, aimed at providing the new Foreign Secretary, Sir John Simon, with a policy cast in the Sargent–Ashton-Gwatkin mould. He pointed out that French reluctance to make concessions had during 1931 played into Hitler's hands, and greatly handicapped Brüning, 'whom we sincerely, and the French Government at least professedly, have desired to sustain'. Vansittart considered French policy short-sighted and disappointing, based upon the belief that Europe 'should remain perpetually divided into immutable sheep and dis-horned goats'. He quoted the blunt opinion of the British Chiefs of Staff that it was questionable whether two out of the three German invasions in the previous hundred years were entirely unprovoked by France and summed up his criticisms of French policy with the claim that:

The historian of the future will not be indulgent to French – and American – post-war policy. Both have been blind and selfish, and the former has been unduly vindictive as well. . . . Fear is, in fact, now to some considerable extent diluted by the human desire to prolong the pleasurable sensation of being on top.

Vansittart emphasized that it was not upon sympathy with

Germany's defeat that Britain should base her policy, but upon 'enlightened self-interest'. He was convinced that if Germany could be given immediate satisfaction, the 'Sargent chain' could be made effective. Treaty revision was in his view the crux of the matter. Monetary crisis – economic chaos – reparations and war debts – disarmament – security – territorial *status quo* of Europe – revision of the peace settlement: such were the problems in the Sargent chain, rearranged by Vansittart.

Vansittart's proposals were bold ones. He wanted Simon to point out to France the dangers that would arise for world peace if Germany were forced to extremes; then to point out that France was militarily so strong as a result of their eastern European alliances that they could easily make concessions without endangering their security; then by means of 'a friend's regretful hint' to warn France that if it came to a show-down over treaty revision, 'neither international policy, nor imperial policy, nor domestic policy will permit any British Government to side with the French against the Germans'. Such a policy would be effective, Vansittart argued, because France would be most unwilling to court isolation. To retain British goodwill, and contribute to the recovery and pacification of Europe, France should, in Vansittart's opinion, be made to accept the following British proposals: the abrogation of the naval clauses of the Treaty of Versailles, to enable the German navy to be built up to a position of equality with France; an ultimate limitation of naval construction on a basis of Franco-German equality; the abrogation of the military clauses of the Treaty of Versailles, to enable Germany to have military aviation, tanks, and heavy guns; the abrogation of all Treaty restrictions on compulsory military service in Germany, allowing Germany to introduce conscription; and a final fixing of the size of all European armies on a population ratio basis. If Britain could not persuade France to make these radical concessions we would have to accept the perpetuation of the present French hegemony, and a return to the pre-1914 balance of power concept, but with the balance firmly in France's favour, and leading inevitably, swiftly, and disastrously to an intensification of German demands.

Vansittart, who had no illusions as to the nature of Germany's capacity for aggression, accepted appeasement as the only policy capable of breaking the European deadlock and averting a war of revenge. He hoped that by satisfying Germany the edge would be taken off German grievances. But he recognized that such a forceful anti-French policy as he proposed, though in his opinion it would lead directly to greater French security, and then to appeasement all along the 'Sargent chain', might be rejected utterly by France. If this happened, Vansittart felt that Britain should withdraw from Europe:

> Europe is now in a number of bad tempers, with prolific sources of quarrel, with little evinced disposition to save her soul and skin by reasonable settlements. She has not hitherto been satisfied or appeased by our large and reasonable contribution both in substance and suggestion during a bitter and fruitless decade; and the jack-o'-lantern improvement is forever a stage further – for *us* – on unsound ground. There must be an end somewhere to this process, and the end had best be now. . . . For us, European politics are mostly other people's feuds and grievances. . . . Beyond a certain point the quarrels of Europe are not our quarrels, and the point may now be reached, when, failing agreement on our contribution, we must say so. This has been the consistent attitude both of our statesmen and of our people.

The 'Sargent chain' and the Vansittart memorandum were too drastic, and too imaginative, to become the basis of British policy. But they undoubtedly influenced the events of 1932, when, at the Lausanne Conference, reparations were finally laid to rest. Although this was a Conference in the old style, taking an issue in isolation and reaching a compromise within a relatively narrow sphere, it did cover a central feature of the chain, and could well be expected to lead on to wider and more politically orientated agreements. In itself, Lausanne was a triumph for Britain's appeasement policy. Its aim was explained to the French Prime Minister Pierre Flandin, by Sir Frederick Leith-Ross, a senior Treasury official:

> I said that my Government (and public opinion felt strongly in the same sense) had hoped for a permanent settlement, but would no doubt be prepared to admit that under present conditions this would be difficult to secure. If only a temporary arrangement could be made it would be essential that the arrangement should be such as to restore confidence and leave open the door for a more permanent settlement later on.[14]

The extreme coercion which Vansittart had proposed was abandoned in favour of gentle persuasion. Unfortunately the Conference was postponed, and before it met, Brüning's Government fell.

The new Chancellor, von Papen, did not have the same stature in British eyes that Brüning had achieved. He was considered a man of dubious antecedents, politically an intriguer, and a poseur. Brüning's fall cast a gloom over the proceedings at Lausanne. Although the end of reparations made a radical improvement in Germany's position, it was feared that without Brüning in power the fruits of the agreement would not ripen. The Conference itself was conducted in an atmosphere of apprehension. Only the British delegation seemed confident that the discussions would serve as a prelude to a series of substantial agreements over a wider range of topics, and thereby set a new tone in international relations. In his opening speech Ramsay MacDonald said:

Today the method of reaching Government agreements by international conference is undergoing its supreme test. We must not forget in all our deliberations and bargainings that the world looks on, not only in need, but in impatience.

It is the essence of our task that we must act with speed. . . . Let us come to business. Despair is a fortress which must be carried by storm and cannot be conquered by a long siege. Despair rarely sinks quietly down to acquiescence. It enlists its decaying strength in frenzied devotion to those movements, not of Divine, but of satanic discontent, which pass hither and thither on the face of the earth in times of unsettlement and hardship such as these.

. . . my desire is that with the gravity of our task in full possession of our minds, its magnificence should also give us courage of heart and determination of will. Men in public life like ourselves must think of public opinion, but in times like these we must never for a moment forget that great issues, even entailing great sacrifices, *can* be put to our people, and, instead of breaking into clamour and revolt, they will respond heroically and play their part nobly. It all depends on us. And so my appeal to this Conference is to fear nothing but weakness.[15]

These were stirring words. They were also sincere. For two weeks MacDonald played the now almost traditional British rôle of seeking to bridge the gulf between opposing French and German positions. When serious differences of opinion arose, MacDonald would argue passionately that 'it must be assumed that all were aware of the terrible consequences of failure and that there would be no failure'.[16] He was equally severe, whether combatting French intransigence or German self-pity. When von Papen pressed relentlessly for the absolute cancellation of reparations, scorning a compromise solution very much in Germany's favour, MacDonald was stern in rebuke:

> It would seem there had been some failure of statesmanship, of leadership, or of courage. . . . Let Herr von Papen clearly understand the situation. Those who were most anxious to help him would be the most shocked. He himself had already overtaxed his strength in his present state of health, and he suggested that it might be well for the conversation to be continued for a little with Mr Chamberlain.[17]

'Mr Chamberlain' was Neville Chamberlain, the Chancellor of the Exchequer. Passing von Papen to him was no move of weakness. Chamberlain fought tenaciously against Papen's stubbornness, and with success. When the Conference ended, Germany had agreed to accept certain token payment. But reparations in all but name were ended. Chamberlain made the concluding remarks for Britain:

> It was impossible that, in discussing a subject so complicated, so bound up with old and painful associations, we should not sometimes have found moments of difficulty, and perhaps even of discouragement, but I believe that, from the first, we have all been sustained by the thought that the future happiness of millions of human beings might depend upon the results that we could achieve here. . . . The British Delegation is proud indeed to have taken part in a work which we believe will prove the beginning of happier times for us all.[18]

With reparations dead, a wave of optimism swept over Brtiain, not perhaps in so joyful a way as at the time of Locarno seven years before, for times were more troubled and German extremism more threatening, but nevertheless in the belief that Europe had been saved at the eleventh hour. But then Von Papen fell from power and the German press derided Lausanne as an insult to the German people. General Schleicher, an army officer, became Chancellor, and Hitler continued to reiterate his intention to destroy every facet of Versailles. Yet the sky did not seem entirely black. Hitler's voice was raucous, but support for his movement seemed to be flagging. German hostility to Lausanne was dismissed as typical German lack of grace, but not dangerous. German rearmament, known by the British Government to be under way, was accepted as inevitable. This optimism was hardly justifiable, but it was grasped firmly by people reluctant to believe that after twelve years of peace there could possibly be a return to the horrors of war. Only a few voices doubted that peace and goodwill would return once more to all men. Churchill told the House of Commons on 23 November 1932:

> Now the demand is that Germany should be allowed to rearm. Do not delude yourselves. Do not let His Majesty's Government believe, I am sure they do not believe, that all that Germany is asking for is equal status. This is not what Germany is seeking. All these bands of sturdy Teutonic youths, marching along the streets and roads of Germany, with the light in their eyes of desire to suffer for their Fatherland, are not looking for status. They are looking for weapons, and, when they have the weapons, believe me they will then ask for the return, the restoration of lost territories and lost colonies. . . .
>
> Compare the state of Europe on the morrow of Locarno with its condition today. Fears are greater, rivalries are sharper, military plans are more closely concerted, military organizations are more carefully and efficiently developed, Britain is weaker: and Britain's hour of weakness is Europe's hour of danger.[19]

Yet even Churchill did not despair entirely. He felt that disarmament was an unreal issue, and that the first task of statesmanship should be to revise the Treaty where it needed revision. This was precisely the point which, inside the Foreign Office, Vansittart, Sargent, and Ashton-Gwatkin had made a year before, and which had failed to influence the cautious, dry mind of Sir John Simon. Churchill declared in the Commons that with 'wisdom and skill' war could be averted, and that the public 'loathing of war' would lend powerful moral support to all Government efforts towards European pacification. He suggested that the Government re-open the question of the German claims in the Polish corridor or Hungarian claims to Transylvania, questions which, he said, should be discussed at once with a view to Treaty revision. It would be better to take up these questions

> . . . with all their delicacy and difficulty, in cold blood and in a calm atmosphere and while the victor nations still have ample superiority, than to wait and drift on, inch by inch and stage by stage, until once again vast combinations, equally matched, confront each other face to face.

Using almost the exact words Vansittart had used nine months before, Churchill suggested that Britain could promote the redress of grievances 'by merely threatening, if our counsels are not attended to, to withdraw ourselves . . . from our present close en-

tanglement in European affairs'. Churchill's theme was relevant
to appeasement, but it was ignored. In words which he had carefully considered, which embodied his profound beliefs, but which
most of his listeners were in no mood to take seriously, he asked
Parliament to follow a new, and as he hoped effective policy:

> Here is my general principle. The removal of the just grievances of
> the vanquished ought to precede the disarmament of the victors. To
> bring about anything like equality of armaments ... while those
> grievances remain unredressed, would be almost to appoint the day for
> another European war – to fix it as if it were a prize fight.

There seemed little reason why Churchill's hopes should be in
vain. Arnold Toynbee wrote from Berlin that

> Germany is, I am sure, on the upgrade.... The 'last gasp' look has
> gone out of the faces of the mass of the people. Schleicher is evidently
> competent and reassuring. I expect he will reap all the fruits of what
> Brüning has done, and will live for ever.[20]

But the reparations concessions at Lausanne were too tardy. The
economic recovery of Germany began too late. The confidence in
Schleicher had no time to grow. The further round of conferences,
some on disarmament and others on a reduction of tariffs was
unable to start soon enough. On 30 January 1933 Adolf Hitler
became Chancellor of Germany. The demagogue who had poured
vitriol upon compromise and obscene ribaldry upon Versailles,
who had sworn to restore Germany to its former glories and to
crush Bolshevism, whose memoirs and manifestos revived in
savage form the anti-semitism that had lain dormant in Germany
for thirty years – that demagogue had come to power, and both
French security and British appeasement seemed doomed. Hitler
ridiculed and despised democracy. He derided the methods of
democratic diplomacy. Would he not consider appeasement the
creed of weaklings, and go about his task without attention to
British whims? Appeasement had had nearly twelve years to
prove itself effective. It had failed, despite all the time and energy
that had been devoted to it. Could it have any relevance in a world
gone mad, dominated by a crude rabble-rouser with no respect
for tradition and no knowledge of moderation? On 30 January
1933 no one in England knew for certain the answer to these
crucial questions.

CHAPTER 14

Nostra Maxima Culpa

Hitler's actions on coming to power confirmed all the worst fears in British minds. He appeared to be a man of violence and irresponsibility, and to be plunging Germany into a cruel orgy of thug rule. The German Ambassador in London, von Hoesch, hastened to assure Sir John Simon that Hitler's Government would not try to change German foreign policy.[1] But he was less successful in allaying fears elsewhere. H. A. L. Fisher met him in March, and described him as 'an exultant Nazi apologizing for everything, even for the exile of Einstein! These Germans always go off the deep end. They are a real danger'.[2] Rumbold reported gloomily from Berlin after the March elections that Hitler's audiences had listened enthusiastically 'to his derogatory remarks about "such nonsensical ideas" as international understanding, peace pacts, and spirit of Locarno, the policy of conciliation and the like'. In Rumbold's view Hitler, despite his lack of success in the elections, would strengthen his power as Chancellor and tighten his grip on the German people. 'A policy of ruthlessness,' Rumbold wrote to Vansittart, 'will always appear in Germany to be a strong policy, and therefore a wise one.'[3] Within a week, the Reichstag passed an Enabling Bill which gave Hitler full dictatorial powers. German democracy, long battered by social discontent, lack of popular appeal, and anti-democratic emergency legislation passed under Brüning, von Papen, and Schleicher, died a sudden death. In May the German trade unions were made illegal. Communists and trade unionists were arrested, maltreated and imprisoned, often without even a semblance of a trial. These acts were widely reported in the British press. Feelings of sympathy towards Germany gave way to feelings of loathing and anxiety. When, on 1 April 1933, a one-day boycott was declared against all Jewish shops, and Jews were beaten up in the streets of Berlin, anti-

German feeling mounted almost to 1914 intensity. 'The German atrocities,' wrote Lady Violet Bonham-Carter to Gilbert Murray, 'make me feel quite ill with rage and shame. They also make me feel foolish at having been so steadfast a pro-German ever since they became under-dogs.'⁴ The *Manchester Guardian* gave prominence to well-substantiated reports of Nazi atrocities.⁵ A debate in the House of Commons on 13 April revealed widespread alarm at the implications of Hitler's methods. Clement Attlee, leader of the Labour Party, urged the Government to say publicly that it would not countenance 'the yielding to Hitler and force what was denied to Stresemann and reason'. If Treaty revision were to be taken up again by Britain, we ought, said Attlee, to 'tell Germany straight out that if she wants any revision she must come with clean hands'. Austen Chamberlain was equally hostile to any discussion of Treaty revision with Nazi Germany:

What is this new spirit of German nationalism? The worst of the all-Prussian Imperialism, with an added savagery, a racial pride, an exclusiveness which cannot allow to any fellow-subject not of 'pure Nordic birth' equality of rights and citizenship within the nation to which he belongs. Are you going to discuss revision with a Government like that?... Germany is afflicted by this narrow, exclusive, aggressive spirit, by which it is a crime to be in favour of peace and a crime to be a Jew. This is not a Germany to which we can afford to make concessions.

This mood of hostility towards the new Germany affected even those who had been most enthusiastic about German recovery. It seemed that a demon had taken hold of the German people, destroying or suppressing all their good instincts, while at the same time feeding and stimulating their bad ones. It was as if the complexities of a national 'character' were being bludgeoned into a single, sinister mould. Evelyn Wrench, the founder of the English-speaking Union, and a man who wrote in 1919 that the Treaty of Versailles 'left the German race no hope but revenge',⁶ found himself horrified that the Germany he had so admired, and for which he had shown such sympathy, should depart from reason so crudely. He was in Berlin on the day of the anti-Jewish demonstrations. 'I had come across anti-semitism in Europe before,' he wrote in retrospect, 'but I thought racial persecution belonged to another age. Half-civilized people might indulge in it, but surely not the Germany that I had known.'⁷

Many Englishmen had done their utmost between 1918 and 1933 to help Germany regain her self-respect, escape from the stigma of defeat, and reach a compromise with France which, by French thinking, could not be to France's advantage. All were shaken by Hitler's actions. Some never recovered their faith in German protestations of goodwill. Vansittart, who had been prepared to press France most severely in Germany's interest, turned fiercely and irrevocably against the new Germany. He was soon convinced that Nazism would lead inexorably to war between Britain and Germany. He became a persistent advocate of British rearmament, and was the centre of Foreign Office hostility to any concessions being made to Hitler which might increase Germany's capacity to make war, or divide the former Allies. These beliefs were strengthened by Rumbold's frequent, perceptive despatches from Berlin, on one of which Vansittart commented sharply:

The present régime in Germany will, on past and present form, loose off another European war just so soon as it feels strong enough. Their only fear is that they may be attacked before they are ready. Meanwhile it will endeavour to cog and lull so as better to eat the artichoke leaf by leaf. This is crude: but we are considering very crude people, who have few ideas in their noddles but brute force, militarism – and hot air to these ends . . . the end being war, for Hitler's fighting man.[8]

During the early months of 1933 J. L. Garvin was writing his biography of Joseph Chamberlain. When Hitler came to power, Garvin was doing research into Chamberlain's desire for an Anglo-German alliance in 1900. Garvin had used *The Observer* since 1918 to advocate peaceful change in Europe, and to give Germany a sympathetic hearing. The 1900 attempts at an Anglo-German rapprochement fascinated him. One question stood out clearly – if Chamberlain's policy had succeeded, Lansdowne's policy of *Entente* with France, and Grey's policy of agreement with Russia might not have been necessary. Britain's sense of moral obligation to the *Entente*, a sense which many had come to consider the crux of British participation in the war, would therefore have been avoided. Here indeed was a root of appeasement even older than the Great War: a feeling that Anglo-German collaboration should have been the 'natural' course of events before 1914, but that Lansdowne and Grey, by incompetence, short-sightedness, or under the influence of the unjustifiable anti-Germanism of their permanent officials, had allowed Britain to drift into the wrong camp, and to link herself with interests that were not her own. Conservative unhappiness at the abandonment of a pro-German policy in 1904, and Liberal dislike of the 'burden' of near-alliances with France and Russia, gave appeasement a strong historical justification in many eyes. If Britain had pushed Germany into enmity between 1900 and 1914, surely it could pull her back into friendship, given frankness and sincerity? When Brüning was Chancellor this question could be answered in the affirmative. Hitler's chancellorship seemed likely to destroy all such hopes. Garvin was disturbed. He wrote to Rumbold that:

I am distraught by what I have to write and by what I foresee. I thought Anglo-German reconciliation was the key to a good European future. For fourteen years from 1919 I worked for it, though sometimes the attempt meant loss for my paper and jeopardy for me. But English generosity has met no return in kind, but has been used for purposes of German self-pity and self-justification.

Like D'Abernon before you, you have represented the sane, constructive spirit of England; but it seems to be the old story. Bismarck, a gigantic exception amongst a heady people, knew and groaned – the Germans, definitely superior in personal industry and in so many aptitudes for combination, seem as definitely inferior in political wisdom. There is no sign of psychological intelligence with regard to any other nation whatever.

Alas, alas! The mistake, as personally I have never ceased to think, was not to have crossed the Rhine in full massiveness in 1919; not to have dictated at Berlin itself a more impressive and competent peace. They would have understood then what indisputable defeat means. They don't now. The psychological infatuation of their hereditary militarism was not thoroughly broken.[9]

These were stern opinions. Yet they reflected both the public mood and official policy in early 1933. Some were to be guided by such severe sentiments until the outbreak of war in 1939. Vansittart never abandoned his new-found conviction that the ultimate German aim was conquest. Rumbold never came to put his trust in Hitler's increasingly frequent protestations that he was not bent upon European war. Lady Violet Bonham-Carter continued to be active in organizations designed to prepare Britain for the war that she felt must come if Nazism continued.[10] But many of those whose anger had been provoked by Nazi domestic violence in 1933, and whose hopes for European peace had been battered by Hitler's wild words against Versailles and Locarno, soon modified their anger and regained their hope. Garvin became a persuasive advocate of making every effort to placate Hitler, and applauded Neville Chamberlain's search for appeasement at the Munich Conference in 1938. Evelyn Wrench began to doubt the wisdom of adopting a censorious tone towards Nazi Germany. The Berlin pogrom had indeed shocked him, but, as he later explained:

After a few days I regained confidence in Germany's good intentions. Perhaps it would be more accurate to say that wishful thinking enabled me to accept the explanations given by supporters of the Nazi régime. I did not abate my intense dislike of many aspects of Nazi policy one iota, but I set it aside in my endeavour to see things from the German point of view.[11]

Before Hitler came to power, it was easy to be in favour of Anglo-German co-operation. Reasons for appeasement were varied. Four stood out most clearly. Firstly, there was the belief in a special Anglo-German affinity, of the sort of which Joseph Chamberlain had spoken, whose origins went back to the days when Angles and Saxons set off in their wattle boats from the mouths of the Rhine, and paddled with the tide towards the Humber, the Wash, and the Thames; a racial unity born before Christ in the mists of legend; a unity of blood which a shared royal dynasty had strengthened in recent times; a belief in a close cultural association, in mutual understanding in the heady realms of philosophic speculation and artistic creation. To accept such a belief needed little mental effort, and only a modicum of self-deception. Secondly, belief in a shared Anglo-German responsibility in the outbreak of war – a belief fostered by British historians and encouraged by German propaganda, casting doubt upon the morality of Britain's action in 1914, and leading to the question: 'Could Britain, by a different foreign policy, have averted an Anglo-German clash?' This disturbing question, if answered in the affirmative, led those that had asked it directly on to a search for a new foreign policy that would make a repetition of 1914 impossible. Thirdly, appeasement seemed justified by the alleged severity of Versailles, a Treaty which was now seen as the 'inevitable' parent of German bitterness and Nazi triumph. Fourthly, appeasement sprang from the desire to find an alternative to a pro-French policy; from fear that France would use Britain as a catspaw to keep Germany weak; and from fear that too close a partnership with France would commit Britain to a permanent policy of encirclement – permanent until Germany, in desperation, chose to break the ring of hostile states by force. Why should Britain participate again in this unfair hampering of natural and legitimate German aspirations? Why should a sentimental attachment to France force Britain into a position where she shunned collaboration with her virile North Sea neighbour? And thence, by a short and nimble jump, one was back with the Angles and Saxons preparing to embark for their island home over a thousand years before. To these arguments Nazism added one more: the need to check communism. This made a strong impact in Britain. It was the basis of a new lease of life for appeasement, temporarily discredited by Nazi tyranny.

Hitler himself claimed to be acting as the principal guardian of Europe against the spread of communism. Although the danger of a communist crusade against capitalist Europe had been averted by the Polish defeat of the Bolshevik armies in 1920, Hitler claimed that the danger was still a serious one. Many Englishmen believed him; and in answer to those who asked how we could possibly side with one tyranny against another, they answered that the evils of communism were eternal, but that the evils of Nazism could be killed by kindness. Fear of communism, and the belief in Nazism's ultimate reformation, were powerful new assets to the appeasement argument. From 1933 –7 they helped to sustain a substantial body of British opinion, and to muddle official thinking at a time when a clear head, a sharp mind, and an honest tongue were more than ever needed by British policy makers.

The new appeasement fed on ignorance. People who had no clear idea about the internal conditions of Germany believed in Hitler's claim that all he wanted for Germany was to restore her self-respect. Those who heard stories of concentration camp brutality were often inclined to attribute them to exaggerated rumours. Among those who controlled national newspapers were some who did not scruple to leave out anti-German material if their policy happened to be rapprochement with Germany. Geoffrey Dawson, Editor of *The Times*, went further, even seeking news items that might show the Germans how eager he was for good relations. 'I spend my nights,' he wrote to Lord Lothian, as late as 1937, 'taking out anything which I think will hurt their susceptibilities, and in dropping in little things which are intended to soothe them.'[12] Lothian himself acted as an independent proponent of the German viewpoint, writing constantly to friends, to the Press, and to critics explaining why appeasement was both sensible and moral, and likely to be effective in preventing the return of war. Lord Lothian was encouraged in his beliefs after a talk with Hitler himself. The two men found that they had much in common. As lapsed Catholics they were able to share an anti-Papal joke. Both feared what they considered the ever-present danger of communism in western Europe, a communism that both believed would not grow naturally, but would spread across Europe by Russian intrigue. Both insisted that the territorial provisions of the Versailles Treaty should be revised. Both considered that Anglo-German friendship was an essential factor in persuading Europe to accept 'peaceful change'.[13] Lothian's views were strengthened by his meeting with Hitler. But they were views held independently and tenaciously. It would be a mistake to think that Hitler hypnotized his many English visitors into accepting his point of view. The majority of those visitors were converted before they arrived. Hitler simply confirmed them in their belief that appeasement was a feasible policy. From 1933 Lothian wrote and spoke in favour of Anglo-German friendship. In November 1933 he addressed a large and appreciative crowd at Nottingham, claiming amid applause that 'in part, at any rate, that régime is the product of our own conduct in trying to exact impossible reparations and in requiring her [Germany] to be disarmed while her neighbours were armed to the teeth for fifteen years'.[14] No one in the meeting pointed out that Britain had successfully fought against the policy of 'impossible reparations', and that these had been virtually abolished at Lausanne in 1932, before the régime they had 'produced' had come to power. No one asked whether it was not perhaps reasonable that Germany's neighbours should hesitate to abandon their arms after a four years' war in which the Germans had invaded and held some of their territory. No one reminded the speaker that immediately after 1919 Britain had disarmed, conduct most unlikely to force Germany to adopt a militaristic attitude. But appeasement could flourish without argument. Its strength often lay in its apparent plausibility, not in its proven accuracy. Lothian's beliefs seemed unchangeable, despite the pressure of some of his friends; his visit to Hitler confirmed them. On his return he wrote in *The Times* that 'Germany does not want war, and is prepared to renounce it absolutely as a method of settling her disputes with her neighbours'.[15] When his friend Abe Bailey, the South African mine owner, telegraphed, 'Go slow. They purchased hundred thousand pounds commercial diamonds last month for military purposes,'[16] Lothian replied by sending him his *Times* articles and telling Bailey that Hitler had told him that Germany's one hope of being able to resist a Russian onslaught was friendship with Britain.[17] To Lord Perth, the British Ambassador in Rome, who wondered whether Lothian might not have been deceived by Hitler's pleasant voice, Lothian replied:

> Hitler is profoundly pre-occupied with Russia. He wants no quarrel with France and I do not think the National Socialists want to absorb the small Eastern European nations because that is contrary to their doctrine of race, though they *are* concerned with frontiers. . . .
> My own view is that Great Britain will get nowhere by joining up with the old encirclement group. That only means war. On the other hand, Germany does not want war.[18]

Lothian, like many advocates of appeasement in the Nazi area, did not base his opinions upon propaganda alone, nor was he entirely reliant upon his own interpretation of recent history. He sought sources that would enable him to make an independent judgement. In 1935 he made contact with Kurt Hahn, a refugee from Nazi persecution. As Private Secretary to Prince Max von Baden from 1917–20, Hahn had some inside knowledge of German policy-making. In England he had already founded Gordonstoun School on the model of the school he had founded at Salem in Germany, in 1920. In it, punishment, which could be severe, was regarded as expiation, and discipline thought to be maintained by creating a strong sense of guilt in every boy. Although Hahn was clearly a bona fide refugee from Nazism he was not entirely, in English terms, liberal-minded.[19] Yet Lothian turned to him for guidance. Hahn responded by encouraging Lothian's hostility towards those who advocated the maintenance of the *status quo* established in 1919:

> The makers and preservers of Versailles kept on denouncing Hitler but these, too, must be regarded as vested interests. I confess: to hear those who ought to be saying 'Nostra culpa, nostra maxima culpa' exploiting the German situation to save themselves from a deservedly bad

F

conscience, to listen to their boast: 'We were right. We always told you so. That is the Bosche' – that makes me feel Nazi[20.]

Hahn was convinced that it was the refusal of the victors to grant Germany 'equality' that made Nazism possible. And he felt certain that Nazism would continue to act irresponsibly for as long as Germany's neighbours failed to make some gesture of amity. In 1935 Churchill asked in public, as Lothian asked in private:

> What manner of man is this grim figure who has performed these superb toils and loosed these frightful evils? Does he still share the passions he has evoked? Does he, in the full sunlight of worldly triumph, at the head of the great nation he has raised from the dust, still feel racked by the hatreds and antagonisms of his desperate struggle; or will they be discarded like the armour and cruel weapons of strife under the mellowing influences of success? Evidently a burning question for men of all nations![21]

Churchill still hoped that the answer might not be an entirely foreboding one. He noted that those who had met Hitler found him 'competent, cool, well-informed', and he concluded that 'the world lives on hopes that the worst is over, and that we may yet live to see Hitler a gentler figure in a happier age'. This was not a lone hope. Appeasement was rooted in the belief that human nature could not be entirely overwhelmed by evil, that even the most dangerous looking situation could be ameliorated and that the most irascible politician could be placated, if treated with respect. As Kurt Hahn explained to Lothian, in words no doubt comforting to so staunch an advocate of appeasement:

> Hitler has a warm, even a soft heart, which makes him over sensitive to suggestions that he is not hard enough. ... The man feels he ought to keep his faith in his mission intact lest he should become' as sounding brass and tinkling cymbals'. This is his mission: cure the hereditary curse of Germany – discord; sweep class war away; and make Germany respected again in the world, as an equal among equals. He does not want war, but he wants a peace in freedom, not a peace from impotence. ... The peace of the world is not safe as long as Germany is surrounded by an atmosphere of distrust and revulsion.[22]

In Lothian's view even Nazi anti-semitism was not necessarily a permanent feature of Hitler's Germany. He felt that 'in some degree the brutality of National Socialism is the reaction to the treatment given to Germany herself since the war', and could be assuaged if

Germany were now given 'her rightful place in Europe.'[23] Lothian reiterated these views as frequently as he could. He had many opportunities. His house at Blickling was a centre of social gatherings with political undertones. He wrote frequently to *The Times*. He spoke often at the Royal Institute of International Affairs at Chatham House, where serious students of contemporary politics met and argued. He spoke in the House of Lords, and corresponded continuously with a widening circle of supporters and sceptics.

Lothian was not alone after 1933 in ascribing German extremism to British action, in supporting German rearmament, and in advocating Treaty revision in Germany's favour. Appeasement was a political philosophy which found adherents in all political parties and in all social classes. It was an attitude of mind common to many politicians, diplomats, civil servants, historians, journalists, industrialists, businessmen, shopkeepers, students, workers, and housewives. It was a policy of hope. Anyone who felt that war with Germany could be avoided, naturally tried to work out the best way of doing so. The most obvious means were conciliation and understanding. The idea, mooted by Churchill, of increasing British armaments until they were large enough to deter Hitler from war revived the belief that it was partly as a result of an 'armaments race' that war had come in 1914. Believing a policy of rearmament to be an almost certain prelude to an inevitable clash of arms, people turned to the idea of discussions and concessions as being more likely to preserve peace. If Hitler could be persuaded that all his aims could be satisfied merely by his presenting them, and without the need for him even to threaten war, he would presumably opt automatically for peace.

Hitler's language was, at first glance, in no way conducive to appeasement. He constantly talked of resorting to force if he could not obtain satisfaction by other means. Yet in this very threat lay the strongest possible incentive to appeasement. Take Hitler at his word. To appease him, offer him satisfaction. Offer to help him in his search for Treaty revision, offer to accept German rearmament and the growing German Navy, illegal according to Versailles, offer to support his claim for the remilitarization of the Rhineland, offer to help him in his search for peaceful *Anschluss* with Austria and a peaceful rectification in Germany's favour of the Czech and Polish frontiers, offer to work out a means of giving Germany, if not a colony, certainly a share in the raw materials and resources of Africa.²⁴ Appeasement had no shortage of suggestions. Often it was Hitler himself, not his British champions, who seemed to hesitate and hold back. Perhaps he could not believe that appeasement was a sincere policy; perhaps he felt that there would come a time when his demands would be challenged, and that too much show of friendship with Britain would make the British think that he was at bottom reliant upon British support. But he continued to see British visitors, and they continued to sing his praises and support his claims on their return to England.

As a public mood, appeasement flourished between 1933 and 1935; as a policy it languished. Foreign policy had to take into account a large number of problems, and relegated the Anglo-German problem to a secondary place. The war between Japan and China, and the war between Italy and Abyssinia, took up an increasing amount of time. Germany caused neither crises nor alarm on such a scale.

Appeasement suffered from another difficulty. In Government circles it failed to make an entirely favourable impression. Rumbold's successor as Ambassador in Berlin, Sir Eric Phipps, was as doubtful as Rumbold had been about the wisdom of accepting Germany's frequent official protestations of peaceful intent. Sir Warren Fisher, the Permanent Under-Secretary of State at the Treasury, considered that British efforts at rearmament were 'ludicrously insubstantial'.²⁵ In 1935 he wrote to Baldwin about the proposed White Paper on rearmament, voicing the fears of many senior civil servants:

We are so convinced (a) of the reality of the danger of war, (b) of the profound ignorance of our own people, (c) of the degree to which they have been misled by so-called pacifist propaganda, that we feel that if any document is to serve a useful purpose it must be downright in its expression, and avoid all half-hearted or unconvincing phraseology. . . .

It seems to me that the one thing of supreme importance is that our public should be warned in no uncertain language.

I do therefore trust that the Cabinet may reconsider its attitude towards the purpose and form of the document, and address its mind not to gilding the pill for German consumption, but to ensuring that the pill provides the effective stimulation so much required by our sluggish-minded people.²⁶

Although Baldwin was reluctant to commit himself to any strong challenge to Germany, and was being pressed by his friends to take more positive action in favour of appeasement, doubts as to the wisdom of too much compromise now permeated British policy-making.[27] The Foreign Office, in particular, showed little enthusiasm from 1933–6 for Anglo-German rapprochement. If any one policy gained general approval it was that of appeasement with Italy, based on the hope of preventing Italy from drifting into the German orbit, and averting the danger of a hostile power in the Mediterranean that might threaten the Suez Canal, Britain's shortest link with the Indian Empire and Malaya. Vansittart was one of the officials most anxious for good relations between Britain and Italy. At the same time, he continued to warn against Germany. Although some politicians found his warnings verbose and repetitive, over-dramatized and over-ornate, they certainly influenced the Foreign Office, and made the appeasement of Germany seem a very risky, if not downright dangerous policy indeed.

Vansittart urged that 'our rearmament is not proceeding fast enough or notoriously enough; and considerable doubt is being cast upon it abroad'.[28] Churchill, with whom Vansittart was in close contact, made this his theme in a series of parliamentary speeches. But the Government would not allow the doubts of a civil servant or the cries of a voice from the political wilderness to detract from what it still considered the practical and moral policy of European appeasement. Neville Chamberlain explained to his sister that in his opinion:

> If we were now to follow Winston's advice and sacrifice our commerce to the manufacture of arms, we should inflict a certain injury on our trade from which it would take generations to recover, we should destroy the confidence which now happily exists, and we should cripple the revenue.[29]

On 21 June 1935 the public desire for appeasement received an official accolade. The British Government announced the conclusion of an Anglo-German Naval Agreement. This Agreement enabled Germany to build a navy up to a third of the size of the British Navy. It also authorized Germany to build, if she considered the circumstances warranted it, an equal number of submarines as Britain. This ended the naval restrictions imposed on Germany at Versailles. As Germany was not a party to the Washington Naval Agreement, no limitation was imposed either – as was imposed on Britain – on the size or armaments of the ships she might build. In return for these major concessions, Hitler promised Britain that Germany would never use submarines against merchant shipping.

The Anglo-German Naval Agreement seemed a moral triumph for appeasement. It was also a political triumph for Baldwin, who succeeded MacDonald as Prime Minister two weeks before the Agreement was announced. It promised to inaugurate a period of positive appeasement. It seemed proof that Britain was determined, irrespective of the opinions of its former allies, to revise Versailles unilaterally, and to take Nazi Germany at its word. The Anglo-German Naval Agreement seemed an ideal form of appeasement. But was it as wise an agreement as the British Government claimed? Churchill was not alone in opposing it at the time, and a growing body of informed criticism grew up around it. Appeasement's most dramatic success, it was also a clear warning of danger if appeasement were pursued further on similar lines. The French, not having been consulted, were seriously offended. Mussolini, with whom we had agreed to consult about matters of mutual interest, saw Britain going cap-in-hand to Germany for bilateral compacts, and saw no reason why he should not now do likewise. The Russians, who, as a result of Barthou's prompting, were preparing the ground for a rapprochement with Britain, looked with alarm at an agreement whereby Britain seemed to hand over control of the seas in the Baltic to a German fleet. As a French diplomat remarked on hearing of the agreement, 'It is not merely treachery, it is folly.' Yet it appeared appeasement's finest hour. The Treaty of Versailles had been revised by the removal of clauses which even Lloyd George had considered imperative; and it had been revised without any concern for French interests or anxieties. It was based upon faith in Hitler's promise to accept an ultimate restriction on the number of ships he built, and in his pledge not to repeat Germany's Great War policy of sinking merchant shipping. If Hitler's promises were those of a rational statesman, in the Stresemann tradition, then the Agreement was clearly a triumph. Nor is there evidence that Baldwin, Neville Chamberlain, Anthony Eden, or Lord Halifax doubted Hitler's trustworthiness when the agreement was signed. They were all prominent members of the Government which had negotiated it. They all believed that it would prove effective. They all chose to ignore the growing signs of danger and deception.

CHAPTER 15

Peace Through Prosperity

The public desire to promote appeasement in the thirties was always stronger than the actual policies pursued by the Government. Although it was clear by 1935 that public feeling might restrict political action, as when the Government justified its reluctance to rearm more rapidly on the grounds of public hostility to rearmament, it was still not true that public sentiment led directly to the initiation of policy. The Government pursued the policy it thought best on evidence available to itself, but not always to the general public. If public whim and official policy happened to coincide, as with the Anglo-German Naval Agreement, a sense of harmony was created. But it was an artificial, accidental harmony. Appeasement advanced in the realm of policy, not because pacifist preachers, Labour orators, or aristocratic conciliators proclaimed it to be the right policy, but because the Government felt that it was the most effective policy they could devise on the evidence at their disposal.

The most serious efforts at appeasement were unknown to the general public. They were in the world of economics and trade. Four days after Hitler came to power Baron Neurath, then Foreign Secretary, asked him whether he had any overall plan for the German economy. Neurath told Rumbold that 'Hitler had replied in the negative, and had added that plans would present themselves as time went on'.[1] Might this not be an opportunity for British policy? If Britain and Germany could seek active co-operation in the economic sphere, mutual advantage would soon accrue. The German sense of isolation would diminish, and, from economic beginnings, appeasement could then move on to the political sphere. Economic co-operation would be a gauge of British good intentions and German common sense. The need for economic co-operation in Europe was still urgent after 1933. The evil effects of the depression did not automatically disappear with the creation of a National Government in Britain and a National Socialist Government in Germany, even though both Governments had come into being largely as a result of the economic crisis.

In 1919 Halford Mackinder, a distinguished politician, geographer, and economist published a book, *Democratic Ideals and Reality*, which among economists had almost as great an impact as the Keynsian broadside. Mackinder examined the influence of geography on political power. He urged the need for the economic union of the nations of each of the great land masses. These unions would then compete with each other economically, and would prosper. Mackinder doubted whether individual states could continue to prosper in the post-war world without such unions. His ideas made an immediate impression in Germany, where they were taken up by the geographer Haushofer, who founded an institute in Munich to study and promote them. There was thus a link between British and German thinking; one which those who accepted Mackinder's thesis hoped would lead to an economic unity in Europe which would make political dissent irrelevant and unnecessary.

The economic situation in Europe after Hitler became Chancellor was in no way conducive to economic appeasement. Each country sought to protect its economy by high tariffs and rigid exchange controls. Each resorted to bilateral agreements and inserted most favoured nation clauses into commercial treaties – a system of preferential tariffs similar to the Imperial Preference which Britain had decided upon at Ottawa in 1932. Those who favoured economic appeasement argued that European political stability could only come through a relaxation of exchange controls and a battering down of tariff walls. It was German economic insecurity and the resultant hardships in the daily lives of individual Germans, which seemed to enable Nazism to trample roughshod over individuals' rights. If Germany could be helped economically, might not Hitler relax his severe grip? If the cruelties and arrogance of Nazism were the outcome of economic distress, might not economic prosperity lead to a change in Nazism for the better?

Little progress in economic appeasement was made between 1933 and 1936. Britain's commitment to imperial preference was consolidated. European free trade was not a concept likely to appeal to protectionist officials in the Treasury and at the Board of

Trade. Some easing of Anglo-German trade relations did take place, and as a result of the Commercial Agreement of May 1933 and the Payments Agreement of August 1934 the volume of trade between the two countries increased, and payments were facilitated. But these were marginal adjustments, unable to affect Nazism in any way, and far from Mackinder's grandiose conception.

In 1935 the Foreign Office set up an Economic Section, to act as a liaison with the Treasury, and to co-ordinate foreign policy and economic developments. The first Head of the Section was Frank Ashton-Gwatkin, who in 1931 had argued with Orme Sargent in favour of a broad-based settlement for Europe. Ashton-Gwatkin had been much influenced by Mackinder's book, and in 1935 sought to effect a revolution in British policy. For two years he wrote a series of notes and memoranda on German expansion which he hoped would convince both the Foreign Office and the Treasury of the need for a bold and unusual policy.[2]

Ashton-Gwatkin pointed out that Nazism had achieved its success in Germany as a result of economic distress which had culminated in 1932 with six million unemployed; but that as a result of the difficult economic situation in Europe, the alleviation of distress since 1933 could lead to an even more severe upheaval unless Germany could find extensive export markets. Without a general economic settlement based upon freer trade with Europe, Hitler might be forced to disguise the distress by resorting to war. Ashton-Gwatkin advocated the gradual breaking down of existing tariffs and quotas; he noted with alarm that Government policy was at that very moment tending towards a raising of duties which would result in a curtailing of German exports and a further reduction in the existing volume of trade.

Germany would be bound by economic pressure to seek some means of escaping the stranglehold of tariff-based systems. Franco-German economic collaboration seemed unlikely, as it would probably involve a gradual transference of economic, and ultimately political power from Paris to Berlin – something France could never be expected to welcome or encourage. Russo-German collaboration was more likely, Ashton-Gwatkin thought; and he pointed out that Russia had made extensive use of German techniques and heavy industry immediately after Rapallo. The likelihood, even the outside chance, of a Russo-German economic bloc ought to be a stimulus to Britain to further economic appeasement on the basis of an Anglo-German bloc. As Ashton-Gwatkin wrote:

It looks as if politics would continue to hold up the achievement of a Russo-German economic bloc with exclusive preferences. If so, this is something for which we should be profoundly grateful, since the formation of such a bloc, whether on capitalist or Communist lines, would not be in the economic interest of this country, while, politically, it might constitute a great danger.

Britain's most sensible policy, he claimed, would be to make the strongest effort to form an Anglo-German economic bloc. Starting with 'a mutual and exclusive reduction of customs barriers' between the two countries, this, although reversing the current commercial policy, would possibly provide 'the key to European peace'. Failing this, Britain should persuade France, and then Holland, Belgium, Switzerland, and Sweden to relieve the internal economic pressures inside Germany by means of a foreign loan. Such a loan could only be effective if German industry, once successfully revived, had somewhere to export its goods to. This reopened the question, and stressed the urgency, of reducing tariff barriers so that German goods could flow cheaply. In theory, Ashton-Gwatkin favoured the abolition of all preference systems in all Colonial Empires. But he realized that as this would be of far greater benefit to Japan than to any other country, those who might suffer from a flood of cheap Japanese exports would not accept such a plan, nor would specific tariff barriers, aimed solely at Japan, be easy to negotiate. Japan's reaction might well lead to a political crisis in the Far East.

The only area in which Ashton-Gwatkin could see it being a question of practical politics for Britain to assist Germany by a British initiative was in Central and Eastern Europe. Britain should renounce her most-favoured-nation rights in this area, which represented 'a "natural" field for German commerce and industry'.

These economic considerations were widely canvassed during 1936. They received strong support from the Treasury, especially from Sir Frederick Leith-Ross, who had known Mackinder from the time when they were both Private Secretaries to Asquith before 1914. Economic appeasement was attractive to businessmen who were anxious to work closely with German industry. In 1935 an Anglo-German society was founded, in which Unilever, Dunlop Rubber, the British Steel Export Association, and Shell-Mex and

BP all participated.[3] Ashton-Gwatkin's suggestions were taken up in the correspondence columns of *The Times* and the *Economist*. It was argued that they could lead to tariff modification, initially on a bilateral but ultimately on a multilateral basis, involving at first small states such as Czechoslovakia, Holland, Switzerland, and Belgium, and finally the creation of a general European common market, tariff-free, in which all economies would flourish, and political pressures, both internal and international, would be relaxed. The alternative to such planning would be to perpetuate the economically unnatural division of Europe, and to reinforce the grip of Nazism inside Germany. If Britain took no action in the pursuit of economic appeasement, wrote Ashton-Gwatkin at the end of 1936:

... in all probability the Germans will rearm until economic difficulties force them to call a halt to rearmament, and then they may embark on some military adventure, the success of which seems to be considerably less doubtful than it previously did, owing to Germany's improved relations with Italy and Japan, and to the course of events in Spain.

In 1937 economic appeasement reached its apogee. It seemed more likely than anything else to be able to end the divisions in Europe which threatened to lead to war. In retrospect, the attempt to reach an economic understanding with Germany, and to bring Germany in on terms of equality to a European economic system has been severely criticized. The idea of any accommodation whatsoever with Nazism has been condemned. The literature flowing out from the printing presses since 1940 has in the main sought to reinforce the initial verdict of *Guilty Men*, that Britain ought to have combined, certainly with France, if necessary with Russia, to encircle, and when challenged, to crush the wicked German State. Often Churchill's calls for rearmament and alliances are cited in favour of this view. But in 1937 Churchill's book *The Unknown War* was reprinted, and in it was a passage dealing with 1914, but relevant to men's schemes and anxieties in the Nazi era:

A war postponed may be a war prevented. The combinations of States vary as years pass. The Ententes or Alliances of one decade may have lost their savour in the next. Time and peace solve many problems, and men's thoughts move on to new spheres. Terrible before the history of a thousand years is the burden of those who let this blast of misery and devastation loose upon the thoughtless world.[4]

The search for economic appeasement was propelled forward, not by fear of Germany, but by the hope that German policy would become rapidly more moderate once the economic situation improved, and once Germany saw that an expanding economy, increased productivity, and wealth would all be hers by peaceful means. In September 1936 Britain, France, and the United States, in their first satisfactory economic collaboration since the end of the war, announced the establishment of equality for the pound, the dollar, and the franc. Other nations were asked to join them. Exchange equalization funds were set up to preserve this 'lasting equilibrium'. The object of the 'triptych', as it was called, was to restore order and stability to international relations. Political calm ought to flow from economic calm. The three countries asserted the importance of 'action being taken without delay to relax progressively the present system of quotas and exchange controls with a view to their abolition'. One goal was uppermost in the minds of these three Governments: if Germany agreed to enter the 'triptych' she could then slacken her rigid exchange controls, tariff reduction would follow, and Germany could afford to buy on the world market the raw materials she so badly needed for her general industry. German anxieties would be reduced, trade would flourish, Franco-Anglo-American profits would rise.

Not all British policy-makers shared this optimism. In November 1937 Neville Chamberlain, who six months earlier had succeeded Baldwin as Prime Minister, sent a strong note of protest to the Chancellor of the Exchequer, Sir John Simon. Chamberlain objected to Britain helping in the release of the Danubian countries from exchange controls, a release which she was going to effect by means of British credits, and which would result in enabling Germany to trade more easily with Central Europe. Chamberlain doubted whether Germany would appreciate Britain's motives in pressing for a relaxation of controls. He feared that 'she would treat it as a favour asked from her rather than offered to her', and he was worried lest Germany 'would begin to think of what conditions she could attach to her acceptance for her further advantage'. Moreover he doubted, in direct contrast to Ashton-Gwatkin's reasoning, whether economic appeasement could possibly succeed until political appeasement had been successful. He does not seem to have believed that a relaxation of economic pressures would of itself play a major part in soothing political tension. At the very moment when 'triptych' was being talked of in economic circles, and by the Treasury, as a possible means of liberalizing European currency and import controls, and leading to a general relaxation of political tensions, Chamberlain was pouring cold water on British ardour. As he wrote to Simon:

> I regard a scheme of this kind as the sort of plan which may some day be practicable and which may then give us something like a solution of the economic difficulties of Europe. But I think it will have to wait until the general political settlement is at least in sight. We should then be working in an atmosphere of goodwill in which every country would be looking for ways of helping instead of examining every new proposal to find the nigger in the woodpile. In such an atmosphere even the USA might be disposed to lend a hand without provoking the virulent hostility of Congress.
> I disagree with those who think you can solve political difficulties by removing economic thorns from the flesh. Politics in international affairs govern actions at the expense of economics, and often of reason.

Chamberlain's instinct was probably a sound one: as a former Chancellor of the Exchequer, and a leading member of Britain's delegation at Lausanne in 1932, he had seen how even on minor matters, political differences had hindered economic agreement. As Prime Minister, determined to play an active part in political appeasement, he was understandably reluctant to consider economic appeasement an indispensable preliminary to a political settlement.

It had also become clear, by the end of 1937, that British goodwill would not on its own solve Europe's economic dilemmas. German co-operation was also needed, and it was realized in the Treasury that this would not be easy to obtain. In June 1937 the International Chamber of Commerce met in Berlin. Superficially, its sessions appeared to show the possibility of useful Anglo-German economic and political co-operation. Goering, in a speech to the Chamber, stated that 'the German defensive forces have not been created to attack or to conquer other nations but to enable the German people to protect its exposed frontiers'. But at the same meeting the Germans gave, as their suggested terms for an economic rapprochement leading to a relaxation of exchange controls and the reduction of armaments expenditure, a set of extremely difficult conditions, including a gold loan of over £300 million and the return of the former German colonies. At this meeting it became evident to most of the British group, and in particular to Sir Frederick Leith-Ross, that 'to the Nazis national prestige was the predominant issue and economic considerations took second place'.

The League of Nations, however, urged the importance of economic collaboration, and of the rapid extension of the 'triptych'. It appointed the Belgian statesman, Van Zeeland, to inquire into trade restrictions in Europe, with a view to seeing how they could be relaxed swiftly and beneficially. Van Zeeland's emissary, M. Frère, made a comprehensive tour of Germany, Italy, Austria, Czechoslovakia, Hungary, and Rumania. He concluded from his inquiries that the dislocation of trade and the high cost of living were created and maintained by the rigid quota systems and high tariffs which had been imposed between 1929 and 1933, during the economic crisis.

In January 1938 Van Zeeland published his report. He recommended, as a matter of urgency, the relaxation of all European tariffs and quotas. His report was greeted everywhere with enthusiasm. For a brief moment Europe seemed on the verge of sanity and salvation. Then, a week after the report was published, Hitler annexed Austria. Politics had stolen a march on economics. The search for economic collaboration was replaced by the search for political protection. Military alliances, or territorial concessions, were henceforth to determine the future of Europe. Economic appeasement, though not entirely neglected, ceased to be a matter of practical politics.[5]

CHAPTER 16

Nationalism Versus Ideology

Appeasement between the wars was always a self-confident creed. It was both utopian and practical. Its aim was peace for all time, or at least for as long as wise men could devise it. Appeasement was never an apologetic, shy, or shameful creed. Its adherents strove openly to organize Europe in a new and unusual way, based, not upon a mere reluctance to go to war again, but upon a fierce determination not to destroy yet another generation of European youth. Appeasement was a search for international relations conducted without resort to armed conflict. It was a search for methods to resolve national grievances without stirring up hatred and fear. If such a world did not exist – and after so vicious a war could not exist – the task of appeasement was to create it. Appeasement sought to satisfy legitimate national aspirations without, in the same process, fomenting aggressive, destructive nationalism.

The Peace Treaties rested upon the principle of independent single-nation states. They fixed the boundaries of two states, Czechoslovakia and Poland, which had not existed, in the first case for 300, in the second for 140 years; they enlarged the frontiers of other states, in particular Rumania and Serbia; they cut back the frontiers of the defeated Germany; and they made the reconstituted Austria and Hungary as small as possible. Whatever the inequalities of this treatment, it was based nevertheless upon a single premise, national self-determination. Appeasement's prime political purpose became the satisfaction of grievances caused by the abuses perpetrated by the 1919 map-makers. Appeasement was designed to perfect their map, and thereby to lead Europe away from war.

Hitler gave appeasement its greatest opportunity. In British eyes he was clearly a fanatic who would if he felt so inclined lead

Germany into war. But he seemed to be a fanatic along reasonable lines. He believed in the right of all German-speaking people to live within the same borders. He only asked, so it seemed, for new frontiers. Such a man had much in common with the old, pre-Nazi advocates of appeasement, for he repeatedly emphasized the 'injustices' of Versailles, while at the same time saying how happy the world would be if the provisions of Versailles were abandoned. His desires seemed reasonable within the Wilsonian framework of national self-determination. Hitler appeared to be a nationalist of the old school, erratic and emotional, but sincere. Britain had championed Greek and Italian independence, and had approved all efforts, however ferocious, to drive out Turkish and Austrian overlords from those lands. Why should she not now help Hitler to 'free' those Germans under Polish or Czech rule, or to make it possible for the German-speaking Austrians to join the new, dynamic society? Hitler seemed only to echo, on behalf of Germans, the national aspirations of other Europeans in the nineteenth century. Was the twentieth century so cynical that it no longer recognized the claims of people struggling to be free? Was it so biased that it could not rid itself of a belief in German aggressiveness and insincerity?

Visitors to Hitler were almost all convinced by him that German territorial claims would be limited to the German-speaking areas of Europe, and to a return of the former German colonies. In conversation he was forceful in expression, yet moderate in his demands. Even when viewed on a public platform neither his methods nor his tone seemed reprehensible. Ashton-Gwatkin, who heard him speak in 1934, felt the force of his personality: 'His speech was clear and easily intelligible. There appeared to be no oratorical or emotional tricks. The emotion came from the crowd.' Ashton-Gwatkin noted that Hitler's ideas, though perhaps 'crude and half baked', represented the deep-seated desire of the 'little fellow' to lead his life free from the fetters imposed by a rigid class system or a regimented socialist one; the 'little fellow' who was opposed to all forms of war and exploitation, and 'wants his children to have more fun out of life than he has had'.[1] Ashton-Gwatkin realized that the hatreds generated by the Nazi movement might lead to war, but he did not believe that war was inevitable. At the end of 1936 he prepared a series of notes for the Foreign Office on the nature of the conflict between totalitarianism and democracy.[2] These notes constitute a most acute assessment, perceptive but not cynical, optimistic but not blind: the epitome of appeasement.

Ashton-Gwatkin saw danger for democracy in both Bolshevism and Fascism, two 'quasi-religious nationalisms controlled by all-powerful individuals whose policy has been to hypnotize their people'. As a precaution, he believed that democracy must seek her immediate protection in adequate armaments and alliances. But a defensive policy was not enough. The dualism between dictatorship and democracy was not necessarily fundamental. It was not so much a symptom of a world gone permanently mad, but rather a result of the breakdown of the nineteenth century politico-economic balance. If the balance could be rectified it would drive the aggressiveness out of the totalitarian mind. Economic inequalities would only make a violent clash between the have and have-not nations more violent. Ashton-Gwatkin pointed out that the German economic situation was getting worse; that ration tickets had been introduced for butter, fats, and bacon. Such growing hardships could lead only to Nazism being forced to justify its domestic impositions by external adventure. In Ashton-Gwatkin's mind the need throughout Europe was to 'foster and develop the spirit and habits of international interdependence'; above all to root out the causes of all inequalities in national wealth, and to rationalize and internationalize the supply of raw materials and the production of manufactured goods:

> Let me have men about me that are fat;
>   Sleek-headed men and such as sleep o'nights;
> Yon Cassius has a lean and hungry look;...
> Such men are dangerous.

Ashton-Gwatkin saw Nazism as a product of economic inequalities. For him appeasement was a doctor's policy; an attempt to heal wounds whose sepsis had been allowed to go unattended for too long. He believed that the whole body would be restored to health if the infected limb were cured. He did not believe in amputation. Such a policy – preventive war – was not even advocated by Vansittart or Churchill, both of whom, like Ashton-Gwatkin, believed in the ultimate deterrent effect of alliances and armaments. Appeasement was an attempt to extend co-operation with Germany, not in spite of Nazism, but because of it; it was a belief in the remedial nature of British friendship. There were some who held it until the very outbreak of war in 1939.

Hitler was able, by his skill as a conversationalist, to convince visitors that Germany would do everything in her power to avoid war, and in particular to avoid war with Britain. His visitors might arrive in a sceptical frame of mind; might think, as they approached his room, of the political murders, the virulent anti-semitism, the concentration camps, or the expansionist urgings in *Mein Kampf*. Most of them left his room convinced that their fears were unjustified, that Hitler was a sincere believer in European peace, and that if he had hatreds, they were towards communism, not Britain. Hitler was skilful in his talk of the communist 'danger'. He posed successfully as the protector of western civilization against eastern barbarism. Thus Lord Halifax, shortly before he became Foreign Secretary, told Hitler that

> Although there was much in the Nazi system that offended British opinion (treatment of the Church; to perhaps a less extent, the treatment of Jews; treatment of Trade Unions), I was not blind to what he had done for Germany and to the achievement from his point of view of keeping Communism out of his country and, as he would feel, of blocking its passage West.[3]

There was some sympathy in England for Hitler's feelings towards communism. In society circles, where wealth and property were important, and class distinctions upheld with religious zeal, communism seemed far more destructive than Nazism. Movements like the Popular Front in France and organizations like the International Brigade in Spain appeared proofs of the ever-widening nature of the communist conspiracy. Against this stood Hitler, so fanatically anti-communist that there was clearly no possibility of his seeking any rapprochement with Russia, as the Weimar Republic had done at Rapallo. In aristocratic circles Hitler's stance as the stalwart guardian and potential crusader against communism was a powerful asset in favour of British sympathy for his regime.

Anti-semitism was another feature of British thought, not confined to any particular class, which was widespread enough to blunt the edge of criticism against Hitler's racial policies. Nor did one have necessarily to be an anti-semite in order to avoid being horrified by Nazi policy towards the Jews. Lord Lothian always tried

Communism in Europe 1917-1939

Communist Russia
Successful Communist Revolution 1919
Unsuccessful Communist Revolution 1919
★ Communist uprisings 1919
Red Army 1920
Large Communist Party 1919-1922
Active Communist Party 1919-1935
Communist participation in Spanish Civil War 1936-1939

to look at this question from what he considered the Jewish point of view, and Jewish interests. As he wrote in 1935:

There is in my view no chance of altering the present régime in Germany by a renewal of revolution as some of our Jewish friends believe. Like most revolutions it will now evolve, and it is essential that its evolution towards moderation should take place under British influences and the best way of ensuring that is to show that people in this country are interested in Germany and prepared to meet them on ordinary terms.[4]

A year later Lothian wrote to H. G. Wells that 'I believe that Germany would now be willing to come to terms with the Jews if the external pressure and denunciation were relaxed', and he claimed that this was also the view of many German Jews.[5] For Lothian, German anti-semitism was a disease which sprang, like all other Nazi illnesses, from Versailles, and from allied short-sightedness. He believed that by helping Hitler to reverse the Versailles Treaty, gather all German-speaking people within his frontiers, expand eastwards, and regain colonial territory, Britain would soon change Nazism from a vicious to an acceptable creed. He saw no fundamental difference between the British and

German systems; indeed he felt that they had more in common than any other two European forms of Government. As he wrote to Asquith's widow in 1936:

My view is quite simple. I loathe all the dictatorships. I think Mussolini and the Pope are the worst. I think after that Litvinov with his intrigue all over Europe to keep the European powers on the edge of war or to drive them into war is the next, and that Hitler, who is a visionary rather than a gangster, is by far the least evil of the lot. . . .

I think the Germans in themselves are much better people than the Italians or the Russians, and are much more likely to insist on recovering some measure of control over their Govt., once we cease the policy of persecuting them because it placates French terrors and pleases Russian aspirations.[6]

These views were shared, with different emphasis on one aspect or another, by a wide range of people who sought to influence policy. Lloyd George visited Hitler in September 1936, discussed world affairs, and came away convinced that Hitler was a reasonable man with acceptable aims and no desire whatsoever to plunge Europe into war.[7] Conservatives, Liberals, and Socialists alike sought out the Führer, and were mesmerized by him. Even Arnold Toynbee was reported to have been won over at his interview to a belief in Hitler's genuine desire for peace in Europe 'and close friendship with England'.[8] George Lansbury, a pacifist, and earlier leader of the Labour Party, was convinced after their personal encounter that Hitler 'will *not* go to war unless pushed into it by others'.[9] Lord Allen of Hurtwood told the *Daily Telegraph* on his return from Germany that 'I watched him with the utmost vigilance throughout our lengthy conversation, and I am convinced he genuinely desires peace'.[10] Halifax recorded after his own visit to Berchtesgaden: 'He struck me as very sincere, and as believing everything he said'.[11] But all Hitler did at these meetings was to repeat to each visitor the same dreary monologue about the insults of Versailles, the need for German unity on an ethnic basis, the evils of communism which he as a German could appreciate more than they could, the stubbornness of the Czechs, the pugnacity of the Poles, and the long-suffering innocence of the Germans. Above all, he reiterated his desire for peace, and in particular for Anglo-German friendship. But he had no concessions of his own to offer, and when Lord Allen of Hurtwood, with greater courage than most of his fellow-visitors, raised the issue of Jewish persecution,

Hitler had nothing to say.[12] He could accept praise, and even argument, but not criticism. Yet few of the visitors bothered to contrast Hitler's reassurances and pledges with what they had heard of German domestic policy. Even *The Times* gave prominence to stories of religious persecution inside Germany. All the newspapers reported Hitler's speeches, and also those of his subordinates, not all of which were as moderate as his own tea-time effusions. Thus Hitler's personal skill gave a new dimension to the appeasement argument. He was the accessible, amiable leader of a hard-working, ill-treated people. If this were true, appeasement was justified; if it were false, appeasement was an act of gross self-deception.

But doubts as to the morality of appeasement grew, for Hitler's régime persisted in its internal persecution. In 1933 many people felt that all revolutions bred initial violence, and that Nazism was no exception. But such a belief implied that the violence would moderate as the revolution settled down. By 1935 it was clear to some that this was not happening in Germany. Refugees told of continuous persecution. Slowly a doubt began to grow in minds long accustomed not to take alarm at dictatorial methods, or to regard extremism as entirely incompatible with good, or at least adequate foreign relations. This doubt concerned the morality of helping Germany, even when her case, on the old Wilsonian grounds, was a good one. If Nazism was not a vigorous, healthy, out-door creed of clean-living Aryan athletes bent on peace, but rather a manifestation of deep evil forces in human thought and behaviour, how could it ever be appeased? If the immorality of Nazism was unchangeable, were not British efforts to treat with it as if it could change not only mistaken, but themselves immoral? If the two ways of life were incompatible, not only in their external aims, which might change, but in their inner motives, which were fixed, how could appeasement work? Statesmen might, by skilful diplomacy, avert a clash for a short while, but the clash would surely come; and if one had meanwhile closed one's eyes and blocked one's ears to all sight and sound of the deep division, would not one's own moral stance, when it came, seem pale and weak?

The basis of positive appeasement was the recognition of Germany's legitimate claims for Treaty revision. This had dominated British policy since 1919. It depended for its justification upon the compatibility of British and German civilization; upon the possibility of mutual acceptance of each other's way of life and philosophic tenets. If Englishmen felt that Nazism was incompatible with the British outlook on life, all justification for appeasement fell to the ground. It could not then be moral to transfer Germans from a democratic to a totalitarian State; it could not then be wise to hand over black Africans to a colonial power which believed them to be racially inferior, rather than merely politically or educationally backward.

Neville Chamberlain became Prime Minister at the very moment when these feelings were gaining momentum. He did not share them, but they dogged his progress towards what he personally still considered was a morally sound policy of supporting German territorial claims. These doubts did not lie dormant in anguished minds. They showed themselves in a growing body of informed criticism. Some of those who had been most willing to accept the possibility of a lasting and constructive appeasement policy asserted boldly that it could not work, not only because Hitler would not be satisfied, but because it was immoral to try to satisfy him. Sir Horace Rumbold wrote forcefully to Geoffrey Dawson in 1936, warning him that the difficulties involved in appeasement were deeper than those of mere arrangements and modifications of adjustable problems:

> One often hears such phrases as 'the Germans are so like us'. Nothing is more untrue. I could quote many points of difference. For one thing Germans have a streak of brutality which is quite absent in the ordinary Englishman. And Germans like to put up with things which are repugnant to the average man of this country.[13]

When Lord Allen of Hurtwood insisted that appeasement was a realistic policy, and in numerous public speeches and letters to *The Times* argued that concessions to Germany would lead the way to a lasting and just peace, Lord Robert Cecil wrote to Gilbert Murray with fierce indignation, and with arguments that a growing number of people, including the leader-writers of the *Daily Telegraph* and the *News Chronicle*, were beginning to share:

> Psychologically I think the whole of Allen's conception is wrong. I do not think that the present grievances of the Germans are genuine so far as Hitler and his entourage are concerned. They are merely being used in order to justify his armaments policy, and if we were successful in

taking away one or more of his grievances, he would only produce others, and at the same time use our concessions as a proof of how well his policy was succeeding.

These people who go to Berlin are really rather a nuisance. They seem to me to be entirely taken in by the Germans. What is the use of Allen assuring us that they mean peace, when Germany never loses an opportunity of arrogant and anti-international action? . . .

My friends on the Right Wing seem to me to be insane in their fear of Communism. Communism is not a danger nationally or internationally at present. The danger is Fascism and Nazi-ism, and that only.[14]

Between the end of 1936 and mid-1938 the position of appeasement was severely shaken. It became the focal point of intense and violent argument. Although much of the public and most of the press believed in maintaining peace at almost any price, the perpetuation and strengthening of the Nazi regime was becoming for more and more people too high a price to pay. Yet any international agreement which benefited Germany at the expense of her neighbours would clearly provide Hitler with greater support inside Germany, and a greater leverage in future international discussions. The nation was divided. Arguments became more bitter and more extreme. G. M. Trevelyan raised his influential voice in favour of accepting the permanence of Nazism, and in advocating the possibility of obtaining lasting agreeements satisfactory to both Britain and Germany. Writing to *The Times* on 12 August 1937 he claimed:

Dictatorship and democracy must live side by side in peace, or civilization is doomed. For this end I believe Englishmen would do well to remember that the Nazi form of government is in large measure the outcome of Allied and British injustice at Versailles in 1919.

As to 1914 and the years before . . . Germans and English will seldom agree, the less so, I would add, because of the egregious folly of the 'guilt' clause of the Treaty of Versailles, which has acted, as might have been foreseen, as a challenge to Germans to prove that their Government was not to blame at all.

But the way to future goodwill does not lie in disputing about 1914. Rather . . . let us 'recognize and appreciate what is good and what is great in the other nation'.

In March 1938 Hitler annexed Austria. Three years earlier this action would have been widely interpreted in England as a necessary revision of the Versailles Treaty, which, as France would not countenance it through negotiations, could only come about through unilateral action by Germany. It would have been seen in 1935 as a long-overdue reunion of German-speaking masses to the main body of Germans. Keynes, Lothian, Geoffrey Dawson, Allen, and a host of other convinced revisionists would have rejoiced unreservedly. But in March 1938 *Anschluss* no longer appeared entirely as the innocent expansion of a much maligned and wrongly circumscribed Germany. Some people asked whether the Austrian socialists, communists, Catholics, Jews, intellectuals, and scholars would now be imprisoned or silenced, as had happened in Germany. Some asked whether Austrian newspapers would at once be censored, Austrian music purged of its 'Jewish elements' and Austrian geniality submerged beneath a mass of heel-clicking, swastika-waving mediocrity. Others asked how anyone could believe that Hitler could possibly have reached the end of his territorial ambition, despite his claim that this was his final extension of territory. Many people were now convinced that German desires could no longer be considered solely within the framework of national self-determination, national dignity, or national aspirations. The moral problem could no longer be ignored. Nazism and democracy were not compatible. As the Bishop of Durham wrote in April 1938 to Lord Londonderry, a strong advocate of appeasement with Nazi Germany:

The suspicion grows on my mind that the well-meant and attractive policy of avoiding the division of Europe or rather of the civilized world into rival 'ideologies' must ultimately fail before the *inherent necessity of agreement in ultimate principle if harmony is to be preserved*. Abraham Lincoln's declaration about the American Union may be justly applied to modern civilization:

'A house divided against a house cannot stand. I believe this government cannot endure half slave and half free. I do not expect the house to fall but I expect it will cease to be divided. It will become all one thing or all the other'.

The *principle* of democracy is personal freedom; the *principle* of dictatorship (No. 1: Bolshevist; No. 2: Fascist) is personal servitude. One or other must be supreme; they cannot co-exist in amiable co-operation in a civilized world so closely linked as is the civilized world today. I wish a clearer expression could be given to the sense of *moral nausea* which is growing in many minds in England, as the abominable oppression of minorities, Jewish and Christian, proceeds and advances in Germany. This is one of the 'imponderables' which Bismarck warned politicians not to neglect. *It will defeat the diplomats of compromise in the long run.*[15]

But Chamberlain, and Sir Nevile Henderson, his Ambassador in Berlin, doubted the wisdom of considering conflict between Britain and Germany as inevitable. Both believed that even Nazi Germany could be appeased, not in order to give Britain a breathing space in which to rearm more rapidly and prepare for war, but to avert the danger of war for all time. Both thought along the same lines and with the same objectives as Lloyd George, Bonar Law, and Ramsay MacDonald. Both felt that Britain still lay under a moral obligation to revise the Treaty of Versailles and to give Germany the benefit of the doubt. As Chamberlain explained to the House of Commons in April 1938:

> Our policy is not one of dividing Europe into two opposing *blocs* of countries, each arming against the other amidst a growing flood of ill-will on both sides, which can only end in war. That seems to us to be a policy which is dangerous and stupid. You may say we may not approve of dictatorships. . . . We have to live with them. . . . We should take any and every opportunity to try to remove any genuine and legitimate grievance that may exist.[16]

Chamberlain, influenced both by Hitler's assertions and Nevile Henderson's dispatches, believed that one final German grievance lay in the way of a permanent settlement in Europe. Three million German-speaking people, living along Germany's frontier in the Sudeten mountain area of Czechoslovakia, who before 1918 had been part of the Habsburg Empire, were demanding a greater voice in their own Government. For twenty years the Czechs had been extremely reluctant to make substantial concessions. In 1938 Hitler announced his support for the Sudeten-Germans, and encouraged them to press for autonomy. Neither Hitler nor the Sudeten-German leaders demanded *Anschluss* with Germany, but merely greater independence for the Sudetens inside Czechoslovakia. By all the original criteria of appeasement and peaceful change, the Sudeten case was unanswerable. They had been incorporated in Czechoslovakia as a result of the Peace Treaties. They had never been consulted about this. Now the British Government had a chance to show Hitler that it was not seeking to challenge him, as he sometimes angrily claimed, in order, as he said, to frustrate his legitimate grievances. Here was an

issue where Britain, by taking the German view, could prove herself not only a true Treaty revisionist, but also a friend of reasonable, 'legitimate' German aspirations. Such proof could only have
one result, or so Chamberlain and Henderson believed, and that
was to show Hitler that he could trust Britain, as his friend, in any
future changes of frontiers that might be needed: that diplomacy,
not war, could further his territorial aspirations. As a result of
such mutual trust, Chamberlain believed that the chances of an
Anglo-German war would rapidly disappear. European peace
would be assured. Germany would feel befriended, and Hitler
would relax internal persecutions.

Chamberlain continued to assert in the House of Commons that
such hopes for appeasement with Nazi Germany were not chi-
meras, and that democratic and totalitarian States did not have
necessarily to resort to war:

> If only we could find some peaceful solution of this Czechoslovakian
> question, I should myself feel that the way was open again for a further
> effort for a general appeasement – an appeasement which cannot be
> obtained until we can be satisfied that no major cause of difference or
> dispute remains unsettled. We have already demonstrated the possi-
> bility of complete agreement between a democratic and a totalitarian
> State, and I do not myself see why that experiment should not be
> repeated ... [The Anglo-German Naval Treaty] stands as a demon-
> stration that it is possible for Germany and ourselves to agree upon
> matters which are vital to both of us. ...
> I do not think that we ought to find it impossible to continue our
> efforts at understanding, which if they were successful, would do so
> much to bring back confidence.[17]

But these opinions no longer went unchallenged. Some of
Chamberlain's supporters, as well as members of the small but
vocal opposition parties, began to feel uneasy at British support
for the proposed Sudeten 'autonomy'. Might not Hitler demand
annexation next, they asked? And would Britain be prepared to
transfer even more non-Nazis to Nazi rule? Josiah Wedgewood, a
Labour MP who had been severely wounded in the Great War,
asked angrily during the same debate:

> What have the Jews to gain, the Jews who have fled from the surround-
> ing Reich into Czechoslovakia and are trying there to build up again a
> life for themselves? Directly Nazi rule comes along what happened in

Austria will be repeated in the Sudeten Deutsch territory – another 20,000 suicides, another great tragedy. . . .

Every time you sacrifice one of your potential allies to this pathetic desire to appease the tyrants you merely bring nearer and make more inevitable that war which you pretend you are trying to avoid.[17]

By mid-1938 appeasement had lost much of its lustre. The morality of revising Versailles in favour of Nazi Germany was no longer asserted as boldly as it had been even a year earlier. Might it not be more moral to check the spread of Nazism, either by warnings or, if the warnings failed, by force ? The influence of a book called *The House that Hitler Built*, published in 1937 by an Australian History Professor, was substantial. The author declared that:

> The whole teaching of Hitlerism is to justify war as a instrument of policy . . . and there is hardly a boy in Germany who does not view the preparation for ultimate war as the most important aspect of his life. . . . . Hitlerism cannot achieve its aims without war; its ideology is that of war. . . . Hitler has worked up Germany to such a state that the people are ready to accept war at any moment.[18]

Chamberlain himself rejected this interpretation, writing to his sister that 'if I accepted the author's conclusions, I should despair, but I don't and won't'.[19] Others, who had been active advocates of appeasement with as much zeal, and for as long as Chamberlain, took Roberts's gloomy forecast more seriously. Lord Lothian ceased his private crusade for Treaty revision. The historian Conwell-Evans, who from 1935–7 had urged Lothian to believe Hitler's protestations of good faith, and who had worked vigorously for an Anglo-German rapprochement, in August 1938, in a series of memoranda, warned the Government not to trust Hitler's pledges. Vansittart put Conwell-Evans's warnings before the Cabinet, and pressed them to take notice. But the warnings, though precise, were ignored. Hitler's mind had been made up, Conwell-Evans declared, when Britain failed to save the Emperor of Abyssinia from Mussolini:

> He scorns the attitude of England, whose fine phrases contributed nothing to the Negus. If England hesitated to tackle the Italians, whom Hitler, like every German, in his heart despises, how much more would the English hesitate to grapple with the Germans – a much tougher proposition, he thinks.[20]

Most powerful of all, Lord Allen of Hurtwood, who had spoken in favour of appeasement for four years, on hundreds of public platforms all over England, and had written myriad letters to *The Times* pleading for a better understanding of Germany's difficult position, needs, problems, and above all sincerity, raised a serious note of alarm in the House of Lords at the end of July:

If this country and Germany should ever drift apart again and should ever find themselves upon the brink of war, I personally do not believe it will be due to some breach of contract or breach of law. It will be due to our discovery in the course of the negotiations that there is a disparity of outlook between our two countries, so far as humanity and cruelty are concerned, and because of the discovery of that disparity of outlook there will be an absence of confidence which will make it exceedingly difficult to carry through to success those negotiations which both Germany and this country so ardently desire.

I look back to the various stages of Anglo-German relationships. I can remember that before the war some of us were admiring and extolling the culture and achievements of the German people. I can remember that we pointed to the geographical position of Germany, situated as she was in the very centre of Europe, and we realized that this geographical disability had affected her history in the past, and must affect it in the future. We realized that Britain, situated as she was, protected by the sea, had been able, because of that security, early to achieve mature political wisdom, and to gather round herself a commonwealth of free peoples. We realized that Germany had desired what we in this country had desired, but had failed in that achievement. Consequently, when the War came, I can well remember that under the leadership of Mr Ramsay MacDonald some of us protested against the proposition that the sole responsibility for that War rested upon the German nation. In 1916 we pleaded for a peace by negotiation, rather than a peace by a knock-out blow, and at the time of the Versailles Treaty we protested, not merely against the terms included in the Treaty, but against the manner in which the Treaty was being negotiated, for we realized that you could not build up the peace of Europe upon the foundation of a humiliated nation. Thereafter, when the War was over, we pleaded for the inclusion of Germany from the beginning in the family of the League of Nations, instead of five years afterwards, as was the case; and at stage after stage of the Disarmament Conference, in your Lordship's House, some of us begged most earnestly for the end of discrimination and of the inequalities that were imposed upon the German people. Finally, even when Herr Hitler introduced into Germany a régime which some of us found difficult to understand,

and which if I may say so was contrary to our British way of looking at the art of government, we have continued to plead for goodwill and understanding between Germany and this country.

I believe that if Germany continues the policy which she is now pursuing with regard to the Jews and other refugees she will bring about an impediment to that peace which we all desire to see established. The moment at which she is carrying on that policy is strangely unfortunate. During the last few years there has grown up amongst every grade of opinion in this country a longing for conciliation with Germany. The British people have realized, and realized with some measure of shame, their part in the responsibility for the last few tragic years, and just at that moment, when goodwill was apparent, Germany has seen fit to impede that growing goodwill by this new barrier of misunderstanding. . . .

We all understand that every government, every nation, will at times impose suffering and persecution upon its political opponents, particularly upon opponents who may seem to it to be guilty of a violent and seditious policy. Persecution of political opponents is something common to all countries. I have myself known [when a conscientious objector] what it is to be the guest of His Majesty's Government in this country for quite a considerable period of my life, and therefore I have reason to understand that all governments see fit at a certain time to consider certain members of the community to be out of order. But the persecution which is being carried on in Germany is not that of persecuting opinion, but of persecuting blood.

I have known myself, as a guest of the German Government, what it is to be taken through the lovely countryside in Germany, and then to feel the profound discomfort which comes from seeing those placards of hatred against the Jews which you encounter as you pass through that country. Some of us have known in Germany, even when we have been the guests of the German Government, what it is to have in our hands the hand of a little German child, a child which in school has been compelled to sit upon benches separate from its school-fellows, an object of contempt, for no other reason than that it is the child of its Jewish parents. I cannot conceive anything more cruel than to try to stir up hatred between child and parent. That is not a persecution of opinion, that is not an attempt to put down sedition, that is persecution of blood, from which there is no escape; and, for a child to be brought up under that form of persecution, I think must stir the heart of anyone who has passed through that experience in Germany.

Germany has said that British democracy is degenerate. Well, I for one was never more proud of British democracy than when Professor Freud, that great scientist, aged and infirm, became an exile from his country and was welcomed within our shores. There was taken to him as an invalid the register of the Royal Society in order that he might inscribe his name therein, an act which I believe has never been carried through in this country except for members of our Royal Family; and thus degenerate democracy linked an exiled and distinguished Jewish scientist with members of our own Royal Family. That seemed to me a cause of pride, and not a sign of degeneracy. I have, I hope, not spoken too unrestrainedly, but this whole attitude of the Germans, with whom we are so longing to see a peace settlement, is affecting issue after issue which comes directly within the purview of any settlement that will have to be made. . . .

I believe that most schools of thought would be eager and anxious to bring about readjustment of the Colonial problem as part of an all-round peace settlement. But do not our German friends realize that just as we have become conscious of an old wrong they now confront us with the dilemma of facing a new wrong, and that we cannot overlook the consequences upon native populations in these Colonial areas when we see the tragic evils which are being perpetrated in Germany so far as German minorities like the Jews are concerned.[21]

The negotiations which Allen feared would break down because of the 'disparity of outlook' between Britain and Germany, began in August 1938, within two weeks of his warning. Chamberlain sent a Mission, led by Lord Runciman, to Czechoslovakia. Its aim was to obtain the basis for an agreement between Czechs and Sudetens, Chamberlain intended the agreement to be reached without German participation, and to be based upon Czech recognition of Sudeten desires. The Runciman Mission was Britain's last exercise in positive appeasement. It set out to mediate between two equally sincere groups; Czechs nervous of the disintegration of the multinational Czech State, and Sudeten-Germans wishing to be their own masters. Ashton-Gwatkin, who was a leading member of the Mission, suggested that the Sudeten-German leader, Conrad Henlein, should go to Germany 'and persuade Hitler . . . not only to support these new negotiations but also to seek a basis of a general settlement with Great Britain'.[22] But Hitler's mind was running more and more along the lines of conquest, not settlement.

Runciman and Ashton-Gwatkin were successful. They obtained concessions from the Czechs and a willingness to accept them from the Sudetens. They proposed a federal system for Czechoslovakia, on the Swiss model. The Czechs and the Sudetens were delighted. Appeasement had won its greatest victory since the Dawes Plan.

But it was not to be: reality was less rational than common-sense. Hitler, angry that the Sudetens were willing to accept autonomy inside Czechoslovakia, incited them to demand more. When they proved reluctant – for Ashton-Gwatkin made a special journey in order to make it quite clear to them that they could expect nothing better for their own interests than the British plan – Hitler publicly and violently denounced the Runciman Mission. On 12 September 1938 he demanded the right of the Sudetens to self-determination. Henlein, caught between the goodwill of his patrons and the threats of his master, at once abandoned the 'Federal' plan which he had been prepared to accept.

Appeasement was dead. Hitler's raucous voice, not the voice of reason, henceforward determined the development of each crisis. If Hitler wished to be conciliatory, there was conciliation in Europe; if he decided to resort to war, there was war. Appeasement could not compete against such whims. Its basis was the reasoned argument, the carefully weighed factors, and the over-riding morality of any proposed change. After 12 September 1938 appeasement became increasingly a nervous, jerky, guilt-en-cumbered affair; not a confident philosophy, but a painful surrender to threats. But Chamberlain himself was not deterred by the failure of the Runciman Mission. He still personally believed in a reconciliation of interests. Yet more and more people doubted whether such a reconciliation could possibly succeed, except in the short term. The Anglo-German Naval Agreement had been welcomed in 1935 as a constructive act of statesmanship from which mutual benefit and satisfaction would steadily accrue. The Munich Agreement of October 1938, which transferred the Sudetenland to Germany, was seen by many former 'appeasers' as a time-saving concession, rather shameful in itself, but essential if Britain were to be able to arm adequately to face an inevitable threat. Chamberlain himself continued to believe most em-phatically that war was not inevitable. At Munich he obtained Hitler's signature to a document which stated that 'we regard the Agreement signed last night, and the Anglo-German Naval Agreement, as symbolic of the desire of our two peoples never to go to war with one another again'. This was a false linking of the two Agreements. The first had its origins in optimism, the second in despair.

Appeasement was a constructive policy. Its aim was the creation

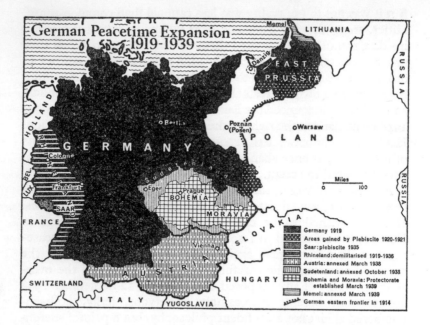

German Peacetime Expansion 1919-1939

Germany 1919
Areas gained by Plebiscite 1920-1921
Saar: plebiscite 1935
Rhineland: demilitarised 1919-1936
Austria: annexed March 1938
Sudetenland: annexed October 1938
Bohemia and Moravia: Protectorate established March 1939
Memel: annexed March 1939
German eastern frontier in 1914

of a Europe better delineated than that of the Peace Treaties; a
Europe in which economic benefits would be shared by all and
political differences settled at the conference table. Hitler's
Germany did not fit into such a plan as Weimar Germany had
done. Yet until 1938 it seemed possible to ignore the fundamental
differences between the British and the Nazi-German way of life.
Even Churchill, who became Nazism's most implacable opponent
during the Second World War, was always reluctant to condemn a
régime that might conceivably change its tone. By early 1938
a growing number of people had come to feel that Nazism was a
fixed, immutable phenomenon that must, ultimately, either
destroy others or be destroyed. Such a belief was seldom held
lightly, for its implications were that Europe must once again
descend into the abyss of war, and that appeasement, in which so
much trust had been placed, had met an obstacle which it could
not surmount. When Churchill suggested early in 1938 that the
clash of ideologies might lead to war, the *Daily Express* challenged
him:

Winston fears that Fascism will engulf our civilization. It won't.
There is no need to try to stamp it out. It is not our business to stamp

it out. Our business is to bring our own form of government to correspond more closely to the urgent needs of our own people.[23]

But Churchill's instinct was the surer. He saw the need, not for attack, but for defence, believing that the German onslaught could not long be delayed. After Munich, Chamberlain still believed a conclusive Anglo-German agreement was possible. Other Cabinet Ministers, including Halifax, sought to delay the day when war with Germany would come, fearing, in contrast to Chamberlain, that conciliation might fail. This was no longer appeasement, but prudence. Many aspects of rearmament and preparation were not ready in November 1938; radar, which played so important a part in the Battle of Britain, was not sufficiently developed for it to have been decisive early in 1939.

After Munich, despite Chamberlain's optimism, the nature and methods of Hitler's policy did not change. He occupied Prague in March 1939 and invaded Poland in September. Chamberlain's hopes that war might be avoided were broken. He could no longer persuade Hitler to return to the earlier basis of appeasement and instead of trying to do so, negotiated alliances with Poland, Rumania, and Greece, pledging Britain's active intervention against Germany should they be attacked. Hitler, who had mistaken appeasement for weakness, tried to convince himself that Britain would not honour her agreement with Poland. But appeasement was never a coward's creed. It never signified retreat or surrender from formal pledges. If, at the last moment, Chamberlain had doubts as to whether war was inevitable, these doubts were not dishonourable, however short-sighted. Germany, not Britain, had gone beyond the bounds of humanity and decency in internal policy. Hitler, not Chamberlain, had made violence the norm of international affairs. Appeasement was not only an approach to foreign policy, it was a way of life, a method of human contact and progress. Hitler chose another method. However nervous he might have been to challenge Britain, however unwilling to commit himself to long-term plans or to blueprints for aggression, it was he who, by destroying the Runciman Mission, and pressing for concessions beyond the bounds of reason, destroyed appeasement. It was Hitler who lost the friendship and sympathy of Germany's most earnest advocate, and propelled Germany into a war which resulted in devastation out of all proportion to that of 1914–18. Hitler's war resulted in a far greater loss

G

of German territory than at Versailles, in the partition of Germany, in the renewed hostility and suspicion of the rest of Europe, and in the westward march of communism, to prevent which so much of his planning had been designed.

Appeasement cannot be held morally responsible for German aggression which led to the invasion of Poland and Britain's declaration of war on Germany.

Epilogue: Munich and the New Appeasement

Appeasement and 'Munich' were quite different phenomena. Appeasement was a traditional policy, based upon concessions made from a position of strength. 'Munich' was much more an emergency plan, intended to buy peace at the expense of the disintegration of Czechoslovakia and the transfer, without plebiscite, of non-Nazis to Nazi rule. Appeasement's justification, whether at the time of the American Revolution or of the Lausanne Conference on reparations, was that it was rooted in a deep concern for considerations of international morality, and that however expedient specific acts of appeasement might be, they were also moral. 'Munich' may have been expedient; but it had less of an aura of morality. Hitler's rejection of the Runciman Mission removed the Czech crisis from the traditional sphere of legitimate Treaty revision to a new world of threats, tension, and emergency.

Certain aspects of the new appeasement had also been present in the old. Fear of communism certainly spanned the two, and the nervousness provoked by the murder of the Tsar, the Red Army's attack on Warsaw and the 'Zinoviev letter' was accentuated by the much publicized Stalinist purges from 1936–8, by the Russian involvement in the Spanish Civil War, albeit in defence of the legitimate republican government, and by the belief that Russia would use a Czechoslovak-German war in order to advance Russian interests in central Europe through her alliance with Prague. Chamberlain may not have been as tempestuously anti-communist in 1937 as Churchill had been in 1919, but he was sufficiently distrustful of Soviet intentions to doubt even Churchill's insistence, as well as that of Lloyd George, that an Anglo-Russian alliance was perhaps the only way of deterring German aggression in 1939.

Suspicion of France was also a link between appeasement old and new. Before 1935 French anti-Germanism was resented as being the supposed cause of European tensions. After 1935, as German rearmament increased, France became an object of derision: surely no reliance could be placed, it was argued, upon a tired nation, weary of war, unwilling to pit her army and resources against the greater power of Germany. French defeatism, much evident after 1935, made alliance and even co-operation with France seem a risky venture, just as, before 1935, French alliances in eastern Europe had queered the value of her friendship. Nor did Léon Blum's Popular Front government improve the French image in British eyes after 1936. It seemed an incitement to overt class antagonism and an invitation to civil war. The cry of the French right, 'better Hitler than Blum', warned British politicians of the dangers of relying in a crisis upon French solidarity or consistency. Churchill insisted, in his public speeches, upon the need to maintain close Anglo-French co-operation. But more than twenty years of anti-French feeling in Britain augmented the arguments of those who at the time of Munich said that France could not be relied upon to act with Britain in any anti-German or pro-Czech policy. The new appeasement lacked the full flavour of international amity and mutual confidence, which, particularly under MacDonald, permeated the old.

A third consistent theme in inter-war foreign policy was the need of successive Governments to work in harmony with the British Empire. The fall of Lloyd George, following Canadian, Australian, and South African hostility to his Chanak policy, seemed to point a warning finger at the dangers of getting out of step with imperial sentiment. Probably these fears were exaggerated: certainly the Locarno agreements, which in theory could have involved Britain in a European war to defend either France or Germany from attack, were negotiated without imperial participation or prior approval, and yet the Empire survived. To strengthen imperial links, Ramsay MacDonald and Baldwin had accepted Imperial Preference in 1932, at the expense, as both Vansittart and Ashton-Gwatkin pointed out at the time, of intervening beneficially, and perhaps decisively, to halt European economic disintegration. Neville Chamberlain seemed to take the wishes of the Empire as seriously as his two immediate predecessors. At the Imperial Conference of 1937 he was struck by the majority view among the Dominion

Prime Ministers that a firm imperial commitment to resist Hitler by force could not be given. General Herzog made South Africa's position plain when he said at the Conference:

I maintain that peace in Europe can be assured today, and should be assured, if Great Britain approached Germany in the same spirit of friendly co-operation that she has shown France since 1919. I sincerely hope that I shall not be accused of unfriendly feelings towards the British government if I say that the impression so far given by Great Britain's attitude towards Germany is far too much one of cold repelling indifference compared with the warm welcome given to France.... If war did come because England continued to associate with France in a policy in respect of central and eastern Europe calculated to threaten Germany's existence through unwillingness to set right the injustices flowing from the Treaty of Versailles, South Africa cannot be expected to take part in the war.[1]

During the Munich crisis the Dominion Prime Ministers made it clear that they did not regard a German attack on Czechoslovakia as an adequate reason for the Empire becoming involved in a European war. No doubt this view, which was expressed forcibly and repeatedly, influenced Chamberlain, and helped to determine British policy. The imperial armies had played a crucial part in the Great War, and had suffered heavy casualties. Passchendaele and Gallipoli were a long way from Toronto, Sydney, and Cape Town. If Chamberlain himself, from London, could describe Czechoslovakia as 'a far-away country', it is not surprising that Dominion politicians could not conceive of it as an acceptable *casus belli*.

Attitudes to Russia, France, and the Empire linked the old appeasement with the new. But the new appeasement was influenced also by factors and emotions absent before 1937, which counteracted the growing belief in German immorality. The new factor was Germany's growing military and air power. The new emotion was fear. Simultaneously, weakness and fear propelled the Government forward, both to the policy of making concessions, and to rearmament. Pro-Germanism, dislike of Versailles, trust in Nazi goodwill, hope in Hitler's reformation; these influences for appeasement all survived. But over them hung the grey cloud of fear, which covered all acts of appeasement after 1937 with a shadow of doubt, hesitation, and uncertainty. All who supported appeasement, but knew Britain's military weakness, and

Chamberlain was one of them, could no longer embark upon a policy beneficial to Germany, even in the short term, without serious anxiety. The firmness of moral purpose that had invigorated appeasement from 1918 to at least 1935, had disappeared almost entirely by the time of the *Anschluss* in 1938.

Lord Allen saw clearly that the new appeasement, in which British military weakness played so large a part, lacked the moral stature of its traditional forerunner. In May 1938, at the outset of the Czech crisis, he wrote to Arnold Toynbee:

I am putting completely on one side my pacifist opinions, and am assuming that force must be put behind law in a world which remains armed. With that premise, my point is that to uphold under every conceivable circumstance the rule of law at a time when there is such a huge margin of doubt as to the capacity of material forces to maintain the law is terribly serious. . . .

Unless force is overwhelming I think one then has to choose between two evils – the evil of a catastrophe in trying to uphold law – and the evil of allowing temporary casualties in morality. It is for that reason that I am willing to take the risks with morality during the transitional period in the hope – perhaps a vain one – that events will play into our hands.[2]

There were other serious difficulties in pursuing the new appeasement. Its supporters were of poor calibre, while its critics had a firm basis of criticism in their constant reiteration that negotiations with Nazi Germany were a special case, not subject to the normal laws of diplomatic pressure and compromise.

The leading politicians and other advocates of the new appeasement were of lesser ability than the majority of their predecessors after 1918. Neville Chamberlain was certainly a man of great determination, but he was also obstinate to the point of blindness, and unimaginative. Lord Halifax, his Foreign Secretary after February 1938, was a man of uncertain judgement and vacillating opinions. Henderson, his principal source of information about German moods and intentions, was erratic, vain, muddle-headed, and at times almost hysterical. All three believed in the possibility of saving Anglo-German relations from the storm, caused by rearmament, *Anschluss*, and anti-semitism, into which international relations had been swept. But these three men did not have the ability or the knowledge to act as successful navigators. Of the Prime Minister himself, Lord Strang, who had accompanied him to Munich, wrote in retrospect:

It can fairly be said of Neville Chamberlain that he was not well versed in foreign affairs, that he had no touch for a diplomatic situation, that he did not fully realize what it was he was doing, and that his naive confidence in his own judgement and powers of persuasion and achievement was misplaced.[3]

This was not the judgement of a hostile or carping critic, but of a man whose sympathies were entirely with the belief in the need for compromise and conciliation in international affairs. The same is true of Lord Birkenhead, Halifax's admirer and biographer, and in 1938 his Parliamentary Private Secretary who, when confronted in 1965 with the evidence of his friend's Foreign Secretaryship wrote of how

His instinct in an explosive situation was to conciliate. When nations or men became inflamed with passion, he did not catch fire ... a certain sluggishness of imagination prevented him ever receiving a blinding realization of terrible events. ... Edward was thus not fitted by nature to preside over the Foreign Office at such a moment of history.[4]

Halifax was not blind. He knew, not only from the newspapers, that Hitler was capable of great brutality. Many of the British protests against concentration camp excesses were sent to Germany through the Foreign Office. Halifax had read of the cruelties perpetrated by the Nazis after the annexation of Austria; he had received full reports on the crude anti-semitic policies by which Jews became 'second-class' citizens and were made to suffer numerous indignities and hardships. At the time of the Munich Agreement he expressed in Cabinet his distaste of a policy which involved forcing a democratic state to make concessions to a totalitarian one. But the troubles of Halifax's conscience were not sufficient to persuade Chamberlain to alter, or even to modify, his policy. As Lord Birkenhead wrote, Halifax, 'failed to induce in the Prime Minister the sense of urgency demanded by the hour, or to exert on him a more powerful influence which he alone in the Cabinet could have commanded'.[4]

The only other source from which a warning might have come was Nevile Henderson, the British Ambassador in Berlin. But Henderson was a man driven by anxiety and prejudice into a pro-German position. He considered the Czechs 'a pig-headed race', on whose behalf Britain should make no efforts whatsoever. Regarding the very existence of Czechoslovakia as a mistake, he wanted Treaty revision in Germany's favour to be the corner-stone of British policy. He felt that it was immoral for Britain to do anything that might keep German-speaking people outside the frontiers of Nazi Germany. He did not pause to ask whether Sudeten Jews, communists, socialists, liberals, or devout Christians would want union with a Germany whose philosophy and actions cast them in the role of unwanted, degenerate 'scum', or would at once restrict, as in the case of authors, actors, musicians or journalists, the things they could publish or perform. According to Henderson:

There can never be appeasement in Europe so long as Czechoslovakia remains the link with Moscow and hostile to Germany. Czechoslovakia can never enjoy a moment's peace so long as she remains the enemy of Germany. It is a case of the inexorable logic of geographic position. If she wants to survive at all she must come economically within the orbit of Germany. We poor mortals can kick against logic but we can never prevail against it in the end.[5]

The appeasement whose 'logic' Henderson upheld was not that which had appealed to his predecessor, Lord D'Abernon; nor were Henderson's reports on the German internal situation as perceptive as those of his two other forerunners in Berlin, Rumbold and Phipps. Orme Sargent, who saw Henderson's dispatches as they reached the Foreign Office, and whose 'Sargent chain' had been a blueprint for appeasement before the advent of Hitler, was horrified by what he read. In retrospect he wrote of Henderson that he

... had no preconceived dislike of authoritarian government as such, and was therefore ready to believe that Great Britain and Germany could be reconciled even if this meant tacit acquiescence by Britain in the adoption by Germany of the Nazi philosophy of life and system of government as well as the aggrandizement of Germany in Central Europe.[6]

This was the gravamen of the contemporary charge against Chamberlain's appeasement; not that conciliation was wrong, or that Treaty revision was wrong, as general guidelines for a liberal and Christian policy, but that such a base was unrealistic when applied to Nazi Germany in 1938. Hitler had been given the benefit of every doubt for five years. He had been offered concessions, including colonial and economic concessions greatly to his advantage, but had preferred the path of unilateral action, surprise, the threat of violence, vituperative language and overt brutality. The old appeasement was rooted in a belief that Britain and Germany had much in common; that their interests often coincided and that their civilizations were in no way incompatible. Neither premise fitted the situation in 1938.

From 1919–1937, the public, the Press, and the politicians could all welcome agreements with Germany as leading to peace. The Munich Agreement was welcomed because it averted war. There was a deep difference between the two attitudes. At bottom, the old appeasement was a mood of hope, Victorian in its optimism, Burkean in its belief that societies evolved from bad to good and that progress could only be for the better. The new appeasement was a mood of fear, Hobbesian in its insistence upon swallowing the bad in order to preserve some remnant of the good, pessimistic in its belief that Nazism was there to stay and, however horrible it might be, should be accepted as a way of life with which Britain ought to deal. But a constructive foreign policy could not be built upon the soft sandstone of nervous tension, nor on the outburst of relief at a war narrowly escaped. Nor could Chamberlain avoid, at the very moment when this relief was at its height, and his reputation as high as that of Lloyd George in 1918, a blast of criticism and doubt. The 'Munich' debate in the House of Commons was an exceptionally bitter one. Many of those who had supported with acclaim the appeasement policies of Chamberlain's predecessors, found the new appeasement galling and humiliating. In the press, warning notes were struck by the *Daily Telegraph*, the *Manchester Guardian*, and the *News Chronicle*. Norman Angell added his voice to the chorus of believers who had lost faith in what they considered to be a perversion of their former creed. Chamberlain was criticized, not because he was an appeaser, for that was a word signifying wisdom, breadth of vision, and stout common sense, but because he had failed to see that appeasement had never been designed as a policy of retreat and weakness, and that an appeaser was meant to be a midwife, not a mortician.

The shadow of dismembered Czechoslovakia hung heavily over the 'Munich' debate. Had the appeasement of Germany reached such a depth of servility that it could only be pursued by the suffering of a country which was in almost every way more suited to be Britain's friend than the Germany on whose behalf that suffering had been allowed? Chamberlain still believed that peace could be preserved. He still doubted the inevitability of an armed clash with Germany. He still resented the suggestion that, in the last resort, British and German interests were incompatible. 'The path which leads to appeasement,' he told the House of Commons after Munich, 'is long and bristles with obstacles. The question of Czechoslovakia is the latest and most dangerous. Now that we have got past it, I feel it may be possible to make further progress along the road to sanity.' *The Times* applauded Chamberlain's realism. The *Daily Express* praised and shared his vision. Lord Londonderry, a dabbler in foreign affairs, who feared communism and had been won over by Hitler's personal charm, wrote enthusiastically of Munich as a prelude to wider, more conclusive settlements.[7] But the new appeasement had lost touch with the respectability, and the plausibility, of the old.

Munich was not appeasement's finest hour, but its most perverted. It was a distortion of all that appeasement stood for. It was a conference without compromise; public speeches without moderation; a final judgement without the principal party, Czechoslovakia, being allowed to be present; a solution which hurt as many people as it benefited and whetted the appetites it had been intended to satisfy; populations transferred without a plebiscite; a sacrifice in interests without a *quid pro quo*; a pandering to immorality without convincing evidence of imminent better times. Clement Attlee, the leader of the Labour Party, and for three years an opponent of rearmament, felt humiliated at 'a victory for brute force .... We have seen today a gallant, civilized, and democratic people betrayed and handed over to a ruthless despotism'.[8] Churchill, who for three years had sensed the danger and been the principal advocate of rearmament, found unendurable 'the sense of our country falling into the power, into the orbit and influence of Nazi Germany, and of our existence becoming dependent upon their will and pleasure'.[9] Among the most telling criticisms were those of Harold Nicolson, whose book *Peacemaking 1919* had done so much, in the very year that Hitler came to power, to confirm public opinion in its belief that Germany had been ill-served at the Paris Peace Conference. Speaking in the House of Commons after Munich, Nicolson criticized those who considered the new appeasement a sign of realism, and who saw compromise with Nazi Germany as a viable, and desirable policy:

> I know that in these days of realism principles are considered as rather eccentric and ideals are identified with hysteria. I know that those of us who believe in the traditions of our policy, who believe in the precepts which we have inherited from our ancestors, who believe that one great function of this country is to maintain moral standards in Europe, to maintain a settled pattern of international relations, not to make friends with people who are demonstrably evil, not to go out of our way to make friends with them but to set up some sort of standard by which the smaller powers can test what is good in international conduct and what is not – I know that those who hold such beliefs are accused of possessing the Foreign Office mind. I thank God that I possess the Foreign Office mind.[10]

'Munich' and appeasement have both become words of disapproval and abuse. For nearly thirty years they have been linked together as the twin symbols of British folly. Together they have been defended as if they were inseparable. Yet 'Munich' was a policy, dictated by fear and weakness, which Neville Chamberlain devised as a means, not of postponing war but, as he personally believed, of making Anglo-German war unnecessary in the future. Appeasement was quite different; it was a policy of constant concessions based on common sense and strength. Whereas the debate over the wisdom of Chamberlain's actions will continue, and the believers in his vision cross swords for many years to come with those who consider his actions short-sighted, unrealistic, and dangerous, the debate over appeasement deserves a different fate.

Although appeasement failed when confronted with the aggressive, irresponsible behaviour of Nazi Germany, it did not, because of this failure become retrospectively mistaken. It was never a misguided policy, even if it became, by 1938, temporarily an unrealistic one. International affairs do from time to time reach an *impasse* on account of the total impossibility of agreement between two conflicting States. But the norm of international affairs remains the assumption that agreement is possible. For as long as this assumption holds good, appeasement is a necessary policy, combining expediency with morality. Just as it was the policy which Britain pursued in Europe after the First World War, so it was with only one exception, Suez, the policy pursued by Britain throughout the world after the Second World War. Only when all the evidence shows, as by 1938 the evidence seemed to show, that the nature of one's protagonist makes appeasement impracticable, should it be abandoned. Nor do those statesmen who abandon it before all its avenues have been explored, all its opportunities tried, and all their energy expended, earn anything but the mistrust of their contemporaries and the censure of history.

Appendix 1

FINAL DRAFT OF THE FONTAINEBLEAU MEMORANDUM

Some considerations for the Peace Conference
before they finally draft their terms
by David Lloyd George

When nations are exhausted by wars in which they have put forth all their strength and which leave them tired, bleeding, and broken, it is not difficult to patch up a peace that may last until the generation which experienced the horrors of the war has passed away. Pictures of heroism and triumph only tempt those who know nothing of the sufferings and terrors of war. It is therefore comparatively easy to patch up a peace which will last for 30 years.

What is difficult, however, is to draw up a peace which will not provoke a fresh struggle when those who have had practical experience of what war means have passed away. History has proved that a peace which has been hailed by a victorious nation as a triumph of diplomatic skill and statesmanship, even of moderation in the long run has proved itself to be short-sighted and charged with danger to the victor. The peace of 1871 was believed by Germany to ensure not only her security but her permanent supremacy. The facts have shown exactly the contrary. France itself has demonstrated that those who say you can make Germany so feeble that she will never be able to hit back are utterly wrong. Year by year France became numerically weaker in comparison with her victorious neighbour, but in reality she became ever more powerful. She kept watch on Europe; she made alliance with those whom Germany had wronged or menaced; she never ceased to warn the world of its danger and ultimately she was able to secure the overthrow of the mightier power which had trampled so brutally upon her. You may strip Germany of her colonies, reduce her armaments to a mere police force and her navy to that of a fifth rate power; all the same in the end if she feels that she has been unjustly treated in the peace of 1919 she will find means of exacting retribution from her conquerors. The impression, the deep impression, made upon the human heart by four years of unexampled slaughter will disappear with the hearts upon which it has been marked by the terrible sword of the great war. The maintenance of peace will then depend upon there being no causes of exasperation constantly stirring up the spirit of patriotism, of justice or of fair play to achieve redress. Our terms may be severe, they may be stern and even ruthless but at the same time they can be so just that the country on which they are imposed will feel in its heart that it has no right to complain. But injustice, arrogance, displayed in the hour of triumph will never be forgotten or forgiven.

For these reasons I am, therefore, strongly averse to transferring more Germans from German rule to the rule of some other nation than can possibly be helped. I cannot conceive any greater cause of future war than that the German people, who have certainly proved themselves one of the most vigorous and powerful races in the world should be surrounded by a number of small states, many of them consisting of people who have never previously set up a stable government for themselves, but each of them containing large masses of Germans clamouring for reunion with their native land. The proposal of the Polish Commission that we should place 2,100,000 Germans under the control of a people which is of a different religion and which has never proved its capacity for stable self-government throughout its history must, in my judgement, lead sooner or later to a new war in the East of Europe. What I have said about the Germans is equally true of the Magyars. There will never be peace in South Eastern Europe if every little state now coming into being is to have a large Magyar Irredenta within its borders. I would therefore take as a guiding principle of the peace that as far as is humanly possible the different races should be allocated to their motherlands, and that this human criterion should have precedence over considerations of strategy or economics or communications which can usually be adjusted by other means. Secondly, I would say that the duration for the payments of reparation ought to disappear if possible with the generation which made the war.

But there is a consideration in favour of a long-sighted peace which influences me even more than the desire to leave no causes justifying a fresh outbreak 30 years hence. There is one element in the present condition of nations which differentiates it from the situation as it was in 1815. In the Napoleonic wars the countries were equally exhausted but the revolutionary spirit had spent its force in the country of its birth and Germany had satisfied the legitimate popular demands for the time being by a series of economic changes which were inspired by courage, foresight and high statesmanship. Even in Russia the Czar had effected great reforms which were probably at that time even too advanced for the half savage population. The situation is very different now. The revolution is still in its infancy. The extreme figures of the Terror are still in command in Russia. The whole of Europe is filled with the spirit of revolution. There is a deep sense not only of discontent, but of anger and revolt amongst the workmen against pre-war conditions. The whole existing order in its political, social, and economic aspects is questioned by the masses of the population from one end of Europe to the other. In some countries, like Germany and Russia, the unrest takes the form of open rebellion, in others like France, Great Britain and Italy it takes the shape of strikes and of general disinclination to settle down to work, symptoms which are just as much concerned with the desire for political and social change as with wage demands.

Much of this unrest is healthy. We shall never make a lasting peace by attempting to restore the conditions of 1914. But there is a danger that we may throw the masses of the population through-out Europe into the arms of the extremists whose only idea for regenerating mankind is to destroy utterly the whole existing fabric of society. These men have triumphed in Russia. They have done so at a terrible price. Hundreds and thousands of the popula-tion have perished. The railways, the roads, the towns, the whole structural organization of Russia has been almost destroyed, but somehow or other they seem to have managed to keep their hold upon the masses of the Russian people, and what is much more significant, they have succeeded in creating a large army which is apparently well directed and well disciplined, and is, as to a great part of it prepared to die for its ideals. In another year Russia inspired by a new enthusiasm may have recovered from her passion for peace and have at her command the only army eager to fight, because it is the only army that believes that it has any cause to fight for.

The greatest danger that I see in the present situation is that Germany may throw in her lot with Bolshevism and place her resources, her brains, her vast organizing power at the disposal of the revolutionary fanatics whose dream it is to conquer the world for Bolshevism by force of arms. This danger is no mere chimera. The present government in Germany is weak; it has no prestige; its authority is challenged; it lingers merely because there is no alternative but the spartacists, and Germany is not ready for spartacism, as yet. But the argument which the spartacists are using with great effect at this very time is that they alone can save Germany from the intolerable conditions which have been bequeathed her by the way. They offer to free the German people from indebtedness to the Allies and indebtedness to their own richer classes. They offer them complete control of their own affairs and the prospect of a new heaven and earth. It is true that the price will be heavy. There will be two or three years of anarchy, perhaps of bloodshed, but at the end the land will remain, the people will remain, the greater part of the houses and the factories will remain, and the railways and the roads will remain, and Germany, having thrown off her burdens, will be able to make a fresh start.

If Germany goes over to the spartacists it is inevitable that she should throw in her lot with the Russian Bolshevists. Once that happens all Eastern Europe will be swept into the orbit of the Bolshevik revolution and within a year we may witness the spectacle of nearly three hundred million organized into a vast red army under German instructors and German generals equipped with German cannon and German machine-guns and prepared for a renewal of the attack on Western Europe. This is a prospect which no one can face with equanimity. Yet the news which came from Hungary yesterday shows only too clearly that this danger is no fantasy. And what are the reasons alleged for this decision? They are mainly the belief that large numbers of Magyars are to be handed over to the control of others. If we are wise, we shall offer to Germany a peace, which, while just, will be preferable for all sensible men to the alternative of Bolshevism. I would, therefore, put it in the forefront of the peace that once she accepts our terms, especially reparation, we will open to her the raw materials and markets of the world on equal terms with ourselves, and will do everything possible to enable the German people to get upon their legs again. We cannot both cripple her and expect her to pay.

Finally, we must offer terms which a responsible Government in Germany can expect to be able to carry out. If we present terms to Germany which are unjust, or excessively onerous, no responsible Government will sign them; certainly the present weak administration will not. If it did, I am told that it would be swept away within 24 hours. Yet if we can find nobody in Germany who will put his hand to a peace treaty, what will be the position? A large army of occupation for an indefinite period is out of the question. Germany would not mind it. A very large number of people in that country would welcome it as it would be the only hope of preserving the existing order of things. The objection would not come from Germany, but from our own countries. Neither the British Empire nor America would agree to occupy Germany. France by itself could not bear the burden of occupation. We should therefore be driven back on the policy of blockading the country. That would inevitably mean spartacism from the Urals to the Rhine, with its inevitable consequence of a huge red army attempting to cross the Rhine. As a matter of fact I am doubtful whether public opinion would allow us deliberately to starve Germany. If the only difference between Germany and ourselves were between onerous terms and moderate terms, I very much doubt if public opinion would tolerate the deliberate condemnation of millions of women and children to death by starvation. If so the Allies would have incurred the moral defeat of having attempted to impose terms on Germany which Germany had successfully resisted.

From every point of view, therefore, it seems to me that we ought to endeavour to draw up a peace settlement as if we were impartial arbiters, forgetful of the passions of the war. This settlement ought to have three ends in view. First of all it must do justice to the Allies, by taking into account Germany's responsibility for the origin of the war, and for the way in which it was fought. Secondly, it must be a settlement which a responsible German Government can sign in the belief that it can fulfil the obligations it incurs. Thirdly, it must be a settlement which will contain in itself no provocations for future wars, and which will constitute an alternative to Bolshevism, because it will commend itself to all reasonable opinion as a fair settlement of the European problem.

It is not, however, enough to draw up a just and far-sighted peace with Germany. If we are to offer Europe an alternative to Bolshevism we must make the League of Nations into something which will be both a safeguard to those nations who are prepared for fair dealing with their neighbours, and a menace to those who would trespass on the rights of their neighbours, whether they are imperialist empires or imperialist Bolshevists. An essential element, therefore, in the peace settlement is the constitution of the League of Nations as the effective guardian of international right and international liberty throughout the world. If this is to happen the first thing to do is that the leading members of the League of Nations should arrive at an understanding between themselves in regard to armaments. To my mind it is idle to endeavour to impose a permanent limitation of armaments upon Germany unless we are prepared similarly to impose a limitation upon our-ourselves. I recognize that until Germany has settled down and given practical proof that she has abandoned her imperialist ambitions, and until Russia has also given proof that she does not intend to embark upon a military crusade against her neighbours, it is essential that the leading members of the League of Nations should maintain considerable forces both by land and sea in order to preserve liberty in the world. But if they are to present an united front to the forces both of reaction and revolution, they must arrive at such an agreement in regard to armaments among themselves as would make it impossible for suspicion to arise between the members of the League of Nations in regard to their intentions towards one another. If the League is to do its work for the world it will only be because the members of the League trust it themselves and because there are no rivalries and jealousies in the matter of armaments between them. The first condition of success for the League of Nations is, therefore, a firm under-standing between the British Empire and the United States of America and France and Italy that there will be no competitive building up of fleets or armies between them. Unless this is arrived at before the Covenant is signed the League of Nations will be a sham and a mockery. It will be regarded, and rightly regarded as a proof that its principal promoters and patrons repose no confidence in its efficacy. But once the leading members of the League have made it clear that they have reached an understanding which will both secure to the League of Nations the strength which is necessary to enable it to protect its members and which at the same time will make misunderstanding and suspicion with regard to competitive armaments impossible between them its future and its authority will be ensured. It will be able to ensure as an essential condition of peace that not only Germany, but all the smaller states of Europe undertake to limit their armaments and abolish conscription. If the small nations are permitted to organize and maintain conscript armies running each to hundreds of thousands, boundary wars will be inevitable and all Europe will be drawn in. Unless we secure this universal limitation we shall achieve neither lasting peace, nor the permanent observance of the limitation of German armaments which we now seek to impose.

I should like to ask why Germany, if she accepts the terms we consider just and fair, should not be admitted to the League of Nations, at any rate as soon as she has established a stable and democratic Government. Would it not be an inducement to her both to sign the terms and to resist Bolshevism? Might it not be safer that she should be inside the League than that she should be outside it?

Finally, I believe that until the authority and effectiveness of the League of Nations has been demonstrated, the British Empire and the United States ought to give to France a guarantee against the possibility of a new German aggression. France has special reason for asking for such a guarantee. She has twice been attacked and twice invaded by Germany in half a century. She has been so attacked because she has been the principal guardian of liberal and democratic civilization against Central European autocracy on the continent of Europe. It is right that the other great Western democracies should enter into an undertaking which will ensure that they stand by her side in time to protect her against invasion, should Germany ever threaten her again or until the League of Nations has proved its capacity to preserve the peace and liberty of the world.

If, however, the peace conference is really to secure peace and prove to the world a complete plan of settlement which all reasonable men will recognize as an alternative preferable to anarchy, it must deal with the Russian situation. Bolshevik imperialism does not merely menace the states on Russia's borders. It threatens the whole of Asia and is as near to America as it is to France. It is idle to think that the Peace Conference can separate, however sound a peace it may have arranged with Germany, if it leaves Russia as it is today. I do not propose, however, to complicate the question of the peace with Germany by introducing a discussion of the Russian problem. I mention it simply in order to remind ourselves of the importance of dealing with it as soon as possible.

Appendix 2

NOTES OF A CONVERSATION BETWEEN LLOYD GEORGE
AND HITLER AT BERCHTESGADEN, 4 SEPTEMBER 1936

from the longhand notes of T. P. Conwell-Evans.

Mr Lloyd George left the Grand Hotel for the Chancellor's
Country House at 3.45 p.m. in the Chancellor's own car. He was
accompanied by Ambassador von Ribbentrop and Dr Schmidt
(the German Foreign Office translator) and Mr T. P. Conwell-
Evans.

As the car approached the house the Chancellor was already
descending the large flight of stone steps leading from his house
to the Alpine Road. Hitler cordially greeted Mr Lloyd George and
they walked up the steps together accompanied by Dr Schmidt,
who made a running translation of their conversation. The Chancellor lead Mr Lloyd George through a very broad corridor to his
sitting-room, where they sat in front of an oil painting. Mr Lloyd
George asked 'Is that Frederick the Great?' This recognition was
astonishing as it was the portrait of a boy. Hitler replied that it
was a painting of Frederick the Great and that it was the only
portrait taken from life. Mr Lloyd George said that Frederick
looked rather as if he suffered from the stern rule of his parents.
The Chancellor laughed and looked at Mr Lloyd George with eyes
beaming with benevolence and admiration.

The Chancellor then said that he was so glad to welcome Mr
Lloyd George to Berchtesgaden and he was particularly glad that
today was a fine one. 'You cannot see,' said Hitler, 'far away over
the mountains except on a fine day. There are times when you
can barely see three yards in front of you when the weather is
bad.'

Mr Lloyd George said that he had found this to be the case when
forty years ago he passed through Berchtesgaden for the first time.

Hitler's bearing seemed very modest and simple. He showed
a veneration for his visitor and could hardly keep his eyes away
from him.

Hitler then suggested with a modest smile that perhaps Mr Lloyd George would like to put questions. Hitler thought that this might be a satisfactory way of beginning.

Thereupon Mr Lloyd George started in a quiet, persuasive way. He said that he had for very many years been convinced of the need for an understanding between the two countries. He had visited Germany as early as 1908 in order to study some of its social schemes, particularly Health Insurance. His interest had always been intense. He had always wished for close co-operation between the two countries. After the tragic upset of the War, he had continued to work to that end. An understanding was necessary not only to promote the well-being of the two countries, but also to preserve Western civilization itself.

Hitler listened with such intensity as if he understood every word. Then came the translation, during which Hitler turned towards Dr Schmidt.

In his reply Hitler insisted that an understanding between the two countries had always been one of his most fervent wishes, and this attitude dated back to the time when he was a young man. This had been his dream. No one who had been following his activities since the War could doubt that it had always been his constant aim in recent years. He had been ready to recognize the vital interests of the British Empire. The Anglo-German Treaty was a proof of his eagerness to respect British vital interests. He thought that England should equally recognize in her turn what the vital interests of Germany required; particularly in regard to Germany's position on the Continent and in regard to her interest to maintain a proper standard of life for her people. He agreed with Mr Lloyd George that on the co-operation of the two countries the future of the civilization of the world depended. He had no need to enlarge upon the qualities of the British and German peoples. His views upon the importance to civilization of co-operation between these two related races were well-known, and on these grounds every German welcomed a strong British Empire. In this connection the Chancellor enlarged upon the dangers of Bolshevism. At the moment, he thought it was more dangerous as a disintegrating force threatening the existence of the national states of Europe than as a military power that aimed at imposing its ideas by the sword, although one could not deny that Russia as a military power was becoming daily more formidable. His emphasis upon the Bolshevik danger might be regarded by some people as an obsession. At the cost of being regarded as a fanatic he was compelled to warn his people to be on their guard against these destructive forces. His experience was that people in England appear to be unable to appreciate what was afoot, but for the German people it was easy to understand the danger of Soviet-ism as he himself had personal experience of what communism meant to a country. The Russian Communistic State and the support it was receiving in every country from sections of the people was a phenomenon which ranked in historical importance with the great events of the migrations of people or with the Mohammedan invasion of Europe. Why did not people see this more clearly. It was of the highest importance that England and Germany should come together; these two countries more than any other could bring about the consolidation of the countries of Western Europe.

Mr Lloyd George expressed cordial approval with these general views. He agreed that Russia was a military danger. Lately, two Englishmen, who had been in Russia, had informed him of the terrific armaments that were proceeding there, although he agreed with Hitler that for some time no military attack was to be feared from that country. But how were we to deal with the immediate situation? What was the immediate task to which England and Germany should apply their energy in order to overcome these dangers? Everything depended clearly upon a successful outcome of the forthcoming Locarno Conference. He did not know whether it would be held in the next month or in November, but of one thing he was certain, that unless an agreement could be reached by these means within the next two or three months, a grave situation would arise and England and Germany would drift rapidly apart. The two Governments should do their utmost to promote the success of this Conference. An Agreement between England, France, Germany and Italy and also Belgium, which, although not a great power, occupied a key position, would give Europe the protection that she needed. The situation urgently required the re-establishment of Locarno on a new basis – on a basis of equality for all the participating powers. Under Stresemann the participat-ing powers did not conclude the original Locarno Treaty on equal terms, but now the situation was different for, through the efforts of the Führer, Germany had achieved equality.

Mr Lloyd George, leading the discussion into a still narrower channel, asked the Chancellor whether he foresaw any difficulties which would hinder the successful outcome of the Conference.

Hitler agreed that the interests of Germany, France, Great Britain and Italy, not to speak of Belgium, urgently required the re-establishment of Locarno on this new basis. As to the equality of Germany, that was an indispensable condition. It was no longer a matter for discussion. He did not anticipate difficulties from the peoples of the countries named. The German people of today had a new outlook, and they were absolutely satisfied with the territorial settlement in the West. That was a condition preliminary to acceptance of any treaty of guarantee.

The success of the Conference might be threatened from other quarters; it would be threatened by the influence of Moscow. Russia would endeavour to bring pressure to bear in order to extend the scope of the Conference and would endeavour to bring into discussion Eastern problems. He could foresee all sorts of questions being brought in if one were not careful – even problems affecting Japan and Russia. The Conference would lose precision and direction and it would degenerate into a Conference discussing almost everything and its purpose would be defeated. It was of the highest importance that its scope should be precisely defined and strictly limited.

Hitler thought that the responsibility in this connection lay precisely upon England. It was essential that the British Government should not give way when an attempt was made to bring in other subjects. England was the power most competent to insist upon this.

Mr Lloyd George here seized the opportunity to make one of his essential points. The best way to meet this difficulty, he said, would be to insist upon the fact that the Conference was a Locarno Conference and concerned only the Locarno Powers. Its aim was solely to secure the *status quo* in Western Europe. Other questions such as Eastern European matters could be raised later at another Conference. The Chancellor, continued Mr Lloyd George, had stated that Germany would return to the League under certain circumstances. 'The League,' Mr Lloyd George went on, 'provided an opportunity to discuss any question including those of Eastern Europe, and Germany could well say that these and other questions, outside the scope of the Locarno Conference, could be discussed at a later stage at the League or, if one preferred it, at another Conference.'

Mr Lloyd George added that if this line were taken Hitler would be able to secure the support of the British Cabinet in limiting the scope of the Conference.

Mr Lloyd George would not deny that the Cabinet was divided. Certain Members were making difficulties as Mr Duff Cooper's lamentable speech delivered recently in Paris had clearly shown. But the Prime Minister was a supporter, though perhaps he lacked power of decision. Mr Lloyd George continued that if the German Government took the natural line which he had proposed the British Government would have no alternative but to support such a policy, and the support of British public opinion would certainly be enlisted. Mr Lloyd George referred to Hitler's speeches on foreign affairs; he had not made a single mistake in regard to their effect on British public opinion. He was most happy to pay tribute to their great value in promoting Anglo-German relations.

With regard to the French Government Mr Lloyd George related that the Franco-Russian Treaty presented a very serious difficulty. In spite of this he urged the German Government with all his energy to work for a successful conclusion of the Locarno Conference. As a Minister who had been at many international conferences and had had long experience of negotiations, he ventured to express these views.

Hitler nodded agreement. If the Locarno Conference was a success, a settlement of Eastern Europe would readily follow, as a solid bloc in the West might bring Czecho-Slovakia, Rumania and Lithuania within its sphere of influence.

Hitler proceeded that he had always favoured a three-power agreement between France, Great Britain and Germany and Mr Lloyd George interposed 'and Italy'.

Hitler replied that Italy was ready to come in at any moment. She would present no difficulty.

Then Mr Lloyd George again interposed, 'Would Germany be prepared to agree to an air pact between the three powers ?'

Hitler replied, 'Yes, provided the three powers were able to reach a common defensive position (*abwehr stellung*) but not otherwise.' He had made attempts to conclude some agreement of this kind and as a first step they had concluded the Naval Treaty with Great Britain which secured Great Britain's supremacy on the High

Seas and the security of Germany in the Baltic. France had not accepted his land armaments proposal and he had accordingly been compelled to take steps to establish the security of his own country, as Germany was very vulnerable.

Mr Lloyd George said that he had given public testimony in the House of Commons and elsewhere to the necessity of these steps and he did not hesitate to repeat this view now. He had declared that these steps had been made necessary because of the failure of the powers to disarm and in view of the recent Franco-Russian Treaty.

Hitler proceeded to say that re-arming was not a pleasant task for him. He would have preferred to devote the increased expenditure to the development of his country. It was true that armaments gave work but they did not give productive work. He would have preferred to develop still further the work of reconstruction. The measures he had taken to increase security did not make him more popular. On the other hand he was not Dictator; the German people regarded him as their Leader and accepted these measures as a disagreeable necessity. If, however, we could set up a European defence system the contribution of each country for its security could be reduced. Agreement between France, England and Germany would alone be capable of meeting the case as the other states were not of decisive importance when one had to consider the preservation of peace in Europe; although Poland had an authoritarian régime it did not enjoy the popular support, which was the backbone of the German Government.

Mr Lloyd George interposed that in the death of Pilsudsky they lost their great Leader.

Hitler continued that the Baltic States were by their size and geographical position far too weak. Czecho-Slovakia was a positive danger on account of her alliance with Soviet Russia. They had photographic evidence of the military facilities afforded to Russia by Czecho-Slovakia. Clearly a Western bloc would be of paramount importance in pacifying Europe.

Hitler, after a slight pause turned to the situation in Spain. Conditions there had made him feel very anxious. The disintegrating forces which were fomented by Russia and to which he had earlier alluded could here be seen in all their tragic significance. Spain illustrated the sort of danger which threatened Europe. The gradual undermining of national traditions and the collapse of law

and order. If the Left succeeded in Spain it would not be a victory
of the Spanish Government but of anarchic Sovietism. In other
words a victory for barbarism. It might spread to France and
Czecho-Slovakia and as an ally Russia would certainly follow.
Germany would be an island in a sea of Bolshevism.

Mr Lloyd George interposed 'and so would England.'

Hitler proceeded that for Germany such a situation would be
extremely dangerous. The Germans lived on a very narrow margin. A slight fall in exports gravely affected their economy and if
the world around collapsed into Sovietism or anarchy, German
economy would be gravely undermined and the country would be
impoverished. Food supplies would be affected and moral infection would spread in areas where distress was acute. We had
seen what had happened in Spain when anarchy triumphed. The
Germans were a disciplined sober people but at a time of acute
distress even they were not immune from infection and might
become a prey to excesses. That they had experienced shortly
after the war. The French were today equally threatened. It was,
therefore, natural that the Germans sympathized with the Right
in France rather than with the Left and also with the Nationalists
in Spain.

Mr Lloyd George in reply stated that he agreed with much that
Hitler had said in regard to Spain but the position in Spain did
not seem very clear to most people in England. The struggle in
Spain seemed to be waged between two sets of extremists. He
alluded to the massacre by the Nationalists of over 1,000 prisoners
at Badajos and said that the fight was between savages on both
sides. Each side, continued Mr Lloyd George, was extremist. The
insurgents were pure militarists. Franco was no statesman and
indeed as a leader he had little or no experience of war. Primo de
Rivera had at least built roads on which motor-cars could travel
with some degree of safety. At this remark Hitler smiled broadly.

Mr Lloyd George continuing said, Franco and his friends were
a purely reactionary and military party. How different was the
situation in Germany where Hitler had grappled with chronic
disorder by hard intensive work conducted over a long period.
After fourteen years of political campaigning and popular education
he had created in the German people a new spirit. He had given
them confidence and faith in the future of the country and a new
outlook affecting every sphere of their life, but in Spain the

military party had nothing to offer except crude force. The struggle was likely to be a long one and on that account the powers should act with the greatest care and circumspection in preserving strict neutrality. He welcomed the German Government's policy in this regard. Indeed, the very success of the Locarno Conference depended on the attitude maintained by the powers regarding events in Spain. The adhesion of France to the new Locarno Treaty was favoured by Blum, the French Prime Minister, although he had to face a great deal of opposition on this point. His position was a very difficult one and it would be made almost intolerable if the other participating powers of the Locarno Conference were to favour the Nationalists in Spain and were not to preserve strict neutrality. Blum had to overcome one obstacle in adhering to a new Locarno system and that obstacle was the Franco-Russian alliance. In adhering to Locarno the French Prime Minister would be in effect side-tracking this alliance and in so doing he would overcome very great opposition. One had to remember that this Franco-Russian Treaty was signed by the French Right and not by Blum, the Socialist. That made his task still more difficult. If then Germany or any of the other Locarno powers, Mr Lloyd George repeated, showed sympathy with the Spanish Nationalists, Blum's position would then be impossible. His burden would be too great and he would not obtain the necessary support for the Locarno Conference. It would end in failure, and chaos would ensue and Russia would have her chance.

Mr Lloyd George continued that he thought that the Spanish struggle would last a long time. If the Locarno Conference was a success the participating powers might co-operate in the positive task of offering their good offices to Spain and to assist them, without going so far as intervention, in the restoration of order in that country.

Hitler seemed impressed by this argument and it was particularly noticeable that he was pleased with the reference to the result of his own fourteen years of hard work. He listened carefully to the translation and said that perhaps they had better now adjourn for tea. On the way downstairs he talked with Mr Lloyd George and agreed that the victory of the Nationalists in Spain would be a purely reactionary dictatorship which was not altogether a pleasant prospect. This clearly showed that Mr Lloyd George's arguments struck home.

At the conclusion of the political talk between Mr Lloyd George and Hitler, the Chancellor proposed that we should all adjourn for tea. Accordingly the five of us – the Chancellor, Mr Lloyd George, Herr von Ribbentrop, Mr Conwell-Evans and Dr Schmidt (the official translator) – proceeded downstairs and were shown into an enormous great drawing-room equipped with one great window – an enormous unbroken sheet of glass quite as large as a theatre curtain, and a very dramatic spectacle was offered by the Bavarian and Austrian Alps with Salzburg in the distance perfectly visible in the valley. The dramatic beauty of the spectacle almost took one's breath away. In a corner of this great room, which looked like some great hall in an old castle, the company sat down to tea – or rather coffee – Mr Lloyd George sitting next to the Chancellor and on Mr Lloyd George's left von Ribbentrop.

The Chancellor after a moment or two asked his attendants who were members of the SS Guard and dressed in military white jackets, to leave everything on the table as they could help themselves. He did not wish, he said, any more formality.

The Chancellor then asked Mr Lloyd George how had he come to Berchtesgaden. Mr Lloyd George answered that he had motored from Munich along the great motor road. With this reply the Chancellor seemed delighted and it was clear that the great motor roads of Germany are one of his favourite plans of reconstruction. With great animation he began to talk about the subject. He said they were making plans which affected three kinds of roads; (1) district or regional roads; (2) national roads about 54,000 kilometres in all and (3) the great motor roads which total 7,000 kilometres. They were proposing to take four years to construct these motor roads. Up to this month (September 1936) they had completed 1,000 kilos. By the spring of 1937 they would have completed 1,500 kilos. Next year 2,500 kilos and the year after they hoped to be ready with the 7,000.

Mr Lloyd George expressed high appreciation and said he had tried to introduce something similar in his country.

It had already been shown, proceeded the Chancellor, that casualties had been greatly diminished by the use of the motor road. It had been observed that motorists in the first eight days of their use of the motor roads drove very quickly, but after fourteen days they realized that it was not necessary to drive at 120 kilos. They found themselves driving at an average of 80 kilos and they reached their destination at this rate in record time as the conditions of the traffic on the motor roads never called upon them to use their brakes or to stop. There was no delay at crossings and so far as the exits and entrances from the motor roads were concerned, they were so devised as to enable on-coming traffic to proceed without lessening speed. Casualties had already fallen on the motor roads and according to the architect (Dr Todt) they were now 35 per cent of other roads – a fall of two-thirds.

The Chancellor proceeded to say that he had introduced a law relieving motor cars of taxation except lorries. The result of this policy was the number of cars in use in Germany had increased already from half a million to 1,800,000.

The Chancellor then proceeded to discuss the financing of the motor roads. This he did with some enthusiasm. He explained in the first place in reply to Mr Lloyd George that the workers employed in constructing the motor roads were mostly unskilled and were formerly unemployed, and they received about 120 Marks per month for their work on the roads. The Chancellor pointed out that as unemployed the State paid them a dole of 60 Marks a month, so that the additional outlay which the State had to expend in the case of each worker was about 55 per cent of the actual sum paid to him.

Now, proceeded the Chancellor, 37 per cent of every sum spent in wages is returned in the form of taxes. In other words one Mark wages represents 37 Pfennig taxation (in other words 1 shilling in wages would represent 3·7 pence taxes). Taking these two factors into consideration – the dole and the return in taxation – the net additional outlay paid to the motor-road worker would then be equal to 25 Marks. In other words, concluded the Chancellor, where, over a given stretch of motor road the State advances 600,000,000 Marks the additional outlay amounts in fact to only 200,000,000 as the difference of 400,000,000 Marks has been saved in unemployment pay and increase of revenue.

The Chancellor pointed out that the higher standard of life enjoyed by the unskilled worker through the provision of work enabled them to stimulate employment in the skilled industries. They could buy shoes and clothes and that gave employment to shoe-makers and tailors. By this progressive stimulation of employment the revenue returns have increased recently 20 per cent above the corresponding four months of last year without raising taxation.

Owing to this increased revenue the Government will no longer need to raise money for the motor roads through loans. The additional outlay for instance to which he had referred as an illustration of 200,000,000 Marks for the stretch of motor road would be met from revenue and in particular from the taxation of petrol and also of lorries and long distance passenger buses – the only kind of car which they tax. The Government also owned all the petrol stations on the motor roads. They would not only be able to meet future additional outlay from revenue but also amortize the loans already issued by the same means. The taxation of lorries was not an additional burden on haulage contractors proceeded the Chancellor because it was saved by using the motor roads. For instance, the distance between Munich and Berlin was 100 kilos lessened and cars saved in petrol and rubber through the use of the roads.

Later the Chancellor talked about his Four-year Plan which he was going to announce at Nuremberg in the coming week. He talked about the artificial raw materials which Germany needed to produce within the next four years; rubber, petrol, of which they were already producing 1,700,000 litres, cotton. It was absolutely necessary for them to produce these raw materials in their country to use all foreign exchange available for the import of the necessaries of life for his people – egg, butter, cheese, meat and fats in which they were not self-sufficient however intensively they cultivated the soil. For the time being until these raw materials were produced his people had to put up with a certain amount of shortage of necessary foods, but he always explained the whole position to them and they understood how necessary it was to put up with these restrictions for the time being. They trusted him as their leader; he was no dictator. They understood under what difficult circumstances the country lay. The Chancellor at this point spoke with great volubility, and made very quickly a passing reference to the fact that England did not understand how difficult it was in Germany to reach and maintain a proper standard of life.

On the next day, 5 September 1936, all the members of Mr Lloyd George's party were invited to tea at Hitler's house. Hitler had again sent his car for Mr Lloyd George and the party was joined by Herr von Ribbentrop, Frau von Ribbentrop and Herr Henckel, von Ribbentrop's brother-in-law. As the car arrived with Mr Lloyd George, Hitler was again waiting on the stone steps to greet him. They both waited for the arrival of the other cars and each member of this party was introduced to the Chancellor in turn. Mr Lloyd George and Hitler then lead the way to the great drawing-room with the large window giving the view of the Bavarian Alps. Presently they all sat down to tea in this order: Mr Lloyd George, von Ribbentrop, Hitler, Miss Lloyd George, Dr Schmidt (the official translator), Lord Dawson of Penn, Mr Tom Jones, Major Gwilym Lloyd George, Mr Henckel, then Herr Meissner, formerly State Secretary to von Hindenberg, President of the Republic, and now State Secretary to Hitler in his capacity as head of the State; next to him Mr Conwell Evans and then Frau von Ribbentrop next to Mr Lloyd George completing the circle. Mr Sylvester walked up and down the room with his Ciné-Kodak and occupied himself all the time taking shots of the company. This was done quite unobtrusively and did not seem to disturb the Chancellor. For some time there was general conversation, then suddenly we all found ourselves listening to a talk between Mr Lloyd George and Hitler. It is difficult to describe the atmosphere. It seemed to become all of a sudden almost solemn. One realized that the great War Leader of the British Empire and the great Leader who had restored Germany to her present position, were meeting on a common ground. One seemed to be witnessing a symbolic act of reconciliation between the two peoples. Everybody listened intensely and it was a moving experience. In a moment or two the Chancellor beckoned to one of his attendants to get something and he brought a signed photograph of the Chancellor in a silver frame with an inscription to Mr Lloyd George. This Hitler handed over to Mr Lloyd George, who got up and shook hands with the Führer and thanked him warmly.

Mr Lloyd George asked the Führer: would he object to his photograph being placed on his desk side by side with that of Foch, Clemenceau and other leaders of the Great War?

The Chancellor replied that he would not object to this. If, however, the photograph was placed by the side of Erzberger and Bauer, he would strongly object. It was not the fact that Germany lost the war that mattered. That might happen to any country and in itself was no disgrace. But what mattered was the manner in which defeat had been accepted by what he called by worst elements of the German nation, who by some unfortunate co-incidence had at that time come to the surface in Germany. There was no hatred for our ex-enemies. We had all realized that they were simply doing their duty as soldiers fighting for their country. We had equally done our duty on the German side, but there was a great deal of resentment and hatred against those unworthy representatives of the German nation who betrayed their country in 1918.

Hitler then turned to Mr Lloyd George and said, 'Furthermore it was realized in Germany that if the war had been won by the Allies, it was not in the first place the soldiers to whom victory was due, but to one great statesman and that yourself Mr Lloyd George,' said Hitler quietly. 'It was you who galvanized the people into a will to victory. I have always thought so and I am glad to tell you in person.' 'Like the soldiers,' Hitler proceeded, he (Mr Lloyd George) had done his duty defending the interests of his country and there was no hatred at all for him on the German side and for that reason he did not in the least object to seeing his photograph side by side with that of great statesmen and soldiers who had served their country well on the other side of the front.

The Führer proceeded that if there had been a statesman on the German side in 1918 things would have been different. If he himself, instead of being one of those eight million private German soldiers liable to be shot at any time even by black troops, had been in the position of a statesman, he thought he might have prevented Germany's downfall.

Mr Lloyd George replied that he was deeply touched by what the Führer had said to him personally and he was particularly proud to have heard it from the greatest German of the age. He was in perfect agreement with the views expressed by Hitler about the possibility of averting the catastrophe had there been a states-man available on the German side; and in the latest Volume of his Memoirs, which he was now preparing, he had stated that if in September, October, and November 1918, Hitler had been Germany's Führer a better Peace would have been negotiated. As it was no real negotiation was possible because the German collapse had been so complete that there was no authority with whom one could negotiate.

Mr Lloyd George related a conversation with Foch in 1919

H

when he asked Foch what he thought of Ludendorff and Hindenburg.

Foch replied that Ludendorff was a 'bon soldat' and Hindenburg was a 'bon patriot'.

Hitler nodded agreement and said that Ludendorff was also a good patriot, but that in his burning love for his country he had become fanatical to the point of being unable to change his opinion on persons and things so that if he hated he would go on hating and if he respected someone he would go on showing respect. He lacked elasticity and he could not adapt himself to changing conditions, but he was certainly a good soldier and if in 1918 he had been assisted on the political side by an able statesman Germany would not have fallen so low.

Mr Lloyd George hereupon talked about the advantage to Europe of strong men being in office. In 1914 weak men were in charge of the Government of Germany and in charge of other Governments. A strong man would not have allowed the nations of Europe to slither into the war. A powerful statesman is in himself a guarantee of peace.

Hitler agreed. He went on 'If the world would only appreciate that his (Hitler's) first and foremost task after Germany's breakdown in 1918 was to restore her international honour and credit, his policy would be better understood. Because Germany had fallen so low he (Hitler) had to insist a little more stubbornly on certain points than would be necessary for a country enjoying normal conditions and that was why he was so glad to meet foreign statesmen who understood this necessity and particularly Mr Lloyd George. Mr Lloyd George was the only great war Minister who understood this necessity; he was also one of the very few statesmen of England today, who in his recent speeches, had shown a very clear understanding of Hitler's special task in this respect.'

Mr Lloyd George replied that the Führer had indeed achieved the task which he had set himself. Germany's honour had been restored and her equality of rights was acknowledged by the whole world. Public opinion in Great Britain was to an increasing degree showing more and more understanding for Hitler's position and the one anxiety of British public opinion today was to bring about the closest co-operation between the two countries.

The Führer replied that he was passionately interested in the furthering of that understanding and the most recent proof of this attitude was the fact that he was sending his best man as Ambassador to London.

Mr Lloyd George replied that the appointment, quite apart from the personal qualities of Herr von Ribbentrop and the personal friendships which he had already acquired in London, had been welcomed by the British people as a clear indication of the Chancellor's intention to do his utmost to give effect to this policy.

After this interchange of views conducted in a very earnest manner, which impressed all members of the party who sat around, everyone got up and moved about admiring the wonderful spectacle of the Bavarian Alps through the large window.

Hitler described to Mr Lloyd George the origin of the tapestry on the wall. At one moment Hitler came to Mr Conwell-Evans and spoke to him about the scenery and his visit to Berchtesgaden the previous Christmas in the Ski Camp. At that moment Mr Lloyd George came up and asked Mr Conwell-Evans to tell the Führer that in his view Hitler should visit England and that he would be acclaimed by the British people. Hitler threw up his hands in a gesture expressing he wished it might be true. Mr Lloyd George continued: 'The time will soon come.'

Hitler again accompanied Mr Lloyd George to the car as before and most cordially wished him good-bye.

Appendix 3

NOTES BY F. T. A. ASHTON-GWATKIN, HEAD OF THE ECONOMIC
SECTION OF THE FOREIGN OFFICE, 21 DECEMBER 1936

Are we perhaps in danger of over-simplification, of seeing things too much in old-school terms of A versus B.

Is the dualism fundamental? Or is it a surface symptom of what is in fact the general breakdown of nineteenth-century ideas and processes – in religion, art, social customs, politics, economics, everything?

'Bolshevism' is the product of the intensified industrialization in the big cities of the nineteenth century; 'Fascism' is the reaction against Bolshevism of those whom the Bolsheviks are going to expropriate.

Both are the result of a failure to secure just and ample division and distribution of the goods, which can now be produced and transported so abundantly.

The quarrel of the twentieth century is therefore a quarrel about the distribution of wealth – between individuals, between classes, between communities, between nations.

Perhaps, this is the eternal problem; but in this twentieth century there is one great difference. Hitherto, there has not been enough wealth to go round; but now, at last, thanks to scientific progress, there really is enough for everybody – if we could only find out the right way of distributing what the world has got to give.

The Bolsheviks believe that they have solved the problem, but in Russia at any rate, they have failed to vindicate their claim.

But, at least, they pointed their policy at the heart of the problem; in this respect, the Fascists have copied them – feebly.

'Democracy' i.e. the Anglo-Saxon Scandinavian political system has also failed so far to solve this problem of distribution; and there is nothing about 'democracy' so sacrosanct that we should fight for her in lands other than our own; that is to introduce that religious spirit which leads to war. Allah! – or the sword!

There is some danger that Bolshevism, Fascism, Democracy even may degenerate into fanatical religion, which sees no reason, just smites.

'For forms of government let fools contest
Whate'er is best administered is best.'

A very sane German said to me the other day: 'There has never been real democracy in Germany.'

Conversely – as Rex Leeper says – 'I do not believe that our democracy can be destroyed by what happens elsewhere'. Nor I think by what happens here – for 'democracy' is our essence.

The danger is in these quasi-religious nationalisms controlled by all-powerful individuals whose policy has been to hypnotize their people.

Against such danger, we must be adequately armed, and have adequate allies.

But we must also seek to foster and develop the spirit and habits of international interdependence which are not only the antidote to 'nationalism' but are the approach to the solution of the ultimate problem of distribution.

International interdependence can be promoted by exchange of culture, sport, tourism etc. but above all by trade.

Intent on our national recovery we have not fully realized that the growth of international interdependence *by trade* depends almost entirely on the economic policy of Great Britain.

Next to Great Britain on Germany; after Germany on the United States of America (which although the second greatest trading nation stands further from the centre of the international complex).

The rough outline of our policy should be:

1 Adequate rearmament.
2 Firm and unmistakable *defensive* alliance with France and Belgium.
3 Political and economic agreement with:

(a) Germany.
(b) Italy.
(c) Japan.

4 General understanding and perhaps commercial treaty with the United States.
5 General world agreement for the rationalization of supplies and production.

The above programme is not intended to ignore the League of Nations; but, I think that for the present time at any rate, the League should give attention especially to economic questions; these can still be based on an ideal of international interdependence.

We must take the risk of a strong Germany ('strong' or 'weak' she is a danger); since by her numbers, her position, and her character she must be strong.

Should Britain modify her tariff system so as to allow greater imports from industrial Europe?

Even apart from the particular German danger, it is a line of policy which His Majesty's Government ought seriously to consider if international trade as a whole is to revive, and our own 'recovery' is not to drift into the doldrums.

There is, however, an opinion fairly widely held that economic recovery in Europe (including Germany) will in itself lessen the danger of war. M. van Zeeland has recently expressed this view in a private conversation here; and M. Imredy, Governor of the National Bank of Hungary, said the same to me when I saw him in Budapest last October.

> Let me have men about me that are fat;
> Sleek-headed men and such as sleep o'nights;
> Yon Cassius has a lean and hungry look;
> Such men are dangerous.

Germany has now been reduced to ration tickets for butter, fats and bacon. It is clear that the economic position in Germany is not improving. Whichever way it be interpreted, the economic position is an important factor.

I should like to see it more fully investigated by our authorities here; and I should like to see it discussed between Sir F. Leith-Ross and Dr Schacht at an early opportunity – not so as to encourage Dr Schacht's more extravagant demands, but so as to show that we are not deaf to reason if Germany will be reasonable, and to explore such lines of compromise as may be open in the economic field.

Appendix 4

It is clear that there are millions of electors – some endorsing and some condemning the Government's policy – who share alike a deep sense of humiliation and shame, sometimes even of fear. Perhaps it may prove impossible to answer all the anxieties that confront every honest thinker, for the situation is far more complex than that of 1914, but I am sure the only way to do so is to state an argument which is a comprehensive whole.

The first essential is that we should not make the starting point of our discussion the breathless events of the final moments in the recent crisis. We must link the present with the past. We must force ourselves to remember that if we have had to buy peace today by what some would call dishonour, it was because twenty years ago we imposed peace by dishonour. If the German people are now ruled by a Government in the grip of passionate and hatefully cruel emotions, it is partly because of what the Allies did at Versailles, and more because of their failure to undo that wrong in the years that followed. Thus the present tragedy had become almost inevitable, and the Prime Minister was right at Munich in refusing to add an even greater tragedy – that of a world war in the name of honour.

Next let us realize that no Great Power and no British party is free from blame. So profound is our sympathy and respect for the gallant Czech people that some of us refuse point-blank to admit the formidable case against them. And yet it is a demonstrable fact that either through an excessive sentiment of nationalism about the 'lands of the Bohemian Crown' or owing to an over-emphasis upon the importance of strategic frontiers against a then prostrate German foe the Czechs did an injury to millions of human beings who wished to be excluded from their rule. They gathered their new State into its final shape by doubtful tactics, in which the French took no small part. This was regretted at the time by the United States Secretary of State and by Mr Arthur Balfour and Lord Milner, not to mention the Labour and peace movements here at home. Had the Czechs been content to create a racially homogeneous State they might today have been at peace reconciled with their great neighbour and possessed both of an area and a population larger than than of many European countries.

From a consideration of the conditions under which the Czecho-Slovak State was created we proceed to the foreign policy that followed. It is true that none of us can look back without a sense of regret to the foreign policy of our own country which failed to give life to the League Covenant. But that sense of regret is even more profound when we come to the policy of France and Czecho-Slovakia, who deliberately created alliances, based on openly declared suspicion of a weak and helpless German Republic at a time when that country was denied entry to the League of Nations in 1924, and, what was worse at the very moment she signed the Locarno Treaty in 1925 and was received into the family of the League. Dr Krofta has described, with his unrivalled authority, how Czecho-Slovakia took particular measures to prevent the incorporation of Austria in Germany (page 171 of his History).

But if few countries are free from blame, certainly no party is. The National Government has in recent years inflicted wound after wound upon the League of Nations. But was it not a Labour Government which was in charge of British policy when Germany and Austria pleaded for the *Anschluss* by voluntary and peaceful consent? Here indeed was an opportunity for firm and un-qualified leadership at Geneva. Instead an elaborate judicial procedure led to the claim being rebuffed by the foes of Germany, and the fate of Czecho-Slovakia was thereby still further sealed in German hatred. We have no right to forget these facts, for they help to explain how ultimately passion over-mastered judgement and fair dealing when the fateful Munich Conference was held.

And now a word about those of us who accepted the theory of armed collective security in an armed world. Are we not also to blame? Have we not thought and spoken far too casually of this dread instrument of war and far too little of the revision of fron-tiers? Collective security, through military action, was rightly held at one time to be as sound in practice as it was in theory. But it is surely doubtful, if we are right, today to go on insisting rigidly upon its application when we know that the one essential condition for its success is missing – namely, the possession of such overwhelming military power as either to prevent war or to win it beyond a shadow of doubt. Armed collective security now – however much we may deplore the circumstances that have led to the present breakdown – is simply one armed alliance against another of almost equal strength, and that at a time when the destructive capacity of scientific war has become more hideous than ever before in history. Nor is this fact any less a fact because we welcome co-operation with Russia. We have no right, under these conditions to resort too rigidly or in too casual a mood to so terrible an instrument as a world war on behalf of lawful procedure.

It was for this and for many other reasons, wise or unwise, that in the past Britain had refused to make a binding declaration that she was willing to go to war over a dispute arising in Czecho-Slovakia. That was so even though it was true that the guarantee sought for was on behalf of lawful procedure rather than on behalf of any territory. Britain refused this guarantee because there was doubt as to the military power of the collective system and doubt as to whether any lawful procedure could at that time have successfully coped with an injustice whose remedy had been delayed too long. In fact a state of affairs internationally had been reached comparable to that existing at a time of civil war within a nation when even domestic judicial procedure is inadequate to release the tension.

And so at Munich the Prime Minister was faced by the fact that the collective system possessed inadequate power to prevent war and by the fact that the decision to vary an unjust frontier had already been arrived at a week earlier. In other words, he was confronted by a choice of catastrophes; either to concede more than he desired to improper threats for speeding up the remedy of a grievance delayed far too long, or a world war. I have no doubt Herr Hitler for his part would have taken this risk of war at that point. And so, having conceded the principle of cession and having regard to the unhappy history of the past, I believe the Prime Minister was right to choose the catastrophe of yielding to improper procedure rather than to choose the terrible catastrophe of war. For otherwise, in order to protect civilization, he would have had to destroy civilization, accepting war not as 'a great illusion' but as the great necessity. The terrible pictures published subsequently in the press headed 'The Price of Peace' are nothing to what those pictures would have been if they had been headed 'The Price of War'.

Ought we not to search our hearts to make sure when we claim to be pro-Czech or pro-lawful procedure that we are not in fact being anti-German? How otherwise could that noblest of international thinkers Lord Cecil have brought himself to write these words:

> But supposing there is a German guarantee, of what is its value? It is unnecessary to accuse Germany of perfidy. Not only the Nazi Government but all previous German Governments from the time of Frederick the Great downwards have made their position perfectly clear. To them an international assurance is no more than a statement of present intention. It has no absolute validity in the future.

I cannot but feel with great respect that this is an appalling view to take of any nation. And is it not also belied by the memories that many of us possess of Stresemann and Brüning and Socialist members of an earlier German Government when the Kaiser was exiled and the Weimar Republic established? If Lord Cecil's statement were accepted as true it could only mean that we have all been playing a hideous farce in trying to build up a League of Nations. For if a State member of the League consisting of over seventy million people at the very heart of the geography of Europe is infected with original sin and predestined to be wicked for all time there never can be a successful League or any hope of a durable peace.

Is not, therefore, the conclusion to be drawn from all this the fact that we have all sinned – every nation, Britain, France, Czecho-Slovakia, and Germany, and every Government National and Labour alike? What useful purpose, then will be served by a bitter campaign waged against the Prime Minister or against each other? Surely we should now all concentrate our minds on the policy which might lead to peace in the future. That duty remains, even if we distrust the word of dictators and believe we shall yet have to fight them in the end, as well we may. We cannot undo the new agreement, but we can make that agreement and the world opinion it has stirred the most formidable moral, and therefore material, barrier that could confront an aggressor contemplating a breach of faith. Hitherto we have missed our chance to resist aggression or put the aggressor in the wrong. Why? Because we have always sought to snatch peace at the eleventh hour out of crisis. Now every one of us should assist and bring pressure to bear upon the Prime Minister in his attempt to seek appeasement forthwith, so that we may not again be caught in the throes of crisis.

And in this new effort it is the British Empire which must make the greatest contribution and take the most vigorous initiative, for it is our nation which first won domestic harmony for herself and it is our Commonwealth which now controls one-quarter of the earth's surface. Somehow or other, indeed, we must resolve this latent conflict between seventy-five million Germans shut within the heart of Europe and the British Commonwealth. It is we, the British, who must be foremost in offering to discuss both economic and colonial readjustments. As for non-self-governing territories, we are under an obligation to offer to extend the area of international administration, but equally we have a duty to insist that any readjustment of sovereignty or mandate shall, in these days of racial discrimination be made dependent upon a final peace settlement that shall include the limitation of armaments and a common code for the treatment of native peoples.

Finally, we must strive as never previously to bring about the entry of all countries into a League of Nations. Perhaps this will mean sacrificing the written text of the cherished Covenant of the League of Nations. In that case, let it be so. For the day upon which the United States of America becomes an active member of the League of Nations – even if it be without the Covenant – may prove to be the most decisive date in contemporary history. The habit of frequent contact at the League table between League members will lead to beneficent action in time of crisis far more surely than any article of obligation.

Whether the Munich Agreement is therefore to be reckoned a great good or a great evil depends not so much upon its own merits as upon what we ourselves and our Prime Minister strengthened by our gratitude and support, do next.

Appendix 5

LETTER FROM SIR ORME SARGENT TO J. W. WHEELER-BENNETT,

ESQ. COMMENTING IN 1946 ON HIS BOOK 'MUNICH:

PROLOGUE TO TRAGEDY'.

The reading of the opening chapter in your book has started me
thinking about what I might call the ethics of appeasement and
now I am going to inflict on you the result of my cogitations,
though I am certain that they will not add anything to what you
already know and think.

Well, to begin with it strikes me it is most unfair that the word
'appeasement' should have been debased to a term of abuse and
condemned without any distinction being made between the many
different forms that appeasement can take.

Many a time both in international affairs as in personal relations,
appeasement is the only wise and prudent course to adopt to break
an immediate deadlock and at the same time achieve an ulterior
aim. It becomes questionable as a method of negotiation only if it
can be shown to be *immoral*; i.e. the appeaser sacrifices the rights
and interests of a third party and not his own when making his
concession; or if it is clearly *dangerous*, i.e. where the concession
made seriously undermines the strength of the appeaser either
internally or internationally; this is especially so when the
concession has to be repeated, for appeasement then becomes
nothing less than blackmail; and lastly when the whole process of
appeasement is just ineffective; i.e. when the appeaser having to
make his concession gets no *quid pro quo* in return.

In point of fact appeasement only stands condemned when it is
proved to be ineffective. For if a position is really critical and if
appeasement will bring salvation, we cannot be expected not to
resort to it just because in normal circumstances it might have
savoured of sharp practice (necessity knows no law), or because it
involves an element of risk which in normal circumstances we
should not have been prepared to run: ('Out of this nettle danger,
we pluck this flower safety.' Chamberlain said this of Munich and

if only it had been true it would have justified his whole policy.) But if appeasement is ineffective it at once loses its whole *raison d'être* and becomes just a mug's game.

Our position at the time of Munich was, thanks to the Baldwin régime, such that we dare not condemn Chamberlain's resort to appeasement merely because it might seem immoral or because it was dangerous. It stands condemned solely because it was ineffective, because it was bound to be ineffective and because Chamberlain ought to have known it would be ineffective. He had only to study Hitler's technique – and he ought to have been studying it ever since 1933 – in order to realize that Hitler would be prevented from responding to any sort of appeasement by his own temperament, by the political philosophy he had evolved, and by all that he stood for in the eyes of the great and fanatical party which he had created and which was governing Germany.

It was not as though Hitler was a blackmailer, and could be bought off as such – dangerous though the process usually is. He was just the reverse of a blackmailer. The blackmailer threatens to do you an injury in order to extort money from you, whereas Hitler did you the injury in the hope, by choosing the right moment and circumstance, of so weakening and demoralizing you that he would be able to repeat the process with progressively less danger each time of your reacting or resisting. In other words, whereas the blackmailer wants your money but does not want to do you the injury he threatens, Hitler did not want your money but was determined as part of a long and carefully worked out plan to do you an injury – in fact one injury after another – and was only concerned as to how he could carry through this process without provoking you to defend yourself before it was too late.

You remember the famous passage in *Mein Kampf* – you probably know it by heart – when Hitler frankly and cynically expounds and justifies his whole method of political and military undermining. If Chamberlain did not know this passage or had forgotten it he showed criminal negligence. If he knew it and chose to ignore it, he was taking a criminal risk which cannot be explained away.

Besides, it was not as though the process of undermining had only just begun. It had been going on for well nigh five years and Hitler had proved the success of his method on at least three occasions; in rearming, in the reoccupation of the Rhineland and in the seizure of Austria. On each of these occasions we and France had either acquiesced tacitly or after a mild protest. Thus the process was working out as Hitler had expected; his theory had been tried and had stood the test; he could continue it therefore in full confidence of further successes.

When he launched his Sudeten campaign, he no doubt expected a protest as before followed by a grudging acceptance of the *fait accompli*. But I doubt whether even he expected Chamberlain to go further than this and in the name of appeasement to coerce the victim and thus legalize and underwrite the rape of Czechoslovakia in return for nothing more than that infamous scrap of paper.

If only we and France had not intervened, had sat back, had washed our hands of the whole business and had accepted under protest the final result, we should have done no more and no less than what we had done when Austria was seized; and we could have justified our inaction and soothed our consciences with the same arguments on that and previous occasions. We should at any rate have avoided the humiliation of going through the process of appeasing Hitler when we knew he could not be appeased, and mark you it was a humiliation, not because it was immoral, not because it was dangerous, but solely because it was ineffective, useless and a sham.

In saying this I ignore the excuse invented subsequently that Hitler gave us a year's grace in return for this our humiliation. It still always will be doubtful whether this year's grace was of greater benefit to us than it was to Hitler and anyhow the argument is a dishonest one as is shown by the way the Munich settlement at the time was in all honesty and sincerity presented by its author to the British people as guaranteeing us peace in our time and the dawn of a new age of concord.

Besides there is nothing to show that Chamberlain's capitulation at Munich led to an alteration in Hitler's timetable. Working as he did on a long-term plan, it is only reasonable to suppose that he had such a timetable and that he did not depart from it; i.e. partition of Czechoslovakia in September 1938, annexation of Czechoslovakia in March 1939 and attack on Poland in September 1939. It would be interesting to know whether the German State documents reveal the existence *before Munich* of such a timetable.

But although Hitler was not propitiated, I do believe that he was deceived by our servile act of abnegation. He must have interpreted it as proof that his method was succeeding even better than he had dared to expect and that we have reached quicker than he had anticipated the ultimate stage of demoralization which is the forerunner of complete capitulation. How could he, poor man, have been expected to understand that this grovelling gesture of ours signified on the contrary that the worm was at last going to make ready to turn. If he had realized this he might have hesitated in 1939 to make his next move as soon as was laid down in his timetable. Calculating Stalin too might have reached other conclusions than he did. But neither Hitler nor Stalin did interpret the Chamberlain intervention at Munich as a warning as they ought to have done, and so our act of appeasement far from delaying the war or enabling us to enter it in improved circumstances, may well have had precisely the opposite effect.

4   *An Appeal to Fair Play* (1924). This pamphlet was probably drafted and organized by Hermann Lutz.

5   Gilbert Murray to the Secretary of the Fichte-Bund, 18 August 1925. Gilbert Murray Papers. The Fichte-Bund was a Hamburg organization which had published a pamphlet, *The Great Fraud*, on the Franco-Russian plot against Germany before 1914.

6   Miss Edith Durham to Dr T. P. Conwell-Evans, 11 December 1924, Conwell-Evans Papers.

7   Arthur Ponsonby, *Falsehood in War-Time*, p. 29.

8   Winston S. Churchill, *The World Crisis*, vol. 6, p. 99.

9   Winston S. Churchill, *Great Contemporaries*, p. 37. In *The World Crisis* Churchill wrote of the Kaiser: 'Those who have wished to judge him should first of all thank God they were not placed in his position.' (Vol. 5, p. 442).

10   D. Lloyd George, *War Memoirs*, p. 57. Chapter Three of this book is devoted to an attack upon Sir Edward Grey.

11   D. Lloyd George, *War Memoirs*, pp. 1995–6.

12   *Manchester Guardian*, 19 May 1935. Quoted in Martin Gilbert, *Britain and Germany Between the Wars*, p. 17.

13   This, and subsequent material on the origin of the 'War Guilt' clause, is in the Lothian Papers at the Scottish Record Office in Edinburgh. The phrase 'the aggression of Germany' replaced 'invasion' on 4 November 1918 at the 8th Session of the Supreme War Council (Annex C of its report).

14   The draft typescript of this letter, corrected in Lord Lothian's handwriting, is in the Lothian Papers, 152/8, folios 754–7.

CHAPTER 4   THE ELUSIVE PEACE

1   Quoted in Julian Symons, *Horatio Bottomley*, p. 165.

2   The same, p. 167.

3   *Rudyard Kipling's Verse*, Inclusive Edition, pp. 587–9.

4   *Hansard*, debate of 21 July 1919.

5   G. Lowes Dickinson, *After the War*, p. 10.

6   H. G. Wells, *A Reasonable Man's Peace*, p. 2.

7   Quoted in *President Wilson's Policy*, ed. G. W. Prothero, p. 54.

8   F. Seymour Cocks, *The Secret Treaties*.

9   D. Lloyd George, *War Memoirs*, p. 1882.

10   I am grateful to the late Lord Beaverbrook for showing me the transcript of this meeting, and for discussing with me the problems which it posed.

11   *Evening Standard*, 17 October 1918. For a discussion of Milner's rôle at this time see A. M. Gollin, *Pro-consul in Politics*, chapter 20.

12   Material in the Lloyd George Papers. The late Lord Beaverbrook kindly made this material available to me.

13 D. Lloyd George, *War Memoirs*, p. 1973.
14 Quoted in Harold Nicolson, *King George V*, pp. 334–5.
15 D. Lloyd George, *War Memoirs*, p. 1987.

CHAPTER 5 APPEASEMENT: THE ESSENTIAL PROSPECT

1 Winston S. Churchill, *The World Crisis*, vol. 5, pp. 41–2.
2 The same, p. 47.
3 Letter of 22 November 1918, the same, p. 7.
4 Lloyd George's policies and performances at this time are discussed in Thomas Jones, *Lloyd George*, Frank Owen, *Tempestuous Journey*, Malcolm Thompson, *David Lloyd George* and Lloyd George's own *Truth About The Peace Treaties*.
5 Quoted in full in Lloyd George, *The Truth About The Peace Treaties* p. 563.
6 *Hansard* debate of 16 April 1919.
7 *The Truth About The Peace Treaties* pp. 404–14. Memorandum dated 25 March 1919.
8 The same, p. 417, Observations drafted by M. Clemenceau, dated 26 March 1919.
9 The same, pp. 420–2.
10 See the full text of the Fontainebleau Memorandum in Appendix I of this volume.
11 Harold Nicolson, *Peacemaking, 1919*, p. 359. Letter dated 8 June 1919.
12 Quoted in Roy Harrod, *John Maynard Keynes*, p. 251. Letter dated 26 May 1919.
13 Memorandum by Lord Cunliffe, Lothian Papers, 139/14. The memorandum is dated 1 June 1919, Paris.
14 Winston S. Churchill, *Great Contemporaries*, p. 326, essay on King George V.
15 *Hansard*, speech delivered on 28 March 1945 in the House of Lords.
16 Lord Beaverbrook, *Men and Power 1917–1918*, p. 344.
17 H. A. L. Fisher to Gilbert Murray, 11 June 1919, quoted in Martin Gilbert, *Britain and Germany Between the Wars*, p. 8.
18 A selection of C. P. Scott's leading articles is given in *C. P. Scott 1846–1932*, published by Frederick Muller in 1946.
19 *Manchester Guardian*, 3 May 1919. Leading article headed 'The Treaty of Peace'.
20 *Manchester Guardian*, 10 May 1919. Leading article headed 'The German Protests'.

CHAPTER 6 VERSAILLES: THE NAGGING DOUBT

1 Lord Vansittart, *The Mist Procession*, p. 220.
2 H. G. Wells, *What Is Coming?* p. 49.

3 The same, p. 94.
4 The same, pp. 202–2.
5 The same, p. 207.
6 The same, p. 271.
7 The same, p. 291.
8 Letter dated 12 November 1918, Lord Esher, *Journals and Letters*, pp. 217–18.
9 Letter dated 23 January 1919, the same, pp. 223–4.
10 Letter dated 1 April 1919. Fisher Papers, Bodleian Library, Oxford. I am grateful to the Principal of St Hilda's College, Oxford, for permission to quote from her father's Letters.
11 Sir Charles Petrie, *Austen Chamberlain*, p. 144.
12 Letter dated 31 July 1919, *Letters From Lord Oxford to a Friend*, p. 98.
13 Letter dated 14 October 1919, Gilbert Murray Papers, Bodleian Library, Oxford.
14 Letter dated 29 November 1919, Lord Esher, *Journals and Letters*, pp. 247–8.
15 *Hansard*, 18 November 1918.
16 Letter dated 5 June 1919, quoted in R. F. Harrod, *John Maynard Keynes*, p. 253.
17 J. M. Keynes, *The Economic Consequences of the Peace*, pp. 4, 5, 25, 33, 38, 39, 47, 48, 50, 102, 173, 190, 251.
18 Lord Robert Cecil to Gilbert Murray, 1 January 1920, Gilbert Murray Papers.
19 Lord Birkenhead, *Turning Points in History*, p. 261.
20 Harold Nicolson, *Peacemaking 1919*, pp. 20, 43, 78, 186.
21 Winston S. Churchill, *The World Crisis*, vol. 5, p. 120
22 Harold Nicolson, *Peacemaking 1919*, p. 188.
23 J. M. Keynes, *The Economic Consequences of the Peace*, p. 209.

CHAPTER 7   THE FIRST APPEASEMENT

1 Harold Nicolson, *Peacemaking 1919*, p. 207.
2 *British Documents on British Foreign Policy*, series 1, vol. 9, no. 601. Record of a Meeting held at the Quai D'Orsay on Friday, 6 February 1920.
3 *Documents on British Foreign Policy*, series 1, vol. 7, No. 1. Notes of an Allied Conference held at 10 Downing Street on Thursday, 12 February 1920.
4 *British Documents*, series 1, vol. 9, No. 292. Account by Lord Curzon of the interview between Cambon and Bonar Law, dated 5 April 1920. See also No. 298, dated 6 April 1920, for the second interview between Cambon and Bonar Law.

5 *British Documents*, series 1, vol. 9, No. 318. Account by Lord Curzon of his interview with Cambon, 8 April 1920.

6 *British Documents*, series 1, vol. 9, No. 322. Lord Curzon to Lord Derby. Marked 'urgent', 8 April 1920.

7 The proceedings of the San Remo Conference are printed in *British Documents*, series 1, vol. 8, Nos. 1–20, pp. 1–252.

8 The proceedings of the Lympne Conference are printed in *British Documents*, series 1, vol. 8, Nos. 26–30, pp. 307–33.

9 *British Documents*, series 1, vol. 8, No. 84, p. 741, 8 August 1920.

10 *Evening News*, 28 July 1920.

11 Harold Temperley. *The Second Year of the League*, pp. 42–3.

12 *British Documents*, series 1, vol. 10, Nos. 386, 387, 397 and 398. The Germans were informed of this on 15 October 1920, a day before the French.

13 *Hansard*, 28 October 1920. Chamberlain's statement is also printed in full in *British Documents*, series 1, vol. 10, No. 397, pp. 542–3.

14 *British Documents*, series 1, vol. 10, No. 397, p. 546. Lord Curzon to Lord Derby, 29 October 1920.

15 Letter dated 15 November 1920. Quoted in Martin Gilbert, *Britain and Germany Between the Wars*, p. 25.

16 *British Documents*, series 1, vol. 10, No. 401, p. 552. Lord D'Abernon to Lord Curzon, 4 November 1920.

17 *British Documents*, series 1, vol. 10, No. 409, p. 558. Lord Hardinge to Lord Curzon, 2 December 1920.

18 Edmund Burke, *Speech on Conciliation with America*, 22 March 1775. Collected Works, 1815 edition, vol. 3, p. 34.

CHAPTER 8 NO VICTOR, NO VANQUISHED

1 Philip Kerr to Lord Curzon, 6 February 1921, Lothian Papers, 144/10.

2 L. S. Amery, *My Political Life*, vol. 2, p. 226.

3 Letter dated 3 May 1921 in *Letters from Lord Oxford To A Friend*, p. 185.

4 Winston S. Churchill, *The World Crisis*, vol. 5, p. 455.

5 Letter dated 23 March 1922, quoted in Lord Beaverbrook, *The Decline and Fall of Lloyd George*, p. 137.

6 Quoted in Frank Owen, *Tempestuous Journey*, p. 615.

7 Quoted in Frank Owen, *Tempestuous Journey*, p. 616.

8 Letter dated 9 May 1922. One of 12 letters sent from Genoa to Miss Stevenson, quoted in Frank Owen, *Tempestuous Journey*, p. 619.

9 *Hansard*, debate of 25 May 1922.

10 *The Times*, 20 May 1922, quoted in T. Jones, *Lloyd George*, p. 186.

11 Lord D'Abernon, *An Ambassador of Peace*, vol. 1, p. 224, diary entry dated 6 November 1921.
12 The same, vol. 2, p. 45, diary entry dated 12 June 1922.
13 The same, vol. 2, pp. 75–6, diary entry dated 5 August 1922.
14 D. Lloyd George, *The Truth About Reparations and War Debts*, pp. 70–1.
15 T. Jones, *Lloyd George*, p. 184.

CHAPTER 9   CRY HAVOC
1 Letter dated 15 September 1922, quoted in full in Lord Beaverbrook, *The Decline and Fall of Lloyd George*, appendix 56, p. 296.
2 See Winston S. Churchill, *The World Crisis*, vol. 5, chapter 19.
3 Quoted in Frank Owen, *Tempestuous Journey*, p. 635. Telegram sent shortly before midnight, 15 September 1922.
4 The same, p. 640.
5 The same, p. 643, letter from Lord Stamfordham to Lloyd George dated 20 September 1922, from Balmoral.
6 Material in the papers of Sir Horace Rumbold. See also Lord Kinross, *Atatürk*, p. 336.
7 Lord Beaverbrook, *The Decline and Fall of Lloyd George*, p. 169.
8 *The Times*, 15 October 1922.
9 The decisive rôle of Stanley Baldwin at this meeting is described in G. M. Young, *Stanley Baldwin*, pp. 39–43.
10 Quoted in L. S. Amery, *My Political Life*, vol. 2, p. 253.
11 H. G. Wells, *Men Like Gods*, p. 20 and p. 116.
12 Quoted in Martin Gilbert, *Plough My Own Furrow*, p. 176.

CHAPTER 10   THE CRISIS WITH FRANCE
1 *British Documents*, series 1, volume 9, No. 50, note 1, dated 20 February 1920.
2 The same, minutes by Lord Hardinge and Lord Curzon dated 23 February 1920.
3 The same, Headlam-Morley to Sir W. Tyrrell, 20 February 1920.
4 *British Documents*, series 1, volume 9, No. 50, note 4, dated 24 February 1920.
5 *British Documents*, series 1, volume 9, No. 79. Memorandum dated 5 March 1920.
6 The same, note 3, dated 9 March 1920.
7 Philip Kerr to Lord D'Abernon, 17 October 1921, Lothian Papers, 144/10.
8 Lord D'Aberon to Philip Kerr, 20 October 1921, Lothian Papers, 144/10.
9 J. M. Keynes. *A Revision of the Treaty*, p. 11.
10 The same, p. 186.

11   The same, p. 55.
12   The same, p. 57.
13   Quoted in Lady D'Abernon, *Red Cross and Berlin Embassy*, pp. 106–7. The letter is dated 19 March 1923.
14   Lord D'Abernon, *An Ambassador of Peace*, vol. 2, pp. 186, 194.
15   The same, p. 225.
16   *Hansard*, debate of 21 January 1924.
17   Lord D'Abernon, *An Ambassador of Peace*, vol. 3, p. 12.

CHAPTER 11   THE NEW LEADER
1   See Richard Lyman *The First Labour Government 1924*, p. 105. There were nine UDC members in Ramsay MacDonald's Cabinet.
2   *Hansard*, 12 February 1924.
3   H. N. Brailsford, *After The Peace*, p. 21.
4   See Lord Elton, *James Ramsay MacDonald*, Chapter Nine, pp. 242–341.
5   On 22 December 1923 the *New Statesman* insisted that Britain must not 'Let France trample on Europe in the name of a fly-blown idol called the *Entente Cordiale*'.
6   *Hansard*, 14 July 1924.
7   *New Leader* editorial, 7 December 1923.
8   British Bureau for Ruhr Information, Bulletin No. 15, 27 February 1924. Charles Roden Buxton was Treasurer of the Bureau and G. P. Gooch one of its Vice-Presidents.
9   The full text of this letter was printed in *The Times* on 3 March 1924.
10   Sir Norman Angell, *After All*, p. 243.
11   The full text of MacDonald's statement was printed in *The Times* on 18 August 1924.
12   Lord D'Abernon, *An Ambassador of Peace*, volume 3, pp. 89–90.
13   *New Leader*, 25 July 1924.
14   The full text of MacDonald's concluding speech was printed in *The Times*.
15   For this, and subsequent negotiations in which D'Abernon was directly involved, see *An Ambassador of Peace*, volume 3, p. 116 *et seq*. In the Austen Chamberlain Papers at Birmingham University is a Memorandum of Churchill's dated 23 February 1925 strongly critical of any Anglo-French pact. As a result of Churchill's opposition to his policy, Chamberlain offered to resign.
16   Sir Charles Petrie, *Austen Chamberlain*, vol. 2, p. 227.
17   Sir Harold Nicolson, *King George V*, p. 407.
18   Nicolson, *George V*, p. 407.
19   Austen Chamberlain to Sir William Tyrrell, 18 October 1925. Quoted in Petrie, *Austen Chamberlain*, vol. 2, pp. 287–90.

20 Lord D'Aberon to Philip Kerr, 24 October 1925. Lothian Papers 145/2.
21 Ramsay MacDonald to Gilbert Murray, 16 June 1925. Gilbert Murray Papers.

CHAPTER 12 LOCARNY BLARNEY

1 Rolf Gardiner, *Meditation on the Future of Northern Europe*, in *Britain and Germany*, edited by R. Gardiner and H. Rocholl, p. 131.
2 The full poem is printed in A. P. Herbert's *A Book of Ballads*, pp. 406–7.
3 Philip Kerr to D. Lloyd George, 13 November 1925. Lothian Papers 145/3.
4 3 June 1926. Quoted in Stanley Baldwin, *Our Inheritance*, pp. 3–6.

CHAPTER 13 THE SARGENT CHAIN

1 Prince Max von Baden to J. Ramsay MacDonald, November 1929. Copy in Lothian Papers 209/5.
2 House of Commons, 11 July 1932. Quoted in *Arms and the Covenant* Compiled by Randolph S. Churchill, p. 31.
3 *British Documents*, series 2, vol. 1, No. 307, Note 5.
4 Quoted by Ian Colvin, *Vansittart in Office*, p. 19.
5 J. L. Garvin to Lord Lothian, 4 April 1930. Lothian Papers 149/3.
6 J. L. Garvin to Lord Lothian, 7 May 1930. Lothian Papers 149/3.
7 *British Documents*, series 2, vol. 1, No. 327. Orme Sargent to Sir Horace Rumbold, 14 October 1930.
8 *British Documents*, series 2, vol. 1, No. 328. Sir Horace Rumbold to Orme Sargent, 16 October 1930.
9 *British Documents*, series 2, vol. 1, No. 329. Sir Horace Rumbold to Arthur Henderson, 23 October 1930.
10 *British Documents*, series 2, vol. 1, No. 350. Arthur Henderson to Sir Horace Rumbold, 19 February 1931.
11 *British Documents*, series 2, vol. 1, No. 352. Sir Horace Rumbold to Arthur Henderson, 26 February 1931.
12 J. L. Hammond to Gilbert Murray, 31 August 1931. Gilbert Murray Papers.
13 I am grateful to the late Sir Orme Sargent for discussing with me the contents and implications of this Memorandum, and also of Vansittart's outspoken and radical sequel; as well as for permission to publish his letter to Sir John Wheeler-Bennett, see Appendix 5 of this volume.
14 *British Documents*, series 2, vol. 2, No. 319. Note received by the Foreign Office, 22 December 1931.
15 *British Documents*, series 2, vol. 3, No. 137, p. 192. 16 June 1932.

16 *British Documents*, series 2, vol. 3, No. 178, p. 393. 6 July 1932.
17 *British Documents*, series 2, vol. 3, No. 182, p. 410. 7 July 1932.
18 *British Documents*, series 2, vol. 3, No. 186, p. 427. 8 July 1932.
19 Quoted in *Arms and the Covenant* compiled by Randolph S. Churchill, pp. 32–48.
20 Arnold Toynbee to Miss Boulter, from Berlin, 3 December 1932. I am grateful to Dr Toynbee for sending me this letter and giving me permission to quote from it.

CHAPTER 14 NOSTRA MAXIMA CULPA

1   *British Documents*, series 2, vol. iv, No. 232. Sir John Simon to Sir Horace Rumbold, 31 January 1933.
2   H. A. L. Fisher to Gilbert Murray, 31 March 1933, Gilbert Murray Papers.
3   *British Documents*, series 2, vol. iv, No. 265. Sir Horace Rumbold to Sir Robert Vansittart, 15 March 1933.
4   Lady Violet Bonham-Carter to Gilbert Murray, 4 April 1933, Gilbert Murray Papers.
5   *Manchester Guardian*, 8 April 1933.
6   Sir Evelyn Wrench, *I Loved Germany*, p. 48.
7   Sir Evelyn Wrench, *I Loved Germany*, p. 286.
8   Quoted in Martin Gilbert, *Britain and Germany Between the Wars*, p. 76.
9   J. L. Garvin to Sir Horace Rumbold, 1 May 1933, Rumbold Papers.
10 See her introduction to *Focus: A Footnote to the History of the Thirties*, by Eugen Spier, pp. 9–12.
11 Sir Evelyn Wrench, *I Loved Germany*, p. 286.
12 Quoted in Martin Gilbert, *Britain and Germany Between the Wars*, p. 82.
13 For full accounts of Lord Lothian's meetings with Hitler see J. R. M. Butler, *Lord Lothian*, Appendix 111, pp. 330–45.
14 *Nottingham Journal*, 13 November 1933.
15 *The Times*, 31 January 1935.
16 Sir Abe Bailey to Lord Lothian, telegram, 3 February 1935, Lothian Papers.
17 Lord Lothian to Sir Abe Bailey, 7 February 1935, Lothian Papers.
18 Lord Perth to Lord Lothian, 7 February 1935, and Lord Lothian's reply, 22 February, Lothian Papers.
19 See *Clifford Allen: The Open Conspirator*, by Arthur Marwick, p. 143, for a discussion of Kurt Hahn's educational methods.
20 Kurt Hahn to Lord Lothian, 1935, Lothian Papers, 209/5.
21 Winston Churchill, *Great Contemporaries*. The Essay on Hitler was written in 1935.

22 Kurt Hahn to Lord Lothian, 1935, Lothian Papers, 209/5.
23 Lord Lothian to Leonard Montefiore, 1 February 1935, Lothian Papers, 209/5.
24 See the British attempt to interest Hitler in Colonial revision, Martin Gilbert and Richard Gott, *The Appeasers*, chapter 4.
25 Quoted in D. C. Watt, *Personalities and Policies*, p. 105.
26 Quoted in G. M. Young, *Stanley Baldwin*, p. 194.
27 Thomas Jones gives examples of unsuccessful pressure on Baldwin in his *A Diary With Letters*, especially in the entries for 1936.
28 Quoted in Martin Gilbert, *Britain and Germany Between the Wars*, p. 63. Memorandum dated 17 May 1936.
29 Quoted in Keith Feiling, *Neville Chamberlain*, p. 314.

CHAPTER 15   PEACE THROUGH PROSPERITY
1 *British Documents*, series 2, vol. 4, No. 235. Sir Horace Rumbold to Sir John Simon, 4 February 1933.
2 I am most grateful to Mr Ashton-Gwatkin for discussing his ideas and proposals with me. Sir Frederick Leith-Ross, Mr Henry Drummond-Wolff, Dr Paul Einzig and Dr Helmuth Wohlthat have also given me valuable advice and materials.
3 Dr T. P. Conwell-Evans to Lord Lothian, 13 March 1935, in which Conwell-Evans describes the inaugural meeting of the Anglo-German society. Lothian Papers.
4 Winston S. Churchill, *The World Crisis*, volume 6, *The Unknown War*, p. 115.
5 The search for economic appeasement after March 1938 is discussed in Martin Gilbert and Richard Gott, *The Appeasers*, Part Three.

CHAPTER 16   NATIONALISM VERSUS IDEOLOGY
1 Quoted in Martin Gilbert, *Britain and Germany Between the Wars*, pp. 97–9.
2 Mr Ashton-Gwatkin has kindly allowed me to study these notes. See also Appendix 3 of this volume.
3 Lord Birkenhead gives Halifax's account of this conversation in *Halifax*, p. 368.
4 Lord Lothian to Reginald Coupland, 11 July 1935, Lothian Papers.
5 Lord Lothian to H. G. Wells, 16 December 1936, Lothian Papers.
6 Lord Lothian to Lady Asquith of Oxford and Asquith, 7 May 1936. Lothian Papers.
7 See Appendix 2 of this volume for the full transcript of Lloyd George's talk with Hitler. I am extremely grateful to Dr T. P. Conwell-Evans for allowing me to publish this record for the first time.

8 See Thomas Jones, *A Diary with Letters*, p. 179, entry for 8 March 1936.
9 Quoted in Martin Gilbert, *Plough My Own Furrow*, p. 381.
10 *Daily Telegraph*, 28 January 1935.
11 Lord Birkenhead, *Halifax*, p. 731.
12 For Lord Allen of Hurtwood's persistent efforts to intervene on behalf of political prisoners in concentration camps in Germany, See Martin Gilbert, *Plough My Own Furrow*, chapters 24 and 25.
13 Quoted in Sir Evelyn Wrench, *Geoffrey Dawson*, pp. 334–5. The letter is dated 19 June 1936.
14 Lord Robert Cecil to Gilbert Murray, 17 November 1936, Gilbert Murray Papers.
15 Quoted in Lord Londonderry, *Ourselves and Germany*, p. 176.
16 *Hansard*, debate of 8 April 1938.
17 *Hansard*, debate of 26 July 1938.
18 Stephen Roberts, *The House That Hitler Built*, p. 363.
19 Quoted in Keith Feiling, *Neville Chamberlain*, p. 328.
20 I am grateful to Dr T. P. Conwell-Evans for permission to quote from his private papers, from which this material is drawn.
21 *Hansard*, debate of 27 July 1938.
22 *British Documents*, series 3, volume 2, No. 687 of 25 August 1938.
23 *Daily Express*, 25 February 1938.

EPILOGUE: MUNICH AND THE NEW APPEASEMENT
1 The influence of the Dominions in policy-making has been much neglected by historians. This quotation and much other material, is in D. C. Watt, *Personalities and Policies*, Part 3.
2 Letter dated 17 May 1938, quoted in Martin Gilbert, *Plough My Own Furrow*, pp. 400–401.
3 Lord Strang, *Britain in World Affairs*, p. 321.
4 Lord Birkenhead, *Halifax*, p. 607.
5 *British Documents*, series 3, vol. 1, No. 534, dated 22 July 1938.
6 Sir Orme Sargent, *Dictionary of National Biography 1941–1950* pp. 376–8.
7 Lord Londonderry, *Ourselves and Germany*, p. 163.
8 *Hansard*, debate of 3 October 1938.
9 *Hansard*, debate of 5 October 1938.
10 *Hansard*, debate of 5 October 1938. For a full defence of the Munich settlement, see Lord Allen of Hurtwood's letter to the *Manchester Guardian* of 20 October 1938, given in full in Appendix 4 of this volume. For a view of appeasement in retrospect, see Sir Orme Sargent's previously unpublished letter, written in 1946, in Appendix 5.

Select Bibliography

The unpublished material in this volume has been drawn from the following collections: the Lothian Papers, at the Scottish Record Office in Edinburgh, the Austen Chamberlain Papers at the University of Birmingham, the Gilbert Murray Papers and the H. A. L. Fisher Papers at the Bodleian Library, Oxford, the Lord Robert Cecil Papers and the Lord D'Abernon Papers at the British Museum; and, in private collections, the papers of Sir Horace Rumbold, Lord Vansittart, Sir Norman Angell, Lord Allen of Hurtwood, F. T. A. Ashton-Gwatkin, Dr T. P. Conwell-Evans, Lord Beaverbrook, and Arnold Toynbee. Other important collections which contain additional material on the origins and course of appeasement are the Duff Cooper Papers, the Simon Papers, the Milner Papers at New College, Oxford, the Lloyd George Papers, the E. D. Morel Papers at the London School of Economics, the diaries of Sir Harold Nicolson, and the Lord Ponsonby of Shulbrede Papers, all of which I have consulted. Most Government archives, including a selection of Cabinet Papers, are open until 1922, and are available for inspection at the Public Record Office in London. The many volumes of *Documents on British Foreign Policy* published by Her Majesty's Stationery Office cover in detail the years 1919–21, 1929–33 and 1938–9. Important documentary material was published by the Royal Institute for International Affairs in their annual *Survey* and *Documents* volumes, covering in detail 1923–39.

CONTEMPORARY WORKS

1914
H. N. Brailsford *The War of Steel and Gold*
Gilbert Murray *How Can War Ever be Right?*
H. A. L. Fisher *The War: Its Causes and Issues*
Clifford Allen *Is Germany Right and Britain Wrong?*
D. Lloyd George *Honour and Dishonour*

1915
H. N. Brailsford *Belgium and the 'Scrap of Paper'*

1915
Norman Angell *The Prussian in Our Midst*
G. Lowes Dickinson *After the War*
Arnold Toynbee *Nationality and the War*

1916
H. G. Wells *What Is Coming?*
E. D. Morel *Truth and the War*

1917
H. G. Wells *A Reasonable Man's Peace*
Arnold Toynbee *The German Terror in Belgium*
Rudyard Kipling *The Children*

1918
Gilbert Murray *Faith, War and Policy*
Seymour Cocks *The Secret Treaties*
Siegfried Sassoon *Counterattack*

1919
Lord Loreburn *How the War Came*
J. L. Garvin *The Economic Foundations of Peace*
Halford Mackinder *Democratic Ideals and Reality*
Charles Sorley *Marlborough and Other Poems*
J. M. Keynes *The Economic Consequences of the Peace*

1920
Lord Haldane *Before the War*
G. W. Prothero (ed.) *President Wilson's Policy*
H. N. Brailsford *After the Peace*

1921
Norman Angell *The Fruits of Victory*
Gilbert Murray *The Problem of Foreign Policy*

1922
J. M. Keynes *A Revision of the Treaty*

1923
Neville Chamberlain *Norman Chamberlain: A Memoir*
Winston S. Churchill *The World Crisis*, vol. I
Lord Robert Cecil *The Moral Basis of the League of Nations*
J. Ramsay MacDonald *The Foreign Policy of the Labour Party*

1924
Joseph King *The Ruhr: History of the French Occupation*

1925
Edith Durham *The Sarajevo Crime*
J. Wheeler-Bennett *Information on the reduction of Armaments*

1926
G. Lowes Dickinson *The International Anarchy*

1928
Lord Morley *Memorandum on Resignation*
Rolf Gardiner and Heinz Rocholl *Britain and Germany*
Austen Chamberlain *Peace in Our Time*
Lord Robert Cecil *The Way of Peace*
H. W. Wilson *The War Guilt*
Stanley Baldwin *Our Inheritance*
Arthur Ponsonby *Falsehood in War-time*

1929
Lord Haldane *Autobiography*
Robert Graves *Goodbye to All That*
Winston S. Churchill *The Aftermath*

1930
Lord D'Abernon *Foreign Policy*
J. Wheeler-Bennett *Information on the Reparation's Settlement*

1932
T. Conwell-Evans *Foreign Policy from a Back Bench*
Winston S. Churchill *Thoughts and Adventures*
D. Lloyd George *The Truth about Reparations and War Debts*
J. Wheeler-Bennett *Disarmament and Security Since Locarno*

1933
Adolf Hitler *Mein Kampf*
Edgar Mowrer *Germany Puts the Clock Back*
Norman Angell *The Great Illusion 1933*
D. Lloyd George *War Memoirs*, vol. 1
J. Wheeler-Bennett *The Wreck of Reparations*
Harold Nicolson *Peacemaking 1919*
W. H. Dawson *Germany Under The Treaty*

1934
Gilbert Murray *The Cult of Violence*
Wickham Steed *Hitler: Whence and Whither*
J. Wheeler-Bennett *The Disarmament Deadlock*
Alfred Zimmern *British Foreign Policy Since the War*

1935
Stanley Baldwin *This Torch of Freedom*
Lord Lothian *Pacifism is not Enough (Nor Patriotism Either)*

1936
Bertrand Russell *Which Way to Peace?*
Wickham Steed *Vital Peace*
Arnold Wilson *Walks and Talks Abroad*
Alfred Zimmern *The League of Nations and the Rule of Law*
Lord Allen of Hurtwood *Peace In Our Time*

1937
Winston S. Churchill *Great Contemporaries*
G. Ward Price *I Know These Dictators*
Stephen Roberts *The House That Hitler Built*

1938
Lord Londonderry *Ourselves and Germany*
Charles Petrie *The Chamberlain Tradition*
Norman Angell *Peace With the Dictators*
D. Lloyd George *The Truth about the Peace Treaties*
George Lansbury *My Quest for Peace*
Louis Macniece *Autumn Journal*
Harold Nicolson *National Character and National Policy*
Eleanor Rathbone *War Can Be Averted*
Lord Esher *Journals and Letters*. 4 vols
Gilbert Murray *Liberality and Civilization*

1939
Anthony Eden *Foreign Affairs*
L. S. Amery *The German Colonial Claim*
Norman Angell *For What Do We Fight?*
A. Duff Cooper *The Second World War*
Winston S. Churchill *Step By Step*
Victor Gollancz *Is Mr. Chamberlain Saving Peace?*
Harold Nicolson *Marginal Comment*
Alfred Zimmern *Spiritual Values and World Affairs*
Ramsay Muir *Future for Democracy*
E. H. Carr *The Twenty Years Crisis*

1940
John F. Kennedy *Why England Slept*
Winston S. Churchill *Into Battle*
Norman Angell *Why Freedom Matters*

George Lansbury *This Way to Peace*
Harold Nicolson *Why Britain Is At War*
H. A. L. Fisher, Harold Nicolson, and others *The Background and Issues of the War*
Evelyn Wrench *I Loved Germany*
Nevile Henderson *Failure of a Mission*
Arthur Greenwood *Why We Fight: Labour's Case*

AUTOBIOGRAPHIES, MEMOIRS AND BIOGRAPHIES

L. S. Amery *My Political Life*
Norman Angell *After All*
Clement Attlee *As It Happened*
A. W. Baldwin *My Father: The True Story*
Lord Birkenhead *Halifax*
Robert Blake *The Unknown Prime Minister* (Bonar Law)
Robert Boothby *I Fight to Live*
J. R. M. Butler *Lord Lothian*
Lord Robert Cecil *A Great Experiment*
Lord Robert Cecil *All The Way*
Ian Colvin *Vansittart in Office*
Alfred Duff Cooper (Lord Norwich) *Old Men Forget*
Sir Colin Coote *Editorial*
Lord D'Abernon *An Ambassador of Peace*
Lady D'Abernon *Red Cross and Berlin Embassy*
Hugh Dalton *The Fateful Years*
Anthony Eden (Lord Avon) *Facing the Dictators*
Paul Einzig *In the Centre of Things*
Keith Feiling *Neville Chamberlain*
Martin Gilbert *Plough My Own Furrow* (Lord Allen of Hurtwood)
A. M. Gollin *Proconsul in Politics* (Lord Milner)
Lord Halifax *Fulness of Days*
Roy Harrod *John Maynard Keynes*
Sir Nevile Henderson *Water Under the Bridges*
Sir Nevile Henderson *Failure of a Mission*
General Ironside *The Ironside Diaries* (ed. R. Macleod)
Leslie Hore-Belisha *Private Papers* (ed. R. J. Minney)
Thomas Jones *Diary With Letters*
Thomas Jones *Lloyd George*
Sir Ivone Kirkpatrick *The Inner Circle*
B. H. Liddell Hart *Memoirs* (2 volumes)
Lord Londonderry *Wings of Destiny*
Iain Macleod *Neville Chamberlain*
Harold Nicolson *Curzon: The Last Phase*

Harold Nicolson *George V*
David Ogg *Herbert Fisher*
Frank Owen *Tempestuous Journey* (Lloyd George)
Charles Petrie *The Life and Letters of the Rt Hon. Sir Austen Chamberlain*
Raymond Postgate *The Life of George Lansbury*
Lord Simon *Retrospect*
Lord Snowdon *An Autobiography*
Dudley Sommer *Haldane of Cloan*
Lord Strang *At Home and Abroad*
Lord Swinton *I Remember*
Julian Symons *Horatio Bottomley*
Lord Templewood (Sir Samuel Hoare) *Nine Troubled Years*
Lord Vansittart *The Mist Procession*
Sir John Wheeler-Bennett *George VI*
Lord Winterton *Orders of the Day*
Sir Evelyn Wrench *Geoffrey Dawson and Our Times*
G. M. Young *Stanley Baldwin*

THE APPEASEMENT DEBATE SINCE 1940

Cato (pseudonym) *Guilty Men (1940)*
Lord Vansittart *Black Record: Germans Past and Present (1941)*
Lord Vansittart *Lessons of My Life (1943)*
V. Wellesley *Diplomacy in Fetters (1944)*
R. B. McCallum *Public Opinion and the Last Peace (1944)*
Lord Elibank *Reflections on Some Aspects of British Foreign Policy Between the Two World Wars (1946)*
J. Wheeler-Bennett *Munich: Prologue to Tragedy (1948)*
Winston S. Churchill *The Gathering Storm (1948)*
L. B. Namier *Diplomatic Prelude (1948)*
F. T. A. Ashton-Gwatkin *The British Foreign Office (1949)*
L. B. Namier *Europe in Decay (1950)*
A History of the Times *volume 4 (1952)*
Walford Selby *Diplomatic Twilight (1953)*
A. J. P. Taylor *The Troublemakers (1957)*
John Connell *The Office: A Study of British Foreign Policy and Its Makers (1958)*
Lord Strang *Britain in World Affairs (1961)*
Sir Charles Webster *The Art and Practice of Diplomacy (1961)*
A. J. P. Taylor *The Origins of the Second World War (1961)*
A. L. Rowse *All Souls and Appeasement (1961)*
W. N. Medlicott *The Coming of War in 1939 (1963)*
Martin Gilbert and Richard Gott *The Appeasers (1963)*

E. M. Robertson *Hitler's Pre-war Policy* (*1963*)
Martin Gilbert *Britain and Germany Between the Wars* (*1964*)
Ivan Maisky *Who Helped Hitler?* (*1964*)
Brigitte Granzow *A Mirror of Nazism* (*1964*)
Lord Francis Williams *A Pattern of Rulers* (*1965*)
D. C. Watt *Personalities and Policies* (*1965*)

Index

Abyssinia, Emperor of (Haile Selassie), British fail to save from defeat, 171

Allen, Clifford, (Lord Allen of Hurtwood), challenges concept of German guilt in 1914, 14–15; reaches small audience, 18; denounces Churchill, 94–5; visits Hitler, 164–5; urges concessions to Germany, 166; on history of pro-Germanism, 172; on Nazi persecution of Jews, 173; on Anglo-German 'disparity of outlook', 174; on immorality of appeasement in 1938, 182; on Munich, 215–19

Amery, Leopold, critical of Lloyd George's Government, 81–2, 93

Angell, (Sir) Norman, on futility of war, 11–12; becomes anti-French, 17; capable of extremism, 18; urges moderate war aims, 36; hostile to French armaments, 107; becomes sympathetic to France, 108; defends MacDonald, 110–11; opposes Munich, 185

Anglo-German Commercial Agreement, marginal in its moderating influence on Nazism 153

Anglo-German Naval Agreement, 'not merely treachery, it is folly', 149–50; creates sense of harmony, 151; seen by Chamberlain as proof of the viability of appeasement, 170, 175

Appeasement, the word used before 1933, by Churchill in 1921, ix; by H. A. L. Fisher in 1919, 52; by the *Manchester Guardian* in 1919, 54; by Austen Chamberlain at the time of Locarno, 1925, 115

Appeasement, only permanent path to peace, xi–xii; chronology of, xv–xvi; and Edmund Burke, 2–4; born of anguish at outbreak of 1914 war, 9; urged as necessary policy in 1919, 52; first triumph of, in 1920, 69–71; and British strength, 78–80; challenged in Asia by Lloyd George, 89–95; revived in Europe by Ramsay MacDonald, 105–11; Austen Chamberlain not enthusiastic about, 111–15; becomes a matter of urgency, 129–130; supported by Sir Robert Vansittart, 131–3; furthered at the Lausanne Conference on Reparations, 134–6; Churchill uneasy about, 136–7; Hitler seems to make impossible, 138–41; Hitler encourages, 142; feeds on ignorance, 143–4; spurred on by British guilt feelings, 145–7; culminates in Anglo-German Naval Agreement, 149–150; sought in economic affairs, 151–8; argues the

245